TWO CENTURIES OF U.S. FOREIGN POLICY

The Documentary Record

Edited by
Stephen J. Valone

PRAEGER

Westport, Connecticut
London

Library of Congress Cataloging-in-Publication Data

Two centuries of U.S. foreign policy : the documentary record / edited
  by Stephen J. Valone.
     p. cm.
  Includes bibliographical references (p.) and index.
  ISBN 0–275–95324–6 (hc : alk. paper).—ISBN 0–275–95325–4 (pbk.)
    1. United States—Foreign relations—Sources. 2. United States—
Foreign relations—20th century—Sources. I. Valone, Stephen J.
E183.7.T88   1995
327.73—dc20   95–13433

British Library Cataloguing in Publication Data is available.

Library of Congress Catalog Card Number: 95–13433
ISBN: 0–275–95324–6
      0–275–95325–4 (pbk.)

First published in 1995

Praeger Publishers, 88 Post Road West, Westport, CT 06881
An imprint of Greenwood Publishing Group, Inc.

Printed in the United States of America

The paper used in this book complies with the
Permanent Paper Standard issued by the National
Information Standards Organization (Z39.48–1984).

10 9 8 7 6 5 4 3 2 1

To my family and the memory of David R. Millar of Hamilton College

Contents

Introduction

When given the opportunity to teach a one-semester survey course on U.S. foreign policy, I hoped to supplement my lectures with a book of documents that would introduce my students to primary source material. I was, however, unable to locate a satisfactory collection. A number of excellent books for the post-1890 period were available, but they were not appropriate for a class beginning in the late eighteenth century. The texts spanning the period from the Washington administration to the present were also not acceptable; some were out of date while others were two-volume collections that included scholarly essays which I thought would be more suitable for an upper-division class. My unsuccessful search ultimately led me to edit my own collection.

As I selected the documents to include in this textbook, I attempted to choose those that accomplished two goals: (1) the document had to be one that shaped and/or reflected a significant episode in the history of U.S. foreign affairs and (2) the document had to be one that helped to define America's place in the world. A brief introduction prefaces each document and serves primarily to place chronologically the issue discussed. A short list of further readings has been included as a starting point for students as they begin their own research.

A brief examination of the Contents will reveal a strong bias toward the twentieth century in the selection of documents. This was my intention from the beginning and reflects the way I structure my class. During the initial month or so of the semester I cover the first century of U.S. foreign policy. This allows me to develop major themes such as neutrality, expansion, and the Monroe Doctrine, and still leave adequate time to cover the progressively complex issues of the second century of U.S. foreign affairs. This approach is not unique and I trust that both colleagues and their students will find it satisfactory.

I would like to acknowledge the assistance I received from many generous individuals: Lin Mocejunas, Barb Mater, and Beth Reabold patiently typed numerous drafts; my colleagues Donald Bain, Mieczyslaw Biskupski, and David Devereux at St. John Fisher College offered valuable suggestions as I selected documents; James Valone and Geraldine Valone, Kimberly Valone, and Daniel Carpenter provided the technical assistance without which this book could not have been completed.

DOCUMENT 1

Treaty of Alliance with France

The British defeat at Saratoga in October 1777 convinced the French government to side openly with the Americans seeking their independence. On 6 February 1778 a Treaty of Amity & Commerce and a Treaty of Alliance "forever" binding the two countries were concluded at Paris.[1]

Article 1. If War should break out betwan [*sic*] france and Great Britain, during the continuence of the present War betwan [*sic*] the United States and England, his Majesty and the said united States, shall make it a common cause, and aid each other mutually with their good Offices, their Counsels, and their forces, according to the exigence of Conjunctures as becomes good and faithful Allies.

Article 2. The essential and direct End of the present defensive alliance is to maintain effectually the liberty, Sovereignty, and independance [*sic*] absolute and unlimited of the said united States, as well in Matters of Gouvernement [*sic*] as of commerce. . . .

Article 5. If the united States should think fit to attempt the Reduction of the British Power remaining in the Northern Parts of America, or the Islands of

---

[1]W. M. Malloy, editor, *Treaties, Conventions, International Acts, Protocols and Agreements between the United States of America and other Powers, 1776–1909* (Washington, D.C.: U.S. Government Printing Office, 1910), 1:479–82.

Bermudas, those Contries [*sic*] or Islands in case of Success, shall be confederated with or dependant [*sic*] upon the said united States.

Article 6. The Most Christian King renounces for ever the possession of the Islands of Bermudas as well as of any part of the continent of North america which before the treaty of Paris in 1763, or in virtue of that Treaty, were acknowledged to belong to the Crown of Great Britain, or to the united States heretofore called British Colonies, or which are at this Time or have lately [*sic*] been under the Power of The King and Crown of Great Britain.

Article 7. If his Most Christian Majesty shall think proper to attack any of the Islands situated in the Gulph [*sic*] of Mexico, or near that Gulph, which are at present under the power of Great Britain, all the said Isles, in case of success, shall appertain to the Crown of france.

Article 8. Neither of the two Parties shall conclude either Truce or Peace with Great Britain, without the formal consent of the other first obtain'd; and they mutually engage not to lay down their arms, until the Independence of the united states shall have been formally or tacitly assured by the Treaty or Treaties that shall terminate the War. . . .

Article 10. The Most Christian King and the united States agree to invite or admit other powers who may have received injuries from England, to make a common cause with them, and to accede to the present alliance. . . .

Article 11. The two Parties guarantee mutually from the present time and forever, against all other powers, to wit, the united states to his most Christian Majesty the present Possessions of the Crown of france in America as well as those which it may acquire by the future Treaty of peace: and his most Christian Majesty guarantees on his part to the united states, their liberty, Sovereignty, and Independence absolute, and unlimited, as well in Matters of Government as commerce and also thair[*sic*] Possessions, and the additions or conquests that their Confederation may obtain during the war, from any of the Dominions now or heretofore possessed by Great Britain in North America, conformable to the 5th & 6th articles above written, the whole as their Possessions shall be fixed and assured to the said States at the moment of the cessation of their present War with England.

FURTHER READINGS

Dull, Jonathan, *A Diplomatic History of the American Revolution* (New Haven, Conn.: Yale University Press, 1985).

Eccles, W. J., "The French Alliance and the American Victory," in John Ferling, *The World Turned Upside Down: The American Victory in the War of Independence* (New York: Greenwood, 1988).

Hoffman, Ronald and Alberts, Peter J., editors, *Diplomacy and the Revolution: The Franco-American Alliance of 1778* (Charlottesville: University Press of Virginia, 1981).

Horsman, Reginald, *The Diplomacy of the New Republic* (Arlington Heights, Ill: Davidson, 1985).

Stinchcombe, William, *The American Revolution and the French Alliance* (Syracuse, N.Y.: Syracuse University Press, 1969).

DOCUMENT 2

George Washington's Neutrality Proclamation

The outbreak of war between France and England in February 1793 raised the possibility that the French government would ask the Washington administration to honor the terms of the Alliance of 1778. After discussion with his cabinet, on 22 April 1793, President George Washington issued a proclamation announcing that the United States would "pursue a conduct friendly and impartial toward the belligerent powers." [2]

BY THE PRESIDENT OF THE UNITED STATES OF AMERICA

A Proclamation

Whereas it appears that a state of war exists between Austria, Prussia, Sardinia, Great Britain, and the United Netherlands of the one part and France on the other, and the duty and interest of the United States require that they should with sincerity and good faith adopt and pursue a conduct friendly and impartial toward the belligerent powers:

I have therefore thought fit by these presents to declare the disposition of the United States to observe the conduct aforesaid toward those powers respectively, and to exhort and warn the citizens of the United States carefully to avoid all acts and proceedings whatsoever which may in any manner tend to contravene such disposition.

And I do hereby also make known that whosoever of the citizens of the United States shall render himself liable to punishment or forfeiture under the law of nations by committing, aiding, or abetting hostilities against any of the said powers, or by carrying to any of them those articles which are deemed contraband by the modern usage of nations, will not receive the protection of

---

[2]Eileen Daney Carzo, editor, *National State Papers of the United States 1789–1817* (Wilmington, Delaware: Michael Glazer, Inc., 1985), part II, Texts of Documents, volume 17:282.

the United States against such punishment or forfeiture; and further, that I have given instructions to those officers to whom it belongs to cause prosecutions to be instituted against all persons who shall, within the cognizance of the courts of the United States, violate the law of nations with respect to the powers at war, or any of them.

FURTHER READINGS

Bowman, Albert H., *The Struggle for Neutrality: Franco-American Diplomacy during the Federal Era* (Knoxville: University of Tennessee Press, 1974).

Boyd, Julian P, *Number 7: Alexander Hamilton's Secret Attempts to Control American Foreign Policy* (Princeton, N.J.: Princeton University Press, 1964).

Cooks, Jacob Ernest, *Alexander Hamilton* (New York: Scribner's, 1982).

Lycan, Gilbert, *Alexander Hamilton and American Foreign Policy* (Norman: University of Oklahoma Press, 1970).

McDonald, Forrest, *The Presidency of George Washington* (Lawrence: University Press of Kansas, 1979).

Peterson, Merrill D., *Thomas Jefferson and the New Nation* (New York: Oxford University Press, 1970).

Ritcheson, Charles, *Aftermath of Revolution: British Policy towards the United States 1783–1795* (Dallas: Southern Methodist Press, 1969).

DOCUMENT 3

George Washington's Farewell Address

George Washington announced that he would not seek a third term as president of the United States in his Farewell Address of 17 September 1796.[3] He also used this opportunity to suggest guidelines for future American foreign and domestic policy.

☙☙☙

As a very important source of strength and security, cherish public credit. One method of preserving it is to use it as sparingly as possible, avoiding occasions of expense by cultivating peace, but remembering also that timely disbursements to prepare for danger frequently prevent much greater disbursements to repel it; avoiding likewise the accumulation of debt, not only by shunning occasions of expense, but by vigorous exertions in time of peace to discharge the debts which unavoidable wars have occasioned, not ungenerously

---

[3]James D. Richardson, editor, *A Compilation of Messages and Papers of the Presidents* (N.p.: Bureau of National Literature and Arts, 1903), 1:212–15.

throwing upon posterity the burthen which we ourselves ought to bear. The execution of these maxims belongs to your representatives; but it is necessary that public opinion should cooperate. To facilitate to them the performance of their duty it is essential that you should practically bear in mind that toward the payment of debts there must be revenue; that to have revenue there must be taxes; that no taxes can be devised which are not more or less inconvenient and unpleasant; that the intrinsic embarrassment inseparable from the selection of the proper objects (which is always a choice of difficulties), ought to be a decisive motive for a candid construction of the conduct of the Government in making it, and for a spirit of acquiescence in the measure for obtaining revenue which the public exigencies may at any time dictate.

Observe good faith and justice toward all nations. Cultivate peace and harmony with all. Religion and morality enjoin this conduct. And can it be that good policy does not equally enjoin it? It will be worthy of a free, enlightened, and at no distant period a great nation to give to mankind the magnanimous and too novel example of a people always guided by an exalted justice and benevolence. Who can doubt that in the course of time and things the fruits of such a plan would richly repay any temporary advantages which might be lost by a steady adherence to it? Can it be that Providence has not connected the permanent felicity of a nation with its virtue? The experiment, at least, is recommended by every sentiment which ennobles human nature. Alas! is it rendered impossible by its vices?

In the execution of such a plan nothing is more essential than that permanent, inveterate antipathies against particular nations and passionate attachments for others should be excluded, and that in place of them just and amicable feelings toward all should be cultivated. The nation which indulges toward another an habitual hatred or an habitual fondness is in some degree a slave. It is a slave to its animosity or to its affection, either of which is sufficient to lead it astray from its duty and its interest. Antipathy in one nation against another disposes each more readily to offer insult and injury, to lay hold of slight causes of umbrage, and to be haughty and intractable when accidental or trifling occasions of dispute occur.

Hence frequent collisions, obstinate, envenomed, and bloody contests. The nation prompted by ill will and resentment sometimes impels to war the government contrary to the best calculations of policy. The government sometimes participates in the national propensity, and adopts through passion what reason would reject. At other times it makes the animosity of the nation subservient to projects of hostility, instigated by pride, ambition, and other sinister and pernicious motives. The peace often, sometimes perhaps the liberty, of nations has been the victim.

So, likewise, a passionate attachment of one nation for another produces a variety of evils. Sympathy for the favorite nation, facilitating the illusion of an imaginary common interest in cases where no real common interest exists, and infusing into one the enmities of the other, betrays the former into a participation in the quarrels and wars of the latter without adequate inducement or justification. It leads also to concessions to the favorite nation of privileges denied to others, which is apt doubly to injure the nation making the concessions by unnecessarily parting with what ought to have been retained, and by exciting jealousy, ill will, and a disposition to retaliate in the parties from whom equal privileges are withheld; and it gives to ambitious, corrupted, or deluded citizens (who devote themselves to the favorite nation) facility to betray or sacrifice the interests of their own country without odium, sometimes even with popularity, gilding with the appearances of a virtuous sense of obligation, a commendable deference for public opinion, or a laudable zeal for public good the base or foolish compliances of ambition, corruption, or infatuation.

As avenues to foreign influence in innumerable ways, such attachments are particularly alarming to the truly enlightened and independent patriot. How many opportunities do they afford to tamper with domestic factions, to practice the arts of seduction, to mislead public opinion, to influence or awe the public councils! Such an attachment of a small or weak toward a great and powerful nation dooms the former to be the satellite of the latter. Against the insidious wiles of foreign influence (I conjure you to believe me, fellow-citizens) the jealousy of a free people ought to be *constantly* awake, since history and experience prove that foreign influence is one of the most baneful foes of republican government. But that jealousy, to be useful, must be impartial, else it becomes the instrument of the very influence to be avoided, instead of a defense against it. Excessive partiality for one foreign nation and excessive dislike of another cause those whom they actuate to see danger only on one side, and serve to veil and even second the arts of influence on the other. Real patriots who may resist the intrigues of the favorite are liable to become suspected and odious, while its tools and dupes usurp the applause and confidence of the people to surrender their interests.

The great rule of conduct for us in regard to foreign nations is, in extending our commercial relations to have with them as little *political* connection as possible. So far as we have already formed engagements let them be fulfilled with perfect good faith. Here let us stop.

Europe has a set of primary interests which to us have none or a very remote relation. Hence she must be engaged in frequent controversies, the causes of which are essentially foreign to our concerns. Hence, therefore, it must be unwise in us to implicate ourselves by artificial ties in the ordinary vicissitudes of her politics or the ordinary combinations and collisions of her friendships or enmities.

Our detached and distant situation invites and enables us to pursue a different course. If we remain one people, under an efficient government, the period is not far off when we may defy material injury from external annoyance; when we may take such an attitude as will cause the neutrality we may at any time resolve upon to be scrupulously respected; when belligerent nations, under the impossibility of making acquisitions upon us, will not lightly hazard the giving us provocation; when we may choose peace or war, as our interest, guided by justice, shall counsel.

Why forego the advantages of so peculiar a situation? Why quit our own to stand upon foreign ground? Why, by interweaving our destiny with that of any part of Europe, entangle our peace and prosperity in the toils of European ambition, rivalship, interest, humor, or caprice?

It is our true policy to steer clear of permanent alliances with any portion of the foreign world, so far, I mean, as we are now at liberty to do it; for let me not be understood as capable of patronizing infidelity to existing engagements. I hold the maxim no less applicable to public than to private affairs that honesty is always the best policy. I repeat, therefore, let those engagements be observed in their genuine sense. But in my opinion it is unnecessary and would be unwise to extend them.

Taking care always to keep ourselves by suitable establishments on a respectable defensive posture, we may safely trust to temporary alliances for extraordinary emergencies.

Harmony, liberal intercourse with all nations are recommended by policy, humanity, and interest. But even our commercial policy should hold an equal and impartial hand, neither seeking nor granting exclusive favors or preferences; consulting the natural course of things; diffusing and diversifying by gentle means the streams of commerce, but forcing nothing; establishing with powers so disposed, in order to give trade a stable course, to define the rights of our merchants, and to enable the Government to support them, conventional rules of intercourse, the best that present circumstances and mutual opinion will permit, but temporary and liable to be from time to time abandoned or varied as experience and circumstances shall dictate; constantly keeping in view that it is folly in one nation to look for disinterested favors from another; that it must pay with a portion of its independence for whatever it may accept under that character; that by such acceptance it may place itself in the condition of having given equivalents for nominal favors, and yet of being reproached with ingratitude for not giving more. There can be no greater error than to expect or calculate upon real favors from nation to nation. It is an illusion which experience must cure, which a just pride ought to discard.

In offering to you, my countrymen, these counsels of an old and affectionate friend I dare not hope they will make the strong and lasting impression I could wish—that they will control the usual current of the passions or prevent our nation from running the course which has hitherto marked the destiny of nations. But if I may even flatter myself that they may be productive of some partial benefit, some occasional good—that they may now and then recur to moderate the fury of party spirit, to warn against the mischiefs of foreign intrigue, to guard against the impostures of pretended patriotism—this hope will be a full recompense for the solicitude for your welfare by which they have been dictated.

FURTHER READINGS

Alden, John, *George Washington* (Baton Rouge: Louisiana State University Press, 1984).
Ferling, John E., *The First of Men* (Knoxville: University of Tennessee Press, 1988).
Flexner, James T., *George Washington and the New Nation* (Boston: Little, Brown, 1970).
———, *George Washington: Anguish and Farewell* (Boston: Little, Brown, 1972).
Lycan, Gilbert, *Alexander Hamilton and American Foreign Policy* (Norman: University of Oklahoma Press, 1970).
McDonald, Forrest, *The Presidency of George Washington* (Lawrence: University Press of Kansas, 1979).

DOCUMENT 4

Thomas Jefferson's Inaugural Address

In his inaugural address on 4 March 1801 Thomas Jefferson announced the "essential principles" of government that would shape his administration and would set the young republic on a new path.[4]

About to enter, fellow-citizens, on the exercise of duties which comprehend everything dear and valuable to you, it is proper you should understand what I deem the essential principles of our Government, and consequently those which ought to shape its Administration. I will compress them within the narrowest compass they will bear, stating the general principle, but not all its limitations. Equal and exact justice to all men, of whatever state or persuasion, religious or political; peace, commerce, and honest friendship with all nations, entangling alliances with none; the support of the State governments in all their rights, as the most competent administrations for our domestic concerns and the surest bulwarks against antirepublican tendencies; the preservation of the General Government in its whole constitutional vigor, as the sheet anchor of our peace at home and safety abroad; a jealous care of the right of election by the people—a mild and safe corrective of abuses which are lopped by the sword of

---

[4]James D. Richardson, editor, *A Compilation of Messages and Papers of the Presidents* (N.p.: Bureau of National Literature and Arts, 1903), 1:311–12.

revolution where peaceable remedies are unprovided; absolute acquiescence in the decisions of the majority, the vital principles of republics, from which is no appeal but to force, the vital principle and immediate parent of despotism; a well-disciplined militia, our best reliance in peace and for the first moments of war, till regulars may relieve them; the supremacy of the civil over the military authority; economy in the public expense, that labor may be lightly burthened; the honest payment of our debts and sacred preservation of the public faith; encouragement of agriculture, and of commerce as its handmaid; the diffusion of information and arraignment of all abuses at the bar of public reason; freedom of religion; freedom of the press, and freedom of person under the protection of the habeas corpus, and trial by juries impartially selected. These principles form the bright constellation which has gone before us and guided our steps through an age of revolution and reformation. The wisdom of our sages and blood of our heroes have been devoted to their attainment. They should be the creed of our political faith, the text of civic instruction, the touchstone by which to try the services of those we trust; and should we wander from them in moments of error or of alarm, let us hasten to retrace our steps and to regain the road which alone leads to peace, liberty, and safety.

Further Readings. See Document 5.

DOCUMENT 5

The Louisiana Purchase

In a letter of 18 April 1802 to Robert Livingston, the United States Minister in France, President Jefferson expressed his concern over the cession of Louisiana to France.[5] Within a year Jefferson solved the problem by purchasing the territory, thus doubling in size the "empire of liberty."

The cession of Louisiana and the Floridas by Spain to France works most sorely on the U.S. On this subject the Secretary of State has written to you fully. Yet I cannot forbear recurring to it personally, so deep is the impression it makes in my mind. It completely reverses all the political relations of the U.S. and will form a new epoch in our political course. Of all nations of any consideration France is the one which hitherto has offered the fewest points on which we could have any conflict of right, and the most points of a communion of

---

[5]Paul Leicester Ford, *The Writings of Thomas Jefferson* (New York: G.P. Putnam's Sons, 1892-99), 8:144–45.

interests. From these causes we have ever looked to her as our *natural friend,* as one with which we never could have an occasion of difference. Her growth therefore we viewed as our own, her misfortunes ours. There is on the globe one single spot, the possessor of which is our natural and habitual enemy. It is New Orleans, through which the produce of three-eighths of our territory must pass to market, and from its fertility it will ere long yield more than half of our whole produce and contain more than half our inhabitants. France placing herself in that door assumes to us the attitude of defiance. Spain might have retained it quietly for years. Her pacific dispositions, her feeble state, would induce her to increase our facilities there, so that her possession of the place would be hardly felt by us, and it would not perhaps be very long before some circumstance might arise which might make the cession of it to us the price of something of more worth to her. Not so can it ever be in the hands of France. The impetuosity of her temper, the energy and restlessness of her character, placed in a point of eternal friction with us, and our character, which though quiet, and loving peace and the pursuit of wealth, is high-minded, despising wealth in competition with insult or injury, enterprising and energetic as any nation on earth, these circumstances render it impossible that France and the U. S. can continue long friends when they meet in so irritable a position. They as well as we must be blind if they do not see this; and we must be very improvident if we do not begin to make arrangements on that hypothesis. The day that France takes possession of N. Orleans fixes the sentence which is to restrain her forever within her low-water mark. It seals the union of two nations who in conjunction can maintain exclusive possession of the ocean. From that moment, we must marry ourselves to the British fleet and nation. We must turn all our attentions to a maritime force, for which our resources place us on very high grounds: and having formed and cemented together a power which may render reinforcement of her settlements here impossible to France, make the first cannon, which shall be fired in Europe the signal for tearing up of any settlement she may have made, and for holding the two continents of America in sequestration for the common purposes of the United British and American nations. This is not a state of things we seek or desire. It is one which this measure, if adopted by France, forces on us, as necessarily as any other cause, by the laws of nature, brings on its necessary effect. It is not from a fear of France that we deprecate this measure proposed by her. For however greater her force is than ours compared in the abstract, it is nothing in comparison of ours when to be exerted on our soil. But it is from a sincere love of peace, and a firm persuasion that bound to France by the interests and the strong sympathies still existing in the minds of our citizens, and holding relative positions which insure their continuance we are secure of a long course of peace. Whereas the change of friends, which will be rendered necessary if France changes that position, embarks us necessarily as a belligerent power in the first war of Europe.

FURTHER READINGS FOR DOCUMENTS 4-5

Johnstone, Jr., Robert, *Jefferson and the Presidency* (Ithaca, N.Y.: Cornell University Press, 1978).

Kaplan, Lawrence S., *Entangling Alliances with None: American Foreign Policy in the Age of Jefferson* (Kent, Ohio: Kent State University Press, 1987).

Malone, Dumas, *Thomas Jefferson as Political Leader* (Berkeley: University of California Press, 1963).

McDonald, Forrest, *The Presidency of Thomas Jefferson* (Lawrence: University Press of Kansas, 1976).

Peterson, Merrill D., *Thomas Jefferson and the New Nation* (New York: Oxford University Press, 1970).

Tucker, Robert W. and Hendrickson, David C., *Empire of Liberty: The Statecraft of Thomas Jefferson* (New York: Oxford University Press, 1990).

Varg, Paul A., *Foreign Policies of the Founding Fathers* (Baltimore: Penguin Books, 1970).

DOCUMENT 6

James Madison's War Message to Congress

The almost constant warfare between England and France presented Americans with the lucrative temptation of wartime profits by trading with the belligerent powers. However, the British with their orders in council and Napoleon with his Continental System sought to prevent such trade from reaching their respective enemies. Ultimately on 1 June 1812 President James Madison addressed Congress to make the case that only war with England could remedy the situation.[6]

☙☙

TO THE SENATE AND HOUSE OF REPRESENTATIVES OF THE UNITED STATES:

I communicate to Congress certain documents, being a continuation of those heretofore laid before them on the subject of our affairs with Great Britain.

Without going back beyond the renewal in 1803 of the war in which Great Britain is engaged, and omitting unrepaired wrongs of inferior magnitude, the

---

[6]James D. Richardson, editor, *A Compilation of Messages and Papers of the Presidents* (N.p.: Bureau of National Literature and Arts, 1903), 2:484–90.

conduct of her Government presents a series of acts hostile to the United States as an independent and neutral nation.

British cruisers have been in the continued practice of violating the American flag on the great highway of nations, and of seizing and carrying off persons sailing under it, not in the exercise of a belligerent right founded on the law of nations against an enemy, but of a municipal prerogative over British subjects. British jurisdiction is thus extended to neutral vessels in a situation where no laws can operate but the law of nations and the laws of the country to which the vessels belong, and a self-redress is assumed which, if British subjects were wrongfully detained and alone concerned, is that substitution of force for a resort to the responsible sovereign which falls within the definition of war. Could the seizure of British subjects in such cases be regarded as within the exercise of a belligerent right, the acknowledged laws of war, which forbid an article of captured property to be adjudged without a regular investigation before a competent tribunal, would imperiously demand the fairest trial where the sacred rights of persons were at issue. In place of such a trial these rights are subjected to the will of every petty commander.

The practice, hence, is so far from affecting British subjects alone that, under the pretext of searching for these, thousands of American citizens, under the safeguard of public law and of their national flag, have been torn from their country and from everything dear to them; have been dragged on board ships of war of a foreign nation and exposed, under the severities of their discipline, to be exiled to the most distant and deadly climes, to risk their lives in the battles of their oppressors, and to be the melancholy instruments of taking away those of their own brethren.

Against this crying enormity, which Great Britain would be so prompt to avenge if committed against herself, the United States have in vain exhausted remonstrances and expostulations, and that no proof might be wanting of their conciliatory dispositions, and no pretext left for a continuance of the practice, the British Government was formally assured of the readiness of the United States to enter into arrangements such as could not be rejected if the recovery of British subjects were the real and the sole object. The communication passed without effect.

British cruisers have been in the practice also of violating the rights and the peace of our coasts. They hover over and harass our entering and departing commerce. To the most insulting pretensions they have added the most lawless proceedings in our very harbors, and have wantonly spilt American blood within the sanctuary of our territorial jurisdiction. The principles and rules enforced by that nation, when a neutral nation, against armed vessels of belligerents hovering near her coasts and disturbing her commerce are well known. When called on, nevertheless, by the United States to punish the greater offenses committed by her own vessels, her Government has bestowed on their commanders additional marks of honor and confidence. . . .

Not content with these occasional expedients for laying waste our neutral trade, the cabinet of Britain resorted at length to the sweeping system of blockades, under the name of orders in council, which has been molded and managed as might best suit its political views, its commercial jealousies, or the avidity of British cruisers. . . .

In reviewing the conduct of Great Britain toward the United States our attention is necessarily drawn to the warfare just renewed by the savages on one of our extensive frontiers—a warfare which is known to spare neither age nor sex and to be distinguished by features peculiarly shocking to humanity. It is difficult to account for the activity and combinations which have for some time been developing themselves among tribes in constant intercourse with British traders and garrisons without connecting their hostility with that influence and without recollecting the authenticated examples of such interpositions heretofore furnished by the officers and agents of that Government. . . .

Other counsels have prevailed. Our moderation and conciliation have had no other effect than to encourage perseverance and to enlarge pretensions. We behold our seafaring citizens still the daily victims of lawless violence, committed on the great common and highway of nations, even within sight of the country which owes them protection. We behold our vessels, freighted with the products of our soil and industry, or returning with honest proceeds of them, wrested from their lawful destinations, confiscated by prize courts no longer the organs of public law but the instruments of arbitrary edicts, and their unfortunate crews dispersed and lost, or forced or inveigled in British ports into British fleets, whilst arguments are employed in support of these aggressions which have no foundation but in a principle equally supporting a claim to regulate our external commerce in all cases whatsoever.

We behold, in fine, on the side of Great Britain a state of war against the United States, and on the side of the United States a state of peace toward Great Britain.

Whether the United States shall continue passive under these progressive usurpations and these accumulating wrongs, or, opposing force to force in defense of their national rights, shall commit a just cause into the hands of the Almighty Disposer of Events, avoiding all connections which might entangle it in the contest or views of other powers, and preserving a constant readiness to concur in an honorable reestablishment of peace and friendship, is a solemn question which the Constitution wisely confides to the legislative department of the Government. In recommending it to their early deliberations I am happy in the assurance that the decision will be worthy the enlightened and patriotic councils of a virtuous, a free, and a powerful nation.

Having presented this view of the relations of the United States with Great Britain and of the solemn alternative growing out of them, I proceed to remark that the communications last made to Congress on the subject of our relations with France will have shewn that since the revocation of her decrees, as they violated the neutral rights of the United States, her Government has authorized illegal captures by its privateers and public ships, and that other outrages have been practiced on our vessels and our citizens. It will have been seen also that no indemnity had been provided or satisfactorily pledged for the extensive spoliations committed under the violent and retrospective orders of the French Government against the property of our citizens seized within the jurisdiction of France. I abstain at this time from recommending to the consideration of Congress definitive measures with respect to that nation, in the expectation that the result of unclosed discussions between our minister plenipotentiary at Paris and the French Government will speedily enable Congress to decide with greater advantage on the course due to the rights, the interests, and the honor of our country.

FURTHER READINGS

Brown, Roger, *The Republic in Peril* (New York: Columbia University Press, 1964).

Coles, Harry, *The War of 1812* (Chicago: University of Chicago Press, 1965).

Hatzenbuehler, Ronald and Ivie, Robert, *Congress Declares War* (Kent, Ohio: Kent State University Press, 1983).

Hickey, Donald R., *The War of 1812: A Forgotten Conflict* (Urbana: University of Illinois Press, 1989).

Ketcham, Ralph, *James Madison* (New York: Macmillan, 1971).

Spivak, Burton, *Jefferson's English Crisis* (Charlottesville: University Press of Virginia, 1979).

Stagg, J.C.A., *Mr. Madison's War: Politics, Diplomacy, and Warfare in the Early American Republic, 1783–1830* (Princeton, N.J.: Princeton University Press, 1983).

Stuart, Reginald, *United States Expansionism and British North America, 1775-1871* (Chapel Hill: University of North Carolina Press, 1988).

DOCUMENT 7

The Monroe Doctrine

In August 1823 British Foreign Minister George Canning sought a joint Anglo-American agreement opposing possible European intervention in Spain's former American empire. Secretary of State John Quincy Adams convinced President James Monroe that a unilateral policy would be "more candid as well as more dignified," and on 2 December 1823 the president announced what would be called "The Monroe Doctrine" to Congress.[7]

FELLOW-CITIZENS OF THE SENATE AND HOUSE OF REPRESENTATIVES:

A precise knowledge of our relations with foreign powers as respects our negotiations and transactions with each is thought to be particularly necessary. Equally necessary is it that we should form a just estimate of our resources, revenue, and progress in every kind of improvement connected with the national prosperity and public defense. It is by rendering justice to other nations that we may expect it from them. It is by our ability to resent injuries and redress wrongs that we may avoid them. . . .

At the proposal of the Russian Imperial Government, made through the minister of the Emperor residing here, a full power and instructions have been transmitted to the minister of the United States at St. Petersburg to arrange by amicable negotiation the respective rights and interests of the two nations on the northwest coast of this continent. A similar proposal had been made by His Imperial Majesty to the Government of Great Britain, which has likewise been acceded to. The Government of the United States has been desirous by this friendly proceeding of manifesting the great value which they have invariably attached to the friendship of the Emperor and their solicitude to cultivate the best understanding with his Government. In the discussions to which this interest has given rise and in the arrangements by which they may terminate the occasion has been judged proper for asserting, as a principle in which the rights and interests of the United States are involved, that the American continents, by the free and independent condition which they have assumed and maintain, are henceforth not to be considered as subjects for future colonization by any European powers. . . .

---

[7]James D. Richardson, editor, *A Compilation of Messages and Papers of the Presidents* (N.p.: Bureau of National Literature and Arts, 1903), 2:776–78.

It was stated at the commencement of the last session that a great effort was then making in Spain and Portugal to improve the condition of the people of those countries, and that it appeared to be conducted with extraordinary moderation. It need scarcely be remarked that the result has been so far very different from what was then anticipated. Of events in that quarter of the globe, with which we have so much intercourse and from which we derive our origin, we have always been anxious and interested spectators. The citizens of the United States cherish sentiments the most friendly in favor of the liberty and happiness of their fellow-men on that side of the Atlantic. In the wars of the European powers in matters relating to themselves we have never taken any part, nor does it comport with our policy so to do. It is only when our rights are invaded or seriously menaced that we resent injuries or make preparations for our defense. With the movements in this hemisphere we are of necessity more immediately connected, and by causes which must be obvious to all enlightened and impartial observers. The political system of the allied powers is essentially different in this respect from that of America. . . . We owe it, therefore, to candor and to the amicable relations existing between the United States and those powers to declare that we should consider any attempt on their part to extend their system to any portion of this hemisphere as dangerous to our peace and safety. With the existing colonies or dependencies of any European power we have not interfered and shall not interfere. But with the Governments who have declared their independence and maintained it, and whose independence we have, on great consideration and on just principles, acknowledged, we could not view any interposition for the purpose of oppressing them, or controlling in any other manner their destiny, by any European power in any other light than as the manifestation of an unfriendly disposition toward the United States.

FURTHER READINGS

Ammon, Harry, *James Monroe* (New York: McGraw-Hill, 1970).

Bemis, Samuel Flagg, *John Quincy Adams and the Foundations of American Foreign Policy* (New York: Knopf, 1949).

Langley, Lester D., *Struggle for the American Mediterranean* (Athens: University of Georgia Press, 1976).

May, Ernest R., *The Making of the Monroe Doctrine* (Cambridge, Mass.: Harvard University Press, 1975).

Perkins, Bradford, *Castlereagh and Adams* (Berkeley: University of California Press, 1964).

Perkins, Dexter, *A History of the Monroe Doctrine* (Boston: Little, Brown, 1963).

DOCUMENT 8

Indian Removal

President Andrew Jackson outlined to Congress on 8 December 1830 his solution to the Indian question recommending that the Native Americans be separated from whites by relocating them west of the Mississippi River.[8]

It gives me pleasure to announce to Congress that the benevolent policy of Government, steadily pursued for nearly thirty years, in relation to the removal of the Indians beyond the white settlements is approaching to a happy consummation. Two important tribes have accepted the provision made for their removal at the last session of Congress, and it is believed that their example will induce the remaining tribes also to seek the same obvious advantages.

The consequences of a speedy removal will be important to the United States, to individual States, and to the Indians themselves. The pecuniary advantages which it promises to the Government are the least of its recommendations. It puts an end to all possible danger of collision between the authorities of the General and State Governments on account of the Indians. It will place a dense and civilized population in large tracts of country now occupied by a few savage hunters. By opening the whole territory between Tennessee on the north and Louisiana on the south to the settlement of the whites it will incalculably strengthen the southwestern frontier and render the adjacent States strong enough to repel future invasions without remote aid. It will relieve the whole State of Mississippi and the western part of Alabama of Indian occupancy, and enable those States to advance rapidly in population, wealth, and power. It will separate the Indians from immediate contact with settlements of whites; free them from the power of the States; enable them to pursue happiness in their own way and under their own rude institutions; will retard the progress of decay, which is lessening their numbers, and perhaps cause them gradually, under the protection of the Government and through the influence of good counsels, to cast off their savage habits and become an interesting, civilized, and Christian community. These consequences, some of them so certain and the rest so probable, make the complete execution of the plan sanctioned by Congress at their last session an object of much solicitude.

Toward the aborigines of the country no one can indulge a more friendly feeling than myself, or would go further in attempting to reclaim them from

---

[8]James D. Richardson, editor, *A Compilation of Messages and Papers of the Presidents* (N.p.: Bureau of National Literature and Arts, 1903), 3:1082–86.

their wandering habits and make them a happy, prosperous people. I have endeavored to impress upon them my own solemn convictions of the duties and powers of the General Government in relation to the State authorities. For the justice of the laws passed by the States within the scope of their reserved powers they are not responsible to this Government. As individuals we may entertain and express our opinions of their acts, but as a Government we have as little right to control them as we have to prescribe laws for other nations. . . .

Humanity has often wept over the fate of the aborigines of this country, and Philanthropy has been long busily employed in devising means to avert it, but its progress has never for a moment been arrested, and one by one have many powerful tribes disappeared from the earth. To follow to the tomb the last of his race and to tread on the graves of extinct nations excite melancholy reflections. But true philanthropy reconciles the mind to these vicissitudes as it does to the extinction of one generation to make room for another. In the monuments and fortresses of an unknown people, spread over the extensive regions of the West, we behold the memorials of a once powerful race, which was exterminated or has disappeared to make room for the existing savage tribes. Nor is there anything in this which, upon a comprehensive view of the general interests of the human race, is to be regretted. Philanthropy could not wish to see this continent restored to the condition in which it was found by our forefathers. What good man would prefer a country covered with forests and ranged by a few thousand savages to our extensive Republic, studded with cities, towns, and prosperous farms, embellished with all the improvements which art can devise or industry execute, occupied by more than 12,000,000 happy people, and filled with all the blessings of liberty, civilization, and religion?

The present policy of the Government is but a continuation of the same progressive change by a milder process. The tribes which occupied the countries now constituting the Eastern States were annihilated or have melted away to make room for the whites. The waves of population and civilization are rolling to the westward, and we now propose to acquire the countries occupied by the red men of the South and West by a fair exchange, and, at the expense of the United States, to send them to a land where their existence may be prolonged and perhaps made perpetual. Doubtless it will be painful to leave the graves of their fathers; but what do they more than our ancestors did or than our children are now doing? To better their condition in an unknown land our forefathers left all that was dear in earthly objects. Our children by thousands yearly leave the land of their birth to seek new homes in distant regions. Does Humanity weep at these painful separations from everything, animate and inanimate, with which the young heart has become entwined? Far from it. It is rather a source of joy that our country affords scope where our young population may range unconstrained in body or in mind, developing the power and faculties of man in their highest perfection. These remove hundreds and almost thousands of miles at their own expense, purchase the lands they occupy, and support themselves at their new homes from the moment of their arrival. Can it be cruel in this Government when, by events which it can not control, the Indian is made discontented in his ancient home to purchase his lands, to give him a new and extensive territory, to pay the expense of his removal, and support him a year in his new abode? How many thousands of our own people would gladly embrace the opportunity of removing to the West on such conditions! If the offers made to the Indians were extended to them, they would be hailed with gratitude and joy.

And is it supposed that the wandering savage has a stronger attachment to his home than the settled, civilized Christian? Is it more afflicting to him to leave the graves of his fathers than it is to our brothers and children? Rightly considered, the policy of the General Government toward the red man is not only liberal, but generous. He is unwilling to submit to the laws of the States and mingle with their population. To save him from this alternative, or perhaps utter annihilation, the General Government kindly offers him a new home, and proposes to pay the whole expense of his removal and settlement. . . .

May we not hope, therefore, that all good citizens, and none more zealously than those who think the Indians oppressed by subjection to the laws of the States, will unite in attempting to open the eyes of those children of the forest to their true condition, and by a speedy removal to relieve them from all the evils, real or imaginary, present or prospective, with which they may be supposed to be threatened.

FURTHER READINGS

Belohlavek, John M., *"Let the Eagle Soar!" The Foreign Policy of Andrew Jackson* (Lincoln: University of Nebraska Press, 1985).

Prucha, Francis P., *American Indian Policy in the Formative Years: Indian Trade and the Intercourse Acts, 1890–1834* (Cambridge, Mass.: Harvard University Press, 1962).

———, *The Great Father: The United States Government and the American Indians* (Lincoln: University of Nebraska Press, 1984).

Remini, Robert V., *Andrew Jackson and the Course of American Freedom, 1822–1832* (New York: Harper & Row, 1981).

Rogin, Michael Paul, *Fathers and Children: Andrew Jackson and the Subjugation of the American Indian* (New York: Knopf, 1975).

Satz, Ronald W., *American Indian Policy in the Jackson Era* (Lincoln: University of Nebraska Press, 1975).

Van Deusen, Glyndon G., *The Jackson Era, 1828–1848* (New York: Harper & Row, 1963).

DOCUMENT 9

The Democratic Party Platform of 1844

In 1844 the Democratic Party adopted an avowedly expansionistic plank in its platform.[9] The party's nominee, James K. Polk, narrowly defeated Henry Clay for the presidency, opening a new era of westward expansion.

꣠꣠

Resolved, That our title to the whole of the Territory of Oregon is clear and unquestionable; that no portion of the same ought to be ceded to England or any other power, and that the re-occupation of Oregon and the re-annexation of Texas at the earliest practicable period are great American measures, which this Convention recommends to the cordial support of the Democracy of the Union.

FURTHER READINGS

Bergeron, Paul H., *The Presidency of James K. Polk* (Lawrence: University Press of Kansas, 1987).

Brown, Charles H., *Agents of Manifest Destiny* (Chapel Hill: University of North Carolina Press, 1980).

Goetzmann, William H., *New Lands, New Men* (New York: Viking Press, 1987).

Hietala, Thomas R., *Manifest Design* (Ithaca, N.Y.: Cornell University Press, 1985).

Merk, Frederick, *The Oregon Question* (Cambridge, Mass.: Harvard University Press, 1967).

Sellers, Charles G., *James K. Polk: Continentalist, 1843–1846* (Princeton, N.J.: Princeton University Press, 1966).

---

[9]Kirk H. Porter and Donald Bruce Johnson, editors, *National Party Platforms 1840–1856* (Urbana, Ill.: University of Illinois Press, 1956), 4.

DOCUMENT 10

Manifest Destiny

John Lewis O'Sullivan gave a name to America's westward expansion in an 1845 issue of The United States Magazine and Democratic Review *when he wrote that "our manifest destiny is to overspread the continent allotted by providence for the free development of our yearly multiplying millions."*[10]

฿฿

ANNEXATION

It is time now for opposition to the Annexation of Texas to cease, all further agitation of the waters of bitterness and strife, at least in connexion with this question,—even though it may perhaps be required of us as a necessary condition of the freedom of our institutions, that we must live on for ever in a state of unpausing struggle and excitement upon some subject of party division or other. But, in regard to Texas, enough has now been given to Party. It is time for the common duty of Patriotism to the Country to succeed;—or if this claim will not be recognized, it is at least time for common sense to acquiesce with decent grace in the inevitable and the irrevocable.

Texas is now ours. Already, before these words are written, her Convention has undoubtedly ratified the acceptance, by her Congress, of our proffered invitation into the Union; and made the requisite changes in her already republican form of constitution to adopt it to its future federal relations. Her star and her stripe may already be said to have taken their place in the glorious blazon of our common nationality; and the sweep of our eagle's wing already includes within its circuit the wide extent of her fair and fertile land. She is no longer to us a mere geographical space—a certain combination of coast, plain, mountain, valley, forest and stream. She is no longer to us a mere country on the map. She comes within the dear and sacred designation of Our Country; no longer a "*pays*," she is a part of "*la patrie*;" and that which is at once a sentiment and a virtue, Patriotism, already begins to thrill for her too within the national heart. It is time then that all should cease to treat her as alien, and even adverse—cease to denounce and vilify all and everything connected with her accession—cease to thwart and oppose the remaining steps for its consummation; or where such efforts are felt to be unavailing, at least to embitter the hour of reception by all the most ungracious frowns of aversion and words of unwelcome. There has been enough of all this. It has had its fitting day during the period when, in common with every other possible

---

[10]*Democratic Review*, 17, no. 85 (July–August 1845): 5–6.

question of practical policy that can arise, it unfortunately became one of the leading topics of party division, of presidential electioneering. But that period has passed, and with it let its prejudices and its passions, its discords and its denunciations, pass away too. The next session of Congress will see the representatives of the new young State in their places in both our halls of national legislation, side by side with those of the old Thirteen. Let their reception into "the family" be frank, kindly, and cheerful, as befits such an occasion, as comports not less with our own self-respect than patriotic duty towards them. Ill betide those foul birds that delight to 'file their own nest, and disgust the ear with perpetual discord of ill-omened croak.

Why, were other reasoning wanting, in favor of now elevating this question of the reception of Texas into the Union, out of the lower region of our past party dissensions, up to its proper level of a high and broad nationality, it surely is to be found, found abundantly, in the manner in which other nations have undertaken to intrude themselves into it, between us and the proper parties to the case, in a spirit of hostile interference against us, for the avowed object of thwarting our policy and hampering our power, limiting our greatness and checking the fulfillment of our manifest destiny to overspread the continent allotted by Providence for the free development of our yearly multiplying millions. This we have seen done by England, our old rival and enemy; and by France, strangely coupled with her against us, under the influence of the Anglicism strongly tinging the policy of her present Prime Minister, Guizot. The zealous activity with which this effort to defeat us was pushed by the representatives of those governments, together with the character of intrigue accompanying it, fully constituted that case of foreign interference, which Mr. Clay himself declared should, and would unite us all in maintaining the common cause of our country against the foreigner and the foe. We are only astonished that this effect has not been more fully and strongly produced, and that the burst of indignation against the unauthorized, insolent and hostile interference against us, has not been more general even among the party before opposed to Annexation, and has not rallied the national spirit and national pride unanimously upon that policy. We are very sure that if Mr. Clay himself were now to add another letter to his former Texas correspondence, he would express this sentiment, and carry out the idea already strongly stated in one of them, in a manner which would tax all the powers of blushing belonging to some of his party adherents.

It is wholly untrue, and unjust to ourselves, the pretence that the Annexation has been a measure of spoliation, unrightful and unrighteous—of military conquest under forms of peace and law—of territorial aggrandizement at the expense of justice, and justice due by a double sanctity to the weak. This view of the question is wholly unfounded, and has been before so amply refuted in these pages, as well as in a thousand other modes, that we shall not again dwell upon it. The independence of Texas was complete and absolute. It was an independence, not only in fact but of right. No obligation of duty towards Mexico tended in the least degree to restrain our right to effect the desired recovery of the fair province once our own—whatever motives of policy might have prompted a more deferential consideration of her feelings and her pride, as involved in the question. If Texas became peopled with an American population, it was by no contrivance of our government, but on the express invitation of that of Mexico herself; accompanied with such guarantees of State independence, and the maintenance of a federal system analogous to our own, as constituted a compact fully justifying the strongest measures of redress on the part of those afterwards deceived in this guaranty, and sought to be enslaved under the yoke imposed by its violation. She was released, rightfully and absolutely released, from all Mexican allegiance, or duty of cohesion to the Mexican political body, by the acts and fault of Mexico herself, and Mexico alone. There never was a clearer case. It was not revolution; it was resistance to revolution; and resistance under such circumstances as left independence the necessary resulting state, caused by the abandonment of those with whom her former federal association had existed. What then can be more preposterous than all this clamor by Mexico and the Mexican interest, against Annexation, as a violation of any rights of hers, any duties of ours?

FURTHER READINGS

Bauer, K. Jack, *Zachary Taylor* (Baton Rouge: Louisiana State University Press, 1985).

Bergeron, Paul H., *The Presidency of James K. Polk* (Lawrence: University Press of Kansas, 1987).

Drinnon, Richard, *Facing West* (Minneapolis: University of Minnesota Press, 1980).

Johannsen, Robert, *To the Halls of Montezuma* (New York: Oxford University Press, 1985).

Merk, Frederick, *Manifest Destiny and Mission in American History* (New York: Knopf, 1963).

————, *The Oregon Question* (Cambridge, Mass.: Belknap Press of Harvard University Press, 1967).

Schroeder, John H., *Mr. Polk's War* (Madison: University of Wisconsin Press, 1973).

DOCUMENT 11

Abraham Lincoln's Blockade Proclamation

On 19 April 1861 President Abraham Lincoln announced that the United States Government would blockade the ports of those states that had seceded from the Union.[11]

☙☙☙

BY THE PRESIDENT OF THE UNITED STATES OF AMERICA

A Proclamation

Whereas an insurrection against the Government of the United States has broken out in the States of South Carolina, Georgia, Alabama, Florida, Mississippi, Louisiana, and Texas, and the laws of the United States for the collection of the revenue cannot be effectually executed therein conformably to that provision of the Constitution which requires duties to be uniform throughout the United States:

And whereas a combination of persons engaged in such insurrection have threatened to grant pretended letters of marque to authorize the bearers thereof to commit assaults on the lives, vessels, and property of good citizens of the country lawfully engaged in commerce on the high seas, and in waters of the United States:

And whereas an executive proclamation has been already issued requiring the persons engaged in these disorderly proceedings to desist therefrom, calling out a militia force for the purpose of repressing the same, and convening Congress in extraordinary session to deliberate and determine thereon:

Now, therefore, I, Abraham Lincoln, President of the United States, with a view to the same purposes before mentioned, and to the protection of the public peace, and the lives and property of quiet and orderly citizens pursuing their lawful occupations, until Congress shall have assembled and deliberated on the said unlawful proceedings, or until the same shall have ceased, have further deemed it advisable to set on foot a blockade of the ports within the States aforesaid, in pursuance of the laws of the United States, and of the law of Nations in such case provided. For this purpose a competent force will be posted so as to prevent entrance and exit of vessels from the ports aforesaid. If, therefore, with a view to violate such blockade, a vessel shall approach or shall attempt to leave either [*sic*] of the said ports, she will be duly warned by the commander of one of the blockading vessels, who will indorse [*sic*] on her

---

[11]Arthur Brooks Lapsley, editor, *The Writings of Abraham Lincoln* (N.Y.: G.P. Putnam's Sons, 1905–06), 286–88.

register the fact and date of such warning, and if the same vessel shall again attempt to enter or leave the blockaded port, she will be captured and sent to the nearest convenient port, for such proceedings against her and her cargo, as prize, as may be deemed advisable.

And I hereby proclaim and declare that if any person, under the pretended authority of the said States, or under any other pretense, shall molest a vessel of the United States, or the persons or cargo on board of her, such person will be held amenable to the laws of the United States for the prevention and punishment of piracy.

FURTHER READINGS

Blumenthal, Henry, *A Reappraisal of Franco-American Relations* (Chapel Hill: University of North Carolina Press, 1959).

Case, Lynn M. and Spencer, Warren F., *The United States and France: Civil War Diplomacy* (Philadelphia: University of Pennsylvania Press, 1970).

Crook, D. P., *Diplomacy during the American Civil War* (New York: Wiley, 1975).

———, *The North, the South, and the Powers, 1861–1865* (New York: Wiley, 1974).

Jenkins, Brian, *Britain and the War for the Union* (Montreal: McGill-Queen's University Press, 1974–80).

Van Deusen, Glyndon, *William H. Seward* (New York: Oxford University Press, 1967).

DOCUMENT 12

Suspension of the Monroe Doctrine

Emperor Napoleon III of France exploited America's distraction with the Civil War by sending troops to Mexico in support of a government headed by Maximilian of Austria. Secretary of State William H. Seward explained the United States position toward this conflict to Minister John L. Motley in Vienna on 9 October 1863.[12]

꙰꙰꙰

I speak next of the relations of France towards Mexico. Until 1860 our prestige was a protection to her and to all the other Republican States on this continent. That prestige has been temporarily broken up by domestic faction and civil war. France has invaded Mexico and war exists between those two countries. The United States holds in regard to those two states and their conflict the same principle that they hold in relation to all other nations and their mutual wars.

---

[12]Seward to Motley, #45, 9 October 1863, Department of State, National Archives.

They have neither a right nor any disposition to intervene by force in the internal affairs of Mexico, whether to establish or to maintain a Republican or even a domestic government there or to overthrow an imperial or a foreign one if Mexico shall choose to establish or accept it. The United States have not a right or a disposition to intervene by force on either side in the lamentable war which is going on between France and Mexico. On the contrary they practise in regard to Mexico in every phase of the war the nonintervention which they require all foreign powers to observe in regard to the United States.

But notwithstanding this self-restraint this Government knows full well that the inherent normal opinion of Mexico favors a government there, republican in form and democratic in its organization in preference to any monarchical institutions to be imposed from abroad.

FURTHER READINGS

Blumenthal, Henry, *A Reappraisal of Franco-American Relations* (Chapel Hill: University of North Carolina Press, 1959).

Callahan, James Morton, *American Foreign Policy in Mexican Relations* (New York: Cooper Square Publishers, 1967).

Case, Lynn M. and Spencer, Warren F., *The United States and France: Civil War Diplomacy* (Philadelphia: University of Pennsylvania Press, 1970).

Van Deusen, Glyndon, *William H. Seward* (New York: Oxford University Press, 1967).

DOCUMENT 13

Reassertion of the Monroe Doctrine

With the end of the Civil War, Secretary of State William H. Seward gradually pressed the French government of Napoleon III to withdraw its support for Maximilian's regime in Mexico. On 6 April 1866 Seward responded to word that Austrian troops might replace the French by sending these instructions to Minister John L. Motley at Vienna.[13]

҂҂

It is thought proper that you should state that, in the event of hostilities being carried on hereafter in Mexico by Austrian subjects, under the command or with the sanction of the government of Vienna, the United States will feel themselves at liberty to regard those hostilities as constituting a state of war by Austria against the republic of Mexico; and in regard to such a war, waged at

---

[13]*Papers Relating to the Foreign Relations of the United States, 1866* (Washington, D.C.: U.S. Government Printing Office, 1866), 3:833.

this time and under existing circumstances, the United States could not engage to remain as silent or neutral spectators.

The President may desire to call the attention of Congress to this interesting subject.

FURTHER READINGS

Blumenthal, Henry, *A Reappraisal of Franco-American Relations* (Chapel Hill: University of North Carolina Press, 1959).

Callahan, James Morton, *American Foreign Policy in Mexican Relations* (New York: Cooper Square Publishers, 1967).

Case, Lynn M. and Spencer, Warren F., *The United States and France: Civil War Diplomacy* (Philadelphia: University of Pennsylvania Press, 1970).

Valone, Stephen J., " 'A Matter of Serious Concern': William H. Seward and the Austrian Crisis of 1866," *Diplomatic History,* forthcoming.

Van Deusen, Glyndon, *William H. Seward* (New York: Oxford University Press, 1967).

DOCUMENT 14

The Influence of Seapower on History

At the close of the nineteenth century a growing number of Americans spoke out in favor of an expansionistic foreign policy. One such advocate was Alfred Thayer Mahan of the Naval War College, who was one of the foremost naval theorists of the nineteenth century. In his book The Influence of Seapower upon History, *Mahan argued that overseas possessions and a navy to protect them were essential for the long-term health of the United States.*[14]

To turn now from the particular lessons drawn from the history of the past to the general question of the influence of government upon the sea career of its people, it is seen that influence can work in two distinct but closely related ways.

First, in peace: The government by its policy can favor the natural growth of a people's industries and its tendencies to seek adventure and gain by way of the sea; or it can try to develop such industries and such sea-going bent, when they do not naturally exist; or, on the other hand, the government may by mistaken action check and fetter the progress which the people left to

---

[14]Alfred Thayer Mahan, *The Influence of Seapower upon History, 1660–1783* (Boston: Little, Brown & Co., 1894), 81–88 passim.

themselves would make. In any one of these ways the influence of the government will be felt, making or marring the sea power of the country in the matter of peaceful commerce; upon which alone, it cannot be too often insisted, a thoroughly strong navy can be based.

Secondly, for war: The influence of the government will be felt in its most legitimate manner in maintaining an armed navy, of a size commensurate with the growth of its shipping and the importance of the interests connected with it. More important even than the size of the navy is the question of its institutions, favoring a healthful spirit and activity, and providing for rapid development in time of war by an adequate reserve of men and of ships and by measures for drawing out that general reserve power which has before been pointed to, when considering the character and pursuits of the people. Undoubtedly under this second head of warlike preparation must come the maintenance of suitable naval stations, in those distant parts of the world to which the armed shipping must follow the peaceful vessels of commerce. The protection of such stations must depend either upon direct military force, as do Gibraltar and Malta, or upon a surrounding friendly population, such as the American colonists once were to England, and, it may be presumed, the Australian colonists now are. Such friendly surroundings and backing, joined to a reasonable military provision, are the best of defences, and when combined with decided preponderance at sea, make a scattered and extensive empire, like that of England, secure; for while it is true that an unexpected attack may cause disaster in some one quarter, the actual superiority of naval power prevents such disaster from being general or irremediable. History has sufficiently proved this. England's naval bases have been in all parts of the world; and her fleets have at once protected them, kept open the communications between them, and relied upon them for shelter.

Colonies attached to the mother-country afford, therefore, the surest means of supporting abroad the sea power of a country. In peace, the influence of the government should be felt in promoting by all means a warmth of attachment and a unity of interest which will make the welfare of one the welfare of all, and the quarrel of one the quarrel of all; and in war, or rather for war, by inducing such measures of organization and defence as shall be felt by all to be a fair distribution of a burden of which each reaps the benefit.

Such colonies the United States has not and is not likely to have. As regards purely military naval stations, the feeling of her people was probably accurately expressed by an historian of the English navy a hundred years ago, speaking then of Gibraltar and Port Mahon. "Military governments," said he, "agree so little with the industry of a trading people, and are in themselves so repugnant to the genius of the British people, that I do not wonder that men of good sense and of all parties have inclined to give up these, as Tangiers was given up." Having therefore no foreign establishments, either colonial or military, the ships of war of the United States, in war, will be like land birds, unable to fly far from their own shores. To provide resting-places for them, where they can coal and repair, would be one of the first duties of a government proposing to itself the development of the power of the nation at sea.

As the practical object of this inquiry is to draw from the lessons of history inferences applicable to one's own country and service, it is proper now to ask how far the conditions of the United States involve serious danger, and call for action on the part of the government, in order to build again her sea power. It will not be too much to say that the action of the government since the Civil War, and up to this day, has been effectively directed solely to what has been called the first link in the chain which makes sea power. Internal development, great production, with the accompanying aim and boast of self-sufficingness, such has been the object, such to some extent the result. In this the government has faithfully reflected the bent of the controlling elements of the country, though it is not always easy to feel that such controlling elements are truly representative, even in a free country. However that may be, there is no doubt that, besides having no colonies, the intermediate link of a peaceful shipping, and the interests involved in it, are now likewise lacking. In short, the United States has only one link of the three. . . .

The question is eminently one in which the influence of the government should make itself felt, to build up for the nation a navy which, if not capable of reaching distant countries, shall at least be able to keep clear the chief approaches to its own. The eyes of the country have for a quarter of a century been turned from the sea; the results of such a policy and of its opposite will be shown in the instance of France and of England. Without asserting a narrow parallelism between the case of the United States and either of these, it may safely be said that it is essential to the welfare of the whole country that the conditions of trade and commerce should remain, as far as possible, unaffected by an external war. In order to do this, the enemy must be kept not only out of our ports, but far away from our coasts.

Can this navy be had without restoring the merchant shipping? It is doubtful. History has proved that such a purely military sea power can be built up by a despot, as was done by Louis XIV; but though so fair seeming, experience showed that his navy was like a growth which having no root soon withers away. But in a representative government any military expenditure must have a strongly represented interest behind it, convinced of its necessity. Such an interest in sea power does not exist, cannot exist here without action by the government. How such a merchant shipping should be built up, whether by subsidies or by free trade, by constant administration of tonics or by free movement in the open air, is not a military but an economical question. Even had the United States a great national shipping, it may be doubted whether a sufficient navy would follow; the distance which separates her from other great powers, in one way a protection, is also a snare. The motive, if any there be, which will give the United States a navy, is probably now quickening in the Central American Isthmus. Let us hope it will not come to the birth too late.

FURTHER READINGS

Cooling, Benjamin F., *Gray Steel and Blue Water Navy* (Hamden, Conn.: Archon Books, 1979).

Drake, Frederick C., *The Empire of the Seas* (Honolulu: University of Hawaii Press, 1984).

Herrick, Walter, *The American Naval Revolution* (Baton Rouge: Louisiana University Press, 1966).

LaFeber, Walter, *The New Empire* (Ithaca, N.Y.: Cornell University Press, 1963).

Seager, Robert, *Alfred Thayer Mahan* (Annapolis, Md.: Naval Institute Press, 1977).

Turk, Richard W., *The Ambiguous Relationship: Theodore Roosevelt and Alfred Thayer Mahan* (New York: Greenwood Press, 1987).

DOCUMENT 15

McKinley's War Message to Congress

On 11 April 1898 President William McKinley outlined to Congress the reasons why he believed that the United States should take steps to end the conflict between Spain and the people of Cuba.[15]

TO THE CONGRESS OF THE UNITED STATES:

It becomes my duty to now address your body with regard to the grave crisis that has arisen in the relations of the United States to Spain by reason of the warfare that for more than three years has raged in the neighboring island of Cuba.

I do so because of the intimate connection of the Cuban question with the state of our own Union and the grave relation the course which it is now incumbent upon the nation to adopt must needs bear to the traditional policy of our Government if it is to accord with the precepts laid down by the founders of the Republic and religiously observed by succeeding Administrations to the present day.

---

[15]James D. Richardson, editor, *A Compilation of Messages and Papers of the Presidents* (N.p.: Bureau of National Literature and Arts, 1909), 14:6281–92, passim.

The present revolution is but the successor of other similar insurrections which have occurred in Cuba against the dominion of Spain, extending over a period of nearly half a century, each of which during its progress has subjected the United States to great effort and expense in enforcing its neutrality laws, caused enormous losses to American trade and commerce, caused irritation, annoyance, and disturbance among our citizens, and, by the exercise of cruel, barbarous, and uncivilized practices of warfare, shocked the sensibilities and offended the humane sympathies of our people.

Since the present revolution began, in February, 1895, this country has seen the fertile domain at our threshold ravaged by fire and sword in the course of a struggle unequaled in the history of the island and rarely paralleled as to the numbers of the combatants and the bitterness of the contest by any revolution of modern times where a dependent people striving to be free have been opposed by the power of the sovereign state.

Our people have beheld a once prosperous community reduced to comparative want, its lucrative commerce virtually paralyzed, its exceptional productiveness diminished, its fields laid waste, its mills in ruins, and its people perishing by tens of thousands from hunger and destitution. We have found ourselves constrained, in the observance of that strict neutrality which our laws enjoin and which the law of nations commands, to police our own waters and watch our own seaports in prevention of any unlawful act in aid of the Cubans.

Our trade has suffered, the capital invested by our citizens in Cuba has been largely lost, and the temper and forbearance of our people have been so sorely tried as to beget a perilous unrest among our own citizens, which has inevitably found its expression from time to time in the National Legislature, so that issues wholly external to our own body politic engross attention and stand in the way of that close devotion to domestic advancement that becomes a self-contained commonwealth whose primal maxim has been the avoidance of all foreign entanglements. All this must needs awaken, and has, indeed, aroused, the utmost concern on the part of this Government, as well during my predecessor's term as in my own. . . .

By the time the present Administration took office, a year ago, reconcentration (so called) had been made effective over the better part of the four central and western provinces—Santa Clara, Matanzas, Havana, and Pinar del Rio.

The agricultural population to the estimated number of 300,000 or more was herded within the towns and their immediate vicinage, deprived of the means of support, rendered destitute of shelter, left poorly clad, and exposed to the most unsanitary conditions. As the scarcity of food increased with the devastation of the depopulated areas of production, destitution and want became misery and starvation. Month by month the death rate increased in an alarming ratio. By March, 1897, according to conservative estimates from official Spanish sources, the mortality among the reconcentrados from starvation and the diseases thereto incident exceeded 50 per cent of their total number.

No practical relief was accorded to the destitute. The overburdened towns, already suffering from the general dearth, could give no aid . . . the increasing destitution of the unfortunate reconcentrados and the alarming mortality among them claimed earnest attention. The success which had attended the limited measure of relief extended to the suffering American citizens among them by the judicious expenditure through the consular agencies of the money appropriated expressly for their succor by the joint resolution approved May 24, 1897, prompted the humane extension of a similar scheme of aid to the great body of sufferers. A suggestion to this end was acquiesced in by the Spanish authorities. . . .

The forcible intervention of the United States as a neutral to stop the war, according to the large dictates of humanity and following many historical precedents where neighboring states have interfered to check the hopeless sacrifices of life by internecine conflicts beyond their borders, is justifiable on rational grounds. It involves, however, hostile constraint upon both the parties to the contest, as well to enforce a truce as to guide the eventual settlement.

The grounds for such intervention may be briefly summarized as follows:

First. In the cause of humanity and to put an end to the barbarities, bloodshed, starvation, and horrible miseries now existing there, and which the parties to the conflict are either unable or unwilling to stop or mitigate. It is no answer to say this is all in another country, belonging to another nation, and is therefore none of our business. It is specially our duty, for it is right at our door.

Second. We owe it to our citizens in Cuba to afford them that protection and indemnity for life and property which no government there can or will afford, and to that end to terminate the conditions that deprive them of legal protection.

Third. The right to intervene may be justified by the very serious injury to the commerce, trade, and business of our people and by the wanton destruction of property and devastation of the island.

Fourth, and which is of the utmost importance. The present condition of affairs in Cuba is a constant menace to our peace and entails upon this Government an enormous expense. With such a conflict waged for years in an island so near us and with which our people have such trade and business relations; when the lives and liberty of our citizens are in constant danger and their property destroyed and themselves ruined; where our trading vessels are liable to seizure and are seized at our very door by war ships of a foreign nation; the expeditions of filibustering that we are powerless to prevent altogether, and the irritating questions and entanglements thus arising—all these and others that I need not mention, with the resulting strained relations, are a constant menace to our peace and compel us to keep on a semi war footing with a nation with which we are at peace.

These elements of danger and disorder already pointed out have been strikingly illustrated by a tragic event which has deeply and justly moved the American people.   I have already transmitted to Congress the report of the naval court of inquiry on the destruction of the battle ship *Maine* in the harbor of Havana during the night of the 15th of February.   The destruction of that noble vessel has filled the national heart with inexpressible horror.   Two hundred and fifty-eight brave sailors and marines and two officers of our Navy, reposing in the fancied security of a friendly harbor, have been hurled to death, grief and want brought to their homes and sorrow to the nation.

The naval court of inquiry, which, it is needless to say, commands the unqualified confidence of the Government, was unanimous in its conclusion that the destruction of the *Maine* was caused by an exterior explosion—that of a submarine mine.   It did not assume to place the responsibility.   That remains to be fixed.

In any event, the destruction of the *Maine*, by whatever exterior cause, is a patent and impressive proof of a state of things in Cuba that is intolerable. That condition is thus shown to be such that the Spanish Government can not assure safety and security to a vessel of the American Navy in the harbor of Havana on a mission of peace, and rightfully there. . . .

The long trial has proved that the object for which Spain has waged the war can not be attained.   The fire of insurrection may flame or may smolder with varying seasons, but it has not been and it is plain that it can not be extinguished by present methods.   The only hope of relief and repose from a condition which can no longer be endured is the enforced pacification of Cuba. In the name of humanity, in the name of civilization, in behalf of endangered American interests which give us the right and the duty to speak and to act, the war in Cuba must stop.

In view of these facts and of these considerations I ask the Congress to authorize and empower the President to take measures to secure a full and final termination of hostilities between the Government of Spain and the people of Cuba, and to secure in the island the establishment of a stable government, capable of maintaining order and observing its international obligations, insuring peace and tranquility and the security of its citizens as well as our own, and to use the military and naval forces of the United States as may be necessary for these purposes.

And in the interest of humanity and to aid in preserving the lives of the starving people of the island I recommend that the distribution of food and supplies be continued and that an appropriation be made out of the public Treasury to supplement the charity of our citizens.

The issue is now with the Congress.   It is a solemn responsibility.   I have exhausted every effort to relieve the intolerable condition of affairs which is at our doors. Prepared to execute every obligation imposed upon me by the Constitution and the law, I await your action.

Yesterday, and since the preparation of the foregoing message, official information was received by me that the latest decree of the Queen Regent of Spain directs General Blanco, in order to prepare and facilitate peace, to proclaim a suspension of hostilities, the duration and details of which have not yet been communicated to me.

This fact, with every other pertinent consideration, will, I am sure, have your just and careful attention in the solemn deliberations upon which you are about to enter. If this measure attains a successful result, then our aspirations as a Christian, peace-loving people will be realized. If it fails, it will be only another justification for our contemplated action.

Further Readings. See Document 18.

DOCUMENT 16

The Teller Amendment and Cuban Resolutions

Congress responded to McKinley's request by passing a joint resolution on 20 April 1898 that declared Cuba to be "free and independent." It furthermore authorized the president to use force to achieve this end and disclaimed any desire to exercise control over the Island.[16]

Whereas the abhorrent conditions which have existed for more than three years in the Island of Cuba, so near our own borders, have shocked the moral sense of the people of the United States, have been a disgrace to Christian civilization, culminating, as they have, in the destruction of a United States battle ship, with two hundred and sixty-six of its officers and crew, while on a friendly visit in the harbor of Havana, and can not longer be endured, as has been set forth by the President of the United States in his message to Congress of April eleventh, eighteen hundred and ninety-eight, upon which the action of Congress was invited: Therefore,

Resolved by the Senate and House of Representatives of the United States of America in Congress assembled, First. That the people of the Island of Cuba are, and of right ought to be, free and independent.

---

[16]*U.S. Statutes at Large* (Washington, D.C.: U.S. Government Printing Office, 1899), 30:738–39.

Second.   That it is the duty of the United States to demand, and the Government of the United States does hereby demand, that the Government of Spain at once relinquish its authority and government in the Island of Cuba and withdraw its land and naval forces from Cuba and Cuban waters.

Third.   That the President of the United States be, and he hereby is, directed and empowered to use the entire land and naval forces of the United States, and to call into the actual service of the United States the militia of the several States, to such extent as may be necessary to carry these resolutions into effect.

Fourth.   That the United States hereby disclaims any disposition or intention to exercise sovereignty, jurisdiction, or control over said Island except for the pacification thereof, and asserts its determination, when that is accomplished, to leave the government and control of the Island to its people.

Further Readings.   See Document 18.

DOCUMENT 17

McKinley Takes the Philippines

The successful war with Spain left McKinley with the question of what to do with the Philippine Islands that had been captured during the conflict.   On 19 November 1898 the president explained the reasons for his decision, which were recorded by Chandler P. Anderson, secretary to the Anglo-American Joint High Commission.[17]

On the question of the Phillipines [*sic*] the President said that he had given the subject most careful and conscientious and profound consideration and that he was unable to arrive at any other conclusion than that we must keep *all* the islands; that we could not give them back to Spain, for the very reasons which justified the war that would be impossible; that we could not give them or dispose of them to any European power for we should have a war on our hands in fifteen minutes, and furthermore why should that be done; the only reason would be to escape responsibility for our own acts and that we could not do; our duty and destiny demanded that we undertake our own responsibilities and the people should not be alarmed or anxious about their ability to fulfil their obligations.

---

[17]Quoted from Ephraim K. Smith, " 'A Question from Which We Could Not Escape': William McKinley and the Decision to Acquire the Philippine Islands," *Diplomatic History*, 9, no. 4 (Fall 1985): 369.

He spoke of the peculiar formation of the islands which were often separated only by a narrow strip of water and consequently if only one of the islands were kept and the rest returned, which was one of the possible alternatives proposed, we should then have a hostile territory, over which we had no control, literally within a stone[']s throw of us and that seemed in itself, apart from other considerations of which there were many, to be sufficient to prevent that disposition of them.

Further Readings. See Document 18.

DOCUMENT 18

The Platt Amendment

President Theodore Roosevelt withdrew United States troops from Cuba in 1902; given, however, America's economic interest in Cuba, as well as the Island's strategic position, the United States Congress had insisted with the Platt Amendment of 2 March 1901 that the Cuban government limit its sovereignty. Cuba and the United States concluded a treaty embodying the provisions of the Platt Amendment in the summer of 1904.[18]

ARTICLE I

The Government of Cuba shall never enter into any treaty or other compact with any foreign power or powers which will impair or tend to impair the independence of Cuba, nor in any manner authorize or permit any foreign power or powers to obtain by colonization or for military or naval purposes, or otherwise, lodgment in or contol over any portion of said island.

ARTICLE II

The Government of Cuba shall not assume or contract any public debt to pay the interest upon which, and to make reasonable sinking-fund provision for the ultimate discharge of which, the ordinary revenues of the Island of Cuba, after defraying the current expenses of the Government, shall be inadequate.

---

[18]*U.S. Statutes at Large* (Washington, D.C.: U.S. Government Printing Office, 1905) 33, part 2:2248–52.

ARTICLE III

The Government of Cuba consents that the United States may exercise the right to intervene for the preservation of Cuban independence, the maintenance of a government adequate for the protection of life, property, and individual liberty, and for discharging the obligations with respect to Cuba imposed by the Treaty of Paris on the United States, now to be assumed and undertaken by the Government of Cuba.

ARTICLE IV

All acts of the United States in Cuba during its military occupancy thereof are ratified and validated, and all lawful rights acquired thereunder shall be maintained and protected.

ARTICLE V

The Government of Cuba will execute, and, as far as necessary, extend the plans already devised, or other plans to be mutually agreed upon, for the sanitation of the cities of the island, to the end that a recurrence of epidemic and infectious diseases may be prevented, thereby assuring protection to the people and commerce of Cuba, as well as to the commerce of the Southern ports of the United States and the people residing therein.

ARTICLE VI

The Island of Pines shall be omitted from the boundaries of Cuba specified in the Constitution, the title thereto being left to future adjustment by treaty.

ARTICLE VII

To enable the United States to maintain the independence of Cuba, and to protect the people thereof, as well as for its own defense, the Government of Cuba will sell or lease to the United States lands necessary for coaling or naval stations, at certain specified points, to be agreed upon with the President of the United States.

ARTICLE VIII

The present Convention shall be ratified by each party in conformity with the respective Constitutions of the two countries, and the ratifications shall be exchanged in the City of Washington within eight months from this date.

FURTHER READINGS FOR DOCUMENTS 15-18

Beisner, Robert L., *From the Old Diplomacy to the New* (Wheeling, Ill.; Harlan
    Davidson, 1986).
———, *Twelve Against Empire* (Chicago: University of Chicago Press, 1985).
Foner, Philip S., *The Spanish-Cuban-American War and the Birth of American
    Imperialism* (New York: Monthly Press Review, 1972).
Gould, Lewis L., *The Spanish-American War and President McKinley* (Lawrence:
    University Press of Kansas, 1983).
Offner, John, *An Unwanted War: The Diplomacy of the United States and Spain Over
    Cuba, 1895–1898* (Chapel Hill: University of North Carolina Press, 1992).
Trask, David F., *The War with Spain in 1898* (New York: Macmillian, 1981).
Williams, William A., *The Roots of the Modern American Empire* (New York: Random
    Hous e, 1969).
———, *The Tragedy of American Diplomacy* (New York: Norton, 1988).

DOCUMENT 19

The Open Door Notes

*Secretary of State John Hay responded to a possible threat to American access
to the China market on 6 September 1899 by asking the governments of
England, France, Germany, Russia, Italy, and Japan "to retain there an open
market for the commerce of the world." While the other Great Powers
generally gave the Open Door policy a cool reception, Hay nonetheless
announced on 20 March 1900 that "final and definitive" assent had been
received.*[19]

✿✿

SECRETARY HAY TO THE AMBASSADOR IN GREAT BRITAIN

Washington, September 6, 1899

Sir: The Government of Her Britannic Majesty has declared that its policy and
its very traditions precluded it from using any privileges which might be
granted it in China as a weapon for excluding commercial rivals, and that
freedom of trade for Great Britain in that Empire meant freedom of trade for all
the world alike. While conceding by formal agreements, first with Germany

---

[19]*The China White Paper* (Stanford, CA.: Stanford University Press, 1967), Annexes,
414–16.

and then with Russia, the possession of "spheres of influence or interest" in China in which they are to enjoy special rights and privileges, more especially in respect of railroads and mining enterprises, Her Britannic Majesty's Government has therefore sought to maintain at the same time what is called the "open-door" policy, to insure to the commerce of the world in China equality of treatment within said "spheres" for commerce and navigation. This latter policy is alike urgently demanded by the British mercantile communities and by those of the United States, as it is justly held by them to be the only one which will improve existing conditions, enable them to maintain their positions in the markets of China, and extend their operations in the future. While the Government of the United States will in no way commit itself to a recognition of exclusive rights of any power within or control over any portion of the Chinese Empire under such agreements as have within the last year been made, it can not conceal its apprehension that under existing conditions there is a possibility, even a probability, of complications arising between the treaty powers which may imperil the rights insured to the United States under our treaties with China.

This Government is animated by a sincere desire that the interests of our citizens may not be prejudiced through exclusive treatment by any of the controlling powers within their so-called "spheres of interest" in China, and hopes also to retain there an open market for the commerce of the world, remove dangerous sources of international irritation, and hasten thereby united or concerted action of the powers at Pekin in favor of the administrative reforms so urgently needed for strengthening the Imperial Government and maintaining the integrity of China in which the whole western world is alike concerned. It believes that such a result may be greatly assisted by a declaration by the various powers claiming "spheres of interest" in China of their intentions as regards treatment of foreign trade therein. The present moment seems a particularly opportune one for informing Her Britannic Majesty's Government of the desire of the United States to see it make a formal declaration and to lend its support in obtaining similar declarations from the various powers claiming "spheres of influence" in China, to the effect that each in its respective spheres of interest or influence[:]

First. Will in no wise interfere with any treaty port or any vested interest within any so-called "sphere of interest" or leased territory it may have in China.

Second. That the Chinese treaty tariff of the time being shall apply to all merchandise landed or shipped to all such ports as are within said "sphere of interest" (unless they be "free ports"), no matter to what nationality it may belong, and that duties so leviable shall be collected by the Chinese Government.

Third. That it will levy no higher harbor duties on vessels of another nationality frequenting any port in such "sphere" than shall be levied on vessels of its own nationality, and no higher railroad charges over lines built, controlled, or operated within its "sphere" on merchandise belonging to citizens or subjects of other nationalities transported through such "sphere" than shall be levied on similar merchandise belonging to its own nationals transported over equal distances.

The recent ukase of His Majesty the Emperor of Russia, declaring the port of Ta-lien-wan open to the merchant ships of all nations during the whole of the lease under which it is to be held by Russia, removing as it does all uncertainty as to the liberal and conciliatory policy of that power, together with the assurances given this Government by Russia, justifies the expectation that His Majesty will cooperate in such an understanding as is here proposed, and our ambassador at the court of St. Petersburg has been instructed accordingly to submit the propositions above detailed to His Imperial Majesty, and ask their early consideration. Copy of my instruction to Mr. Tower is herewith inclosed for your confidential information.

The action of Germany in declaring the port of Kiaochao a "free port," and the aid the Imperial Government has given China in the establishment there of a Chinese custom-house, coupled with the oral assurance conveyed the United States by Germany that our interests within its "sphere" would in no wise be affected by its occupation of this portion of the province of Shang-tung, tend to show that little opposition may be anticipated from that power to the desired declaration.

The interests of Japan, the next most interested power in the trade of China, will be so clearly served by the proposed arrangement, and the declaration of its statesmen within the last year are so entirely in line with the views here expressed, that its hearty cooperation is confidently counted on.

*   *   *   *   *   *   *   *

SECRETARY HAY TO AMERICAN DIPLOMATIC REPRESENTATIVES AT LONDON, PARIS, BERLIN, ST. PETERSBURG, ROME, AND TOKYO

WASHINGTON, MARCH 20, 1900

Sir: The _____ Government having accepted the declaration suggested by the United States concerning foreign trade in China, the terms of which I transmitted to you in my instruction No.___ of ___, and like action having been taken by all the various powers having leased territory or so-called "spheres of interest" in the Chinese Empire, as shown by the notes which I herewith transmit to you, you will please inform the Government to which you are accredited that the condition originally attached to its acceptance—that all other powers concerned should likewise accept the proposals of the United States—having been complied with, this Government will therefore consider the assent given to it by ____ as final and definitive.

You will also transmit to the minister for foreign affairs copies of the present inclosures, and by the same occasion convey to him the expression of the sincere gratification which the President feels at the successful termination of these negotiations, in which he sees proof of the friendly spirit which animates the various powers interested in the untrammeled development of commerce and industry in the Chinese Empire, and a source of vast benefit to the whole commercial world.

FURTHER READINGS

Cohen, Warren I., *America's Response to China* (New York: Columbia University Press, 1990).

Dudden, Arthur Power, *The American Pacific: From the Old China Trade to the Present* (New York: Oxford University Press, 1992).

Fairbank, John K., *The United States and China* (Cambridge, Mass.: Harvard University Press, 1983).

Hunt, Michael, *The Making of a Special Relationship: The United States and China to 1914* (New York: Columbia University Press, 1983).

Iriye, Akira, *Across the Pacific* (New York: Harcourt, Brace & World, 1967).

McCormack, Thomas, *China Market: America's Quest for Informal Empire, 1893-1901* (Chicago: Quadrangle Books, 1967).

Schaller, Michael, *The United States and China in the Twentieth Century* (New York: Oxford University Press, 1990).

Varg, Paul, *The Making of a Myth: The United States and China, 1897–1912* (Westport, Conn.: Greenwood Press, 1980).

DOCUMENT 20

The Roosevelt Corollary to the Monroe Doctrine

In an address to Congress on 6 December 1904 President Theodore Roosevelt outlined not only his famous corollary to the Monroe Doctrine, but also several general principles that he believed should guide the foreign and military policies of the United States.[20]

In treating of our foreign policy and of the attitude that this great Nation should assume in the world at large, it is absolutely necessary to consider the Army and the Navy, and the Congress, through which the thought of the Nation finds

---

[20]James D. Richardson, editor, *A Compilation of Messages and Papers of the Presidents* (N.p.: Bureau of National Literature and Arts, 1909), 16:7051–54.

its expression, should keep ever vividly in mind the fundamental fact that it is impossible to treat our foreign policy, whether this policy takes shape in the effort to secure justice for others or justice for ourselves, save as conditioned upon the attitude we are willing to take toward our Army, and especially toward our Navy. It is not merely unwise, it is contemptible, for a nation, as for an individual, to use high-sounding language to proclaim its purposes, or to take positions which are ridiculous if unsupported by potential force, and then to refuse to provide this force. If there is no intention of providing and of keeping the force necessary to back up a strong attitude, then it is far better not to assume such an attitude.

The steady aim of this Nation, as of all enlightened nations, should be to strive to bring ever nearer the day when there shall prevail throughout the world the peace of justice. There are kinds of peace which are highly undesirable, which are in the long run as destructive as any war. Tyrants and oppressors have many times made a wilderness and called it peace. Many times peoples were slothful or timid or shortsighted, who had been enervated by ease or by luxury, or misled by false teachings, have shrunk in unmanly fashion from doing duty that was stern and that needed self-sacrifice, and have sought to hide from their own minds their shortcomings, their ignoble motives, by calling them love of peace. The peace of tyrannous terror, the peace of craven weakness, the peace of injustice, all these should be shunned as we shun unrighteous war. The goal to set before us as a nation, the goal which should be set before all mankind, is the attainment of the peace of justice, of the peace which comes when each nation is not merely safe-guarded in its own rights, but scrupulously recognizes and performs its duty toward others. Generally peace tells for righteousness; but if there is conflict between the two, then our fealty is due first to the cause of righteousness. Unrighteous wars are common, and unrighteous peace is rare; but both should be shunned. The right of freedom and the responsibility for the exercise of that right can not be divorced. One of our great poets has well and finely said that freedom is not a gift that tarries long in the hands of cowards. Neither does it tarry long in the hands of those too slothful, too dishonest, or too unintelligent to exercise it. The eternal vigilance which is the price of liberty must be exercised, sometimes to guard against outside foes; although of course far more often to guard against our own selfish or thoughtless shortcomings.

If these self-evident truths are kept before us, and only if they are so kept before us, we shall have a clear idea of what our foreign policy in its larger aspects should be. It is our duty to remember that a nation has no more right to do injustice to another nation, strong or weak, than an individual has to do injustice to another individual; that the same moral law applies in one case as in the other. But we must also remember that it is as much the duty of the Nation to guard its own rights and its own interests as it is the duty of the individual so to do. Within the Nation the individual has now delegated this right to the State, that is, to the representative of all the individuals, and it is a maxim of the law that for every wrong there is a remedy. But in international law we have not advanced by any means as far as we have advanced in municipal law. There is as yet no judicial way of enforcing a right in international law. When one nation wrongs another or wrongs many others, there is no tribunal before which the wrongdoer can be brought. Either it is necessary supinely to acquiesce in the wrong, and thus put a premium upon brutality and aggression, or else it is necessary for the aggrieved nation valiantly to stand up for its rights. Until some method is devised by which there shall be a degree of international control over offending nations, it would be a wicked thing for the most civilized powers, for those with most sense of international obligations and with keenest and most generous appreciation of the difference between right and wrong, to disarm. If the great civilized nations of the present day should completely disarm, the result would mean an immediate recrudescence of barbarism in one form or another. Under any circumstances a sufficient armament would have to be kept up to serve the purposes of international police; and until international cohesion and the sense of international duties and rights are far more advanced than at present, a nation desirous both of securing respect for itself and of doing good to others must have a force adequate for the work which it feels is allotted to it as part of the general world duty. Therefore it follows that a self-respecting, just, and far-seeing nation should on the one hand endeavor by every means to aid in the development of the various movements which tend to provide substitutes for war, which tend to render nations in their actions toward one another, and indeed towards their own peoples, more responsive to the general sentiment of humane and civilized mankind; and on the other hand that it should keep prepared, while scrupulously avoiding wrongdoing itself, to repel any wrong, and in exceptional cases to take action which in a more advanced stage of international relations would come under the head of the exercise of the international police. A great free people owes it to itself and to all mankind not to sink into helplessness before the powers of evil. . . .

It is not true that the United States feels any land hunger or entertains any projects as regard the other nations of the Western Hemisphere save such as are for their welfare. All that this country desires is to see the neighboring countries stable, orderly, and prosperous. Any country whose people conduct themsevles well can count upon our hearty friendship. If a nation shows that it knows how to act with reasonable efficiency and decency in social and political matters, if it keeps order and pays its obligations, it need fear no interference from the United States. Chronic wrongdoing, or an impotence which results in a general loosening of the ties of civilized society, may in America, as elsewhere, ultimately require intervention by some civilized nation, and in the Western Hemisphere the adherence of the United States to the Monroe Doctrine may force the United States, however reluctantly, in flagrant cases of such wrongdoing or impotence, to the exercise of an international police power. If every country washed by the Caribbean Sea would show the progress in stable and just civilization which with the aid of the Platt amendment Cuba has shown since our troops left the island, and which so many of the republics in both Americas are constantly and brilliantly showing, all question of interference by this Nation with their affairs would be at an end. Our interests and those of our southern neighbors are in reality identical. They have great natural riches, and if within their borders the reign of law and justice obtains, prosperity is sure to come to them. While they thus obey the primary laws of civilized society they may rest assured that they will be treated by us in a spirit of cordial and helpful sympathy. We would interfere with them only in the last resort, and then only if it became evident that their inability or unwillingness to do justice at home and abroad had violated the rights of the United States or had invited foreign aggression to the detriment of the entire body of American nations. It is a mere truism to say that every nation, whether in America or anywhere else, which desires to maintain its freedom, its independence, must ultimately realize that the right of such independence can not be separated from the responsibility of making good use of it.

FURTHER READINGS

Beale, Howard K., *Theodore Roosevelt and the Rise of America to World Power* (Baltimore: Johns Hopkins University Press, 1956).

Burton, David, *Theodore Roosevelt: Confident Imperialist* (Philadelphia: University of Pennsylvania Press, 1968).

Collin, Richard H., *Theodore Roosevelt, Culture, Diplomacy, and Expansionism* (Baton Rouge: Louisiana State University Press, 1985).

————, *Theodore Roosevelt's Caribbean: The Panama Canal, the Monroe Doctrine, and the Latin American Context* (Baton Rouge: Louisiana State University Press, 1991).

Esthus, Raymond A., *Theodore Roosevelt and the International Rivalries* (Waltham, Mass.: Ginn-Blaisdell, 1970).

Harbaugh, William H., *The Life and Times of Theodore Roosevelt* (New York: Oxford University Press, 1975).

Schoonover, Thomas, *The United States in Central America, 1860–1911* (Durham, N.C.: Duke University Press, 1991).

DOCUMENT 21

Woodrow Wilson and Latin America

On 12 March 1913 Woodrow Wilson issued a statement on relations with Latin America which aptly foreshadowed his idealistic, as well as interventionist attitude towards that region.[21]

One of the chief objects of my administration will be to cultivate the friendship and deserve the confidence of our sister republics of Central and South America, and to promote in every proper and honorable way the interests which are common to the peoples of the two continents. I earnestly desire the most cordial understanding and cooperation between the peoples and leaders of America and, therefore, deem it my duty to make this brief statement.

Cooperation is possible only when supported at every turn by the orderly processes of just government based upon law, not upon arbitrary or irregular force. We hold, as I am sure all thoughtful leaders of republican government everywhere hold, that just government rests always upon the consent of the governed, and that there can be no freedom without order based upon law and upon the public conscience and approval. We shall look to make these principles the basis of mutual intercourse, respect, and helpfulness between our sister republics and ourselves. We shall lend our influence of every kind to the realization of these principles in fact and practice, knowing that disorder, personal intrigue and defiance of constitutional rights weaken and discredit government and injure none so much as the people who are unfortunate enough to have their common life and their common affairs so tainted and disturbed. We can have no sympathy with those who seek to seize the power of government to advance their own personal interests or ambition. We are the friends of peace, but we know that there can be no lasting or stable peace in such circumstances. As friends, therefore, we shall prefer those who act in the interest of peace and honor, who protect private rights and respect the restraints of constitutional provision. Mutual respect seems to us the indispensable foundation of friendship between states, as between individuals.

The United States has nothing to seek in Central and South America except the lasting interests of the peoples of the two continents, the security of governments intended for the people and for no special group or interest, and the development of personal and trade relationships between the two continents

---

[21]Arthur Link, editor, *The Papers of Woodrow Wilson* (Princeton, N.J.: Princeton University Press, 1978), 27:172–73.

which shall redound to the profit and advantage of both and interfere with the rights and liberties of neither.

From these principles may be read so much of the future policy of this government as it is necessary now to forecast; and in the spirit of these principles I may, I hope, be permitted with as much confidence as earnestness to extend to the governments of all the republics of America the hand of genuine disinterested friendship and to pledge my own honor and the honor of my colleagues to every enterprise of peace and amity that a fortunate future may disclose.

FURTHER READINGS

Calhoun, Frederick S., *Power and Principle: Armed Interventionism in Wilsonian Foreign Policy* (Kent, Ohio: Kent State University Press, 1986).

Cooper, Jr., John M., *The Warrior and the Priest: Woodrow Wilson and Theodore Roosevelt* (Cambridge, Mass.: Harvard University Press, 1983).

Gardner, Lloyd C., *Safe for Democracy* (New York: Oxford University Press, 1984).

Gilderhus, Mark T., *Pan American Vision: Woodrow Wilson in the Western Hemisphere, 1913–1921* (Tucson: University of Arizona Press, 1986).

Healy, David, *Gunboat Diplomacy in the Wilson Era* (Madison: University of Wisconsin Press, 1976).

DOCUMENT 22

Wilson Renounces Dollar Diplomacy

The administration of William Howard Taft had pursued economic and political advantages for the United States by encouraging American bankers to participate in an international loan to the Chinese government. Woodrow Wilson announced his reasons for renouncing "Dollar Diplomacy" in a statement issued on 18 March 1913.[22]

We are informed that at the request of the last administration a certain group of American bankers undertook to participate in the loan now desired by the government of China (approximately $125,000,000). Our government wished American bankers to participate along with the bankers of other nations, because it desired that the good will of the United States towards China should be exhibited in this practical way, that American capital should have access to

---

[22]Arthur Link, editor, *The Papers of Woodrow Wilson* (Princeton, N.J.: Princeton University Press, 1978), 27:192–94.

that great country, and that the United States should be in a position to share with the other powers any political responsibilities that might be associated with the development of foreign relations of China in connection with her industrial and commercial enterprises. The present administration has been asked by this group of bankers whether it would also request them to participate in the loan.   The representatives of the bankers through whom the administration was approached declared that they would continue to seek their share of the loan under the proposed agreements only if expressly requested to do so by the government. The administration has declined to make such request because it did not approve the conditions of the loan or the implications of responsibilty on its own part which it was plainly told would be involved in the request.

The conditions of the loan seem to us to touch very nearly the administrative independence of China itself; and this administration does not feel that it ought, even by implication, to be a party to those conditions.   The responsibility on its part which would be implied in requesting the bankers to undertake the loan might conceivably go the length in some unhappy contingency of forcible interference in the financial, and even the political, affairs of that great oriental State, just now awakening to a consciousness of its power and of its obligation to its people. The conditions include not only the pledging of particular taxes, some of them antiquated and burdensome, to secure the loan, but also the administration of those taxes by foreign agents. The responsibility on the part of our government implied in the encouragement of a loan thus secure and administered is plain enough and is obnoxious to the principles upon which the government of our people rests.

The government of the United States is not only willing, but earnestly desirous, of aiding the great Chinese people in every way that is consistent with their untrammeled development and its own immemorial principles.   The awakening of the people of China to a consciousness of their possibilities under free government is the most significant, if not the most momentous, event of our generation. With this movement and aspiration the American people are in profound sympathy.   They certainly wish to participate, and participate very generously, in opening to the Chinese and to the use of the world the almost untouched and perhaps unrivalled resources of China.

The government of the United States is earnestly desirous of promoting the most extended and intimate trade relationships between this country and the Chinese republic.   The present administration will urge and support the legislative measures necessary to give American merchants, manufacturers, contractors, and engineers the banking and other financial facilities which they now lack, and without which they are at a serious disadvantage as compared with their industrial and commercial rivals. This is its duty. This is the main material interest of its citizens in the development of China. Our interests are those of the open door—a door of friendship and mutual advantage. This is the only door we care to enter.

FURTHER READINGS

Cohen, Warren I., *America's Response to China* (New York: Columbia University Press, 1990).

Dudden, Arthur Power, *The American Pacific: From the Old China Trade to the Present* (New York: Oxford University Press, 1992).

Fairbank, John K., *The United States and China* (Cambridge, Mass.: Harvard University Press, 1983).

Hunt, Michael, *The Making of a Special Relationship: The United States and China to 1914* (New York: Columbia University Press, 1983).

Iriye, Akira, *Across the Pacific* (New York: Harcourt, Brace and World, 1967).

Schaller, Michael, *The United States and China in the Twentieth Century* (New York: Oxford University Press, 1990).

Scholes Walter, and Scholes, Marie, *Foreign Policies of the Taft Administration* (Columbia: University of Missouri Press, 1970).

DOCUMENT 23

Wilson and U.S. Neutrality

On 18 August 1914 President Woodrow Wilson appealed to the people of the United States to be "impartial in thought as well as in action" toward the belligerent powers fighting World War I.[23]

MY FELLOW COUNTRYMEN:

I suppose that every thoughtful man in America has asked himself during these last troubled weeks what influence the European war may exert upon the United States, and I take the liberty of addressing a few words to you in order to point out that it is entirely within our own choice what its effects upon us will be and to urge very earnestly upon you the sort of speech and conduct which will best safeguard the nation against distress and disaster.

The effect of the war upon the United States will depend upon what American citizens say and do. Every man who really loves America will act

---

[23]Arthur Link, editor, *The Papers of Woodrow Wilson* (Princeton, N.J.: Princeton University Press, 1978), 30:393–94.

and speak in the true spirit of neutrality, which is the spirit of impartiality and fairness and friendliness to all concerned. The spirit of the nation in this critical matter will be determined largely by what individuals and societies and those gathered in public meetings do and say, upon what newspapers and magazines contain, upon what ministers utter in their pulpits, and men proclaim as their opinions on the street.

The people of the United States are drawn from many nations, and chiefly from the nations now at war. It is natural and inevitable that there should be the utmost variety of sympathy and desire among them with regard to the issues and circumstances of the conflict. Some will wish one nation, others another, to succeed in the momentous struggle. It will be easy to excite passion and difficult to allay it. Those responsible for exciting it will assume a heavy responsibility, responsibility for no less a thing than that the people of the United States, whose love of their country and whose loyalty to its government should unite them as Americans all, bound in honor and affection, to think first of her and her interests—may become divided in camps of hostile opinion, hot against each other, involved in the war itself in impulse and opinion, if not in action. Such divisions among us would be fatal to our peace of mind and might seriously stand in the way of the proper performance of our duty as the one great nation at peace, the one people holding itself ready to play a part of impartial mediation and speak the counsels of peace and accommodation, not as a partisan, but as a friend.

I venture, therefore, my fellow countrymen, to speak a solemn word of warning to you against that deepest, most subtle, most essential breach of neutrality which may spring out of partisanship, out of passionately taking sides. The United States must be neutral in fact as well as in name during these days that are to try men's souls. We must be impartial in thought as well as in action, must put a curb upon our sentiments as well as upon every transaction that might be construed as a preference of one party to the struggle before another.

My thought is of America. I am speaking, I feel sure, the earnest wish and purpose of every thoughtful American that this great country of ours, which is, of course, the first in our thoughts and in our hearts, should show herself in this time of peculiar trial a nation fit beyond others to exhibit the fine poise of undisturbed judgment, the dignity of self-control, the efficiency of dispassionate action; a nation that neither sits in judgment upon others nor is disturbed in her own counsels and which keeps herself fit and free to do what is necessary and disinterested and truly serviceable for the peace of the world.

Shall we not resolve to put upon ourselves the restraints which will bring to our people the happiness and the great and lasting influence for peace we covet for them?

FURTHER READINGS

Ambrosius, Lloyd E., *Wilsonian Statecraft* (Wilmington, Del.: SR Books, 1991).

Burk, Kathleen, *Britain, America, and the Sinews of War, 1914–1918* (Boston: Allen Unwin, 1985).

Clements, Kendrick A., *Woodrow Wilson: World Statesman* (Boston: Twayne, 1987).

Cooper, Jr., John M., *The Warrior and the Priest: Woodrow Wilson and Theodore Roosevelt* (Cambridge, Mass.: Harvard University Press, 1983).

Devlin, Patrick, *Too Proud to Fight* (New York: Oxford University Press, 1975).

Ferrell, Robert H., *Woodrow Wilson and World War I* (New York: Harper & Row, 1985).

Gardner, Lloyd C., *Safe for Democracy* (New York: Oxford University Press, 1984).

Heckscher, August, *Woodrow Wilson: A Biography* (New York: Scribner, 1991).

Knock, Thomas J., *To End All Wars: Woodrow Wilson and the Quest for a New World Order* (New York: Oxford University Press, 1992).

May, Ernest R., *The World War and American Isolation* (Cambridge, Mass.: Harvard University Press, 1959).

Smith, Daniel M., *Robert Lansing and American Neutrality, 1914–1917* (Berkeley: University of California Press, 1958).

DOCUMENT 24

Wilson's War Message

In February 1917 the Imperial German government informed the United States government that its submarines would attack all vessels approaching its enemies' ports. President Woodrow Wilson, who prominently cited unrestricted submarine warfare as "warfare against mankind," asked Congress for a declaration of war on 2 April 1917. Congress overwhelmingly complied four days later.[24]

I have called the Congress into extraordinary session because there are serious, very serious, choices of policy to be made, and made immediately, which it was neither right nor constitutionally permissible that I should assume the responsibility of making.

On the third of February last I officially laid before you the extraordinary announcement of the Imperial German Government that on and after the first day of February it was its purpose to put aside all restraints of law or of

---

[24]Ray S. Baker, *War and Peace* (Garden City, N.Y.: Doubleday Page & Co., 1927–39), 1:6–16, passim.

humanity and use its submarines to sink every vessel that sought to approach either the ports of Great Britain and Ireland or the western coasts of Europe or any of the ports controlled by the enemies of Germany within the Mediterranean. That had seemed to be the object of the German submarine warfare earlier in the war, but since April of last year the Imperial Government had somewhat restrained the commanders of its undersea craft in conformity with its promise then given to us that passenger boats should not be sunk and that due warning would be given to all other vessels which its submarines might seek to destroy, when no resistance was offered or escape attempted, and care taken that their crews were given at least a fair chance to save their lives in their open boats. The precautions taken were meager and haphazard enough, as was proved in distressing instance after instance in the progress of the cruel and unmanly business, but a certain degree of restraint was observed. The new policy has swept every restriction aside. Vessels of every kind, whatever their flag, their character, their cargo, their destination, their errand, have been ruthlessly sent to the bottom without warning and without thought of help or mercy for those on board, the vessels of friendly neutrals along with those of belligerents. Even hospital ships and ships carrying relief to the sorely bereaved and stricken people of Belgium, though the latter were provided with safe conduct through the proscribed areas by the German Government itself and were distinguished by unmistakable marks of identity, have been sunk with the same reckless lack of compassion or of principle.

I was for a little while unable to believe that such things would in fact be done by any government that had hitherto subscribed to the humane practices of civilized nations. International law had its origin in the attempt to set up some law which would be respected and observed upon the seas, where no nation had right of dominion and where lay the free highways of the world. By painful stage after stage has that law been built up, with meager enough results, indeed, after all was accomplished that could be accomplished, but always with a clear view, at least, of what the heart and conscience of mankind demanded. This minimum of right the German Government has swept aside under the plea of retaliation and necessity and because it had no weapons which it could use at sea except these which it is impossible to employ as it is employing them without throwing to the winds all scruples of humanity or of respect for the understandings that were supposed to underlie the intercourse of the world. I am not now thinking of the loss of property involved, immense and serious as that is, but only of the wanton and wholesale destruction of the lives of non-combatants, men, women, and children, engaged in pursuits which have always, even in the darkest periods of modern history, been deemed innocent and legitimate. Property can be paid for; the lives of peaceful and innocent people cannot be. The present German submarine warfare against commerce is a warfare against mankind.

It is a war against all nations. American ships have been sunk, American lives taken, in ways which it has stirred us very deeply to learn of, but the ships and people of other neutral and friendly nations have been sunk and overwhelmed in the waters in the same way. There has been no discrimination. The challenge is to all mankind. Each nation must decide for itself how it will meet it. The choice we make for ourselves must be made with a moderation of counsel and a temperateness of judgment befitting our character and our motives as a nation. We must put excited feeling away. Our motive will not be revenge or the victorious assertion of the physical might of the nation, but only the vindication of right, of human right, of which we are only a single champion. . . .

With a profound sense of the solemn and even tragical character of the step I am taking and of the grave responsibilities which it involves, but in unhesitating obedience to what I deem my constitutional duty, I advise that the Congress declare the recent course of the Imperial German Government to be in fact nothing less than war against the government and people of the United States; that it formally accept the status of belligerent which has thus been thrust upon it; and that it take immediate steps not only to put the country in a more thorough state of defense but also to exert all its power and employ all its resources to bring the Government of the German Empire to terms and end the war. . . .

While we do these things, these deeply momentous things, let us be very clear, and make very clear to all the world what our motives and objects are. My own thought has not been driven from its habitual and normal course by the unhappy events of the last two months, and I do not believe that the thought of the Nation has been altered or clouded by them. I have exactly the same things in mind now that I had in mind when I addressed the Senate on the twenty-second of January last; the same that I had in mind when I addressed the Congress on the third of February and on the twenty-sixth of February. Our object now, as then, is to vindicate the principles of peace and justice in the life of the world as against selfish and autocratic power and to set up amongst the really free and self-governed peoples of the world such a concert of purpose and of action as will henceforth insure the observance of those principles. Neutrality is no longer feasible or desirable where the peace of the world is involved and the freedom of its peoples, and the menace to that peace and freedom lies in the existence of autocratic governments backed by organized force which is controlled wholly by their will, not by the will of their people. We have seen the last of neutrality in such circumstances. We are at the beginning of an age in which it will be insisted that the same standards of conduct and of responsibility for wrong done shall be observed among nations and their governments that are observed among the individual citizens of civilized states.

We have no quarrel with the German people. We have no feeling towards them but one of sympathy and friendship. It was not upon their impulse that their government acted in entering this war. It was not with their previous knowledge or approval. It was a war determined upon as wars used to be determined upon in the old, unhappy days when peoples were nowhere consulted by their rulers and wars were provoked and waged in the interest of dynasties or of little groups of ambitious men who were accustomed to use their fellow men as pawns and tools. Self-governed nations do not fill their neighbor states with spies or set the course of intrigue to bring about some critical posture of affairs which will give them an opportunity to strike and make conquest. Such designs can be successfully worked out only under cover and where no one has the right to ask questions. Cunningly contrived plans of deception or aggression, carried, it may be, from generation to generation, can be worked out and kept from the light only within the privacy of courts or behind the carefully guarded confidences of a narrow and privileged class. They are happily impossible where public opinion commands and insists upon full information concerning all the nation's affairs.

A steadfast concert for peace can never be maintained except by a partnership of democratic nations. No autocratic government could be trusted to keep faith within it or observe its covenants. It must be a league of honor, a partnership of opinion. Intrigue would eat its vitals away; the plottings of inner circles who could plan what they would and render account to no one would be a corruption seated at its very heart. Only free peoples can hold their purpose and their honor steady to a common end and prefer the interests of mankind to any narrow interest of their own.

Does not every American feel that assurance has been added to our hope for the future peace of the world by the wonderful and heartening things that have been happening within the last few weeks in Russia? Russia was known by those who knew it best to have been always in fact democratic at heart, in all the vital habits of her thought, in all the intimate relationships of her people that spoke their natural instinct, their habitual attitude towards life. The autocracy that crowned the summit of her political structure, long as it had stood and terrible as was the reality of its power, was not in fact Russian in origin, character, or purpose; and now it has been shaken off and the great, generous Russian people have been added in all their naive majesty and might to the forces that are fighting for freedom in the world, for justice, and for peace. Here is a fit partner for a League of Honor. . . .

It is a distressing and oppressive duty, Gentlemen of the Congress, which I have performed in thus addressing you. There are, it may be, many months of fiery trial and sacrifice ahead of us. It is a fearful thing to lead this great peaceful people into war, into the most terrible and disastrous of all wars, civilization itself seeming to be in the balance. But the right is more precious than peace, and we shall fight for the things which we have always carried nearest our hearts,—for democracy, for the right of those who submit to authority to have a voice in their own Governments, for the rights and liberties of small nations, for a universal dominion of right by such a concert of free peoples as shall bring peace and safety to all nations and make the world itself at last free.   To such a task we can dedicate our lives and our fortunes, everything that we are and everything that we have, with the pride of those who know that the day has come when America is privileged to spend her blood and her might for the principles that gave her birth and happiness and the peace which she has treasured. God helping her, she can do no other.

FURTHER READINGS

Ambrosius, Lloyd E., *Wilsonian Statecraft* (Wilmington, Del.: SR Books, 1991).

Burk, Kathleen, *Britain, America, and the Sinews of War, 1914–1918* (Boston: Allen Unwin, 1985).

Clements, Kendrick A., *Woodrow Wilson: World Statesman* (Boston: Twayne, 1987).

Coogan, John W., *The End of Neutrality* (Ithaca, N.Y.: Cornell University Press, 1981).

Cooper, Jr., John M., *The Warrior and the Priest: Woodrow Wilson and Theodore Roosevelt* (Cambridge, Mass.: Harvard University Press, 1983).

Devlin, Patrick, *Too Proud to Fight* (New York: Oxford University Press, 1975).

Ferrell, Robert H., *Woodrow Wilson and World War I* (New York: Harper & Row, 1985).

Gardner, Lloyd C., *Safe for Democracy* (New York: Oxford University Press, 1984).

Heckscher, August, *Woodrow Wilson: A Biography* (New York: Scribner, 1991).

Jonas, Manfred, *The United States and Germany* (Ithaca, N.Y.: Cornell University Press, 1984).

Knock, Thomas J., *To End All Wars: Woodrow Wilson and the Quest for a New World Order* (New York: Oxford University Press, 1992).

May, Ernest R., *The World War and American Isolation* (Cambridge, Mass.: Harvard University Press, 1959).

Smith, Daniel M., *Robert Lansing and American Neutrality, 1914–1917* (Berkeley: University of California Press, 1958).

Stevenson, David, *The First World War and International Politics* (New York: Oxford University Press, 1988).

DOCUMENT 25

The Lansing-Ishii Agreement

The great power rivalry in China intensified during World War I. In an effort to ease tensions that could complicate the war effort against Germany, on 2 November 1917 Japan and the United States accepted the Lansing-Ishii

Agreement, which reaffirmed the Open Door policy while conceding that Japan had "special interests in China."[25]

🙟🙟🙟

SECRETARY LANSING TO VISCOUNT ISHII, JAPANESE AMBASSADOR ON SPECIAL MISSION

Washington, November 2, 1917

EXCELLENCY: I have the honor to communicate herein my understanding of the agreement reached by us in our recent conversations touching the questions of mutual interest to our Governments relating to the Republic of China.

In order to silence mischievous reports that have from time to time been circulated, it is believed by us that a public announcement once more of the desires and intentions shared by our two Governments with regard to China is advisible.

The Governments of the United States and Japan recognize that territorial propinquity creates special relations between countries, and, consequently, the Government of the United States recognizes that Japan has special interests in China, particularly in the part to which her possessions are contiguous.

The territorial sovereignty of China, nevertheless, remains unimpaired and the Government of the United States has every confidence in the repeated assurances of the Imperial Japanese Government that while geographical position gives Japan such special interests they have no desire to discriminate against the trade of other nations or to disregard the commercial rights heretofore granted by China in treaties with other powers.

The Governments of the United States and Japan deny that they have any purpose to infringe in any way the independence or territorial integrity of China and they declare, furthermore, that they always adhere to the principle of the so-called "open door" or equal opportunity for commerce and industry in China.

Moreover, they mutually declare that they are opposed to the acquisition by any Government of any special rights or privileges that would affect the independence or territorial integrity of China or that would deny to the subjects or citizens of any country the full enjoyment of equal opportunity in the commerce and industry of China.

I shall be glad to have your excellency confirm this understanding of the agreement reached by us.

---

[25]*The China White Paper* (Stanford, CA.: Stanford University Press, 1967), Annexes, 437.

FURTHER READINGS

Beers, Burton, *Vain Endeavor: Robert Lansing's Attempts to End the American-Japanese Rivalry* (Durham, N.C.: Duke University Press, 1962).

Dudden, Arthur Power, *The American Pacific: From the Old China Trade to the Present* (New York: Oxford University Press, 1992).

Fairbank, John K., *The United States and China* (Cambridge, Mass.: Harvard University Press, 1979).

Schaller, Michael, *The United States and China in the Twentieth Century* (New York: Oxford University Press, 1979).

DOCUMENT 26

The Fourteen Points

President Woodrow Wilson presented his vision of a new postwar international order to a joint session of Congress on 8 January 1918.[26] *Ten months later the German government would sue for peace on the basis of Wilson's Fourteen Points.*

It will be our wish and purpose that the processes of peace, when they are begun, shall be absolutely open and that they shall involve and permit henceforth no secret understandings of any kind. The day of conquest and aggrandizement is gone by; so is also the day of secret covenants entered into in the interest of particular governments and likely at some unlooked-for moment to upset the peace of the world. It is this happy fact, now clear to the view of every public man whose thoughts do not still linger in an age that is dead and gone, which makes it possible for every nation whose purposes are consistent with justice and the peace of the world to avow now or at any other time the objects it has in view.

We entered this war because violations of right had occurred which touched us to the quick and made the life of our own people impossible unless they were corrected and the world secured once for all against their recurrence. What we demand in this war, therefore, is nothing peculiar to ourselves. It is that the world be made fit and safe to live in; and particularly that it be made safe for every peace-loving nation which, like our own, wishes to live its own life, determine its own institutions, be assured of justice and fair dealing by the other peoples of the world as against force and selfish aggression. All the

---

[26]Arthur Link, editor, *The Papers of Woodrow Wilson* (Princeton, N.J.: Princeton University Press, 1978), 45:536–38.

peoples of the world are in effect partners in this interest, and for our own part we see very clearly that unless justice be done to others it will not be done to us. The programme of the world's peace, therefore, is our programme; and that programme, the only possible programme, as we see it, is this:

I.   Open covenants of peace, openly arrived at, after which there shall be no private international understandings of any kind but diplomacy shall proceed always frankly and in the public view.

II. Absolute freedom of navigation upon the seas, outside territorial waters, alike in peace and in war, except as the seas may be closed in whole or in part by international action for the enforcement of international covenants.

III. The removal, so far as possible, of all economic barriers and the establishment of an equality of trade conditions among all the nations consenting to the peace and associating themselves for its maintenance.

IV. Adequate guarantees given and taken that national armaments will be reduced to the lowest point consistent with domestic safety.

V.   A free, open-minded, and absolutely impartial adjustment of all colonial claims, based upon a strict observance of the principle that in determining all such questions of sovereignty the interests of the populations concerned must have equal weight with the equitable claims of the government whose title is to be determined.

VI. The evacuation of all Russian territory and such a settlement of all questions affecting Russia as will secure the best and freest cooperation of the other nations of the world in obtaining for her an unhampered and unembarrassed opportunity for the independent determination of her own political development and national policy and assure her of a sincere welcome into the society of free nations under institutions of her own choosing; and, more than a welcome, assistance also of every kind that she may need and may herself desire. The treatment accorded Russia by her sister nations in the months to come will be the acid test of their good will, of their comprehension of her needs as distinguished from their own interests, and of their intelligent and unselfish sympathy.

VII. Belgium, the whole world will agree, must be evacuated and restored, without any attempt to limit the sovereignty which she enjoys in common with all other free nations. No other single act will serve as this will serve to restore confidence among the nations in the laws which they have themselves set and determined for the government of their relations with one another. Without this healing act the whole structure and validity of international law is forever impaired.

VIII. All French territory should be freed and the invaded portions restored, and the wrong done to France by Prussia in 1871 in the matter of Alsace-Lorraine, which has unsettled the peace of the world for nearly fifty years, should be righted, in order that peace may once more be made secure in the interests of all.

IX. A readjustment of the frontiers of Italy should be effected along clearly recognizable lines of nationality.

X. The peoples of Austria-Hungary, whose place among the nations we wish to see safeguarded and assured, should be accorded the freest opportunity of autonomous development.

XI. Rumania, Serbia, and Montenegro should be evacuated; occupied territories restored; Serbia accorded free and secure access to the sea; and the relations of the several Balkan states to one another determined by friendly counsel along historically established lines of allegiance and nationality; and international guarantees of the political and economic independence and territorial integrity of the several Balkan states should be entered into.

XII. The Turkish portions of the present Ottoman Empire should be assured a secure sovereignty, but the other nationalities which are now under Turkish rule should be assured an undoubted security of life and an absolutely unmolested opportunity of autonomous development, and the Dardanelles should be permanently opened as a free passage to the ships and commerce of all nations under international guarantees.

XIII. An independent Polish state should be erected which should include the territories inhabited by indisputably Polish populations, which should be assured a free and secure access to the sea, and whose political and economic independence and territorial integrity should be guaranteed by international covenant.

XIV. A general association of nations must be formed under specific covenants for the purpose of affording mutual guarantees of political independence and territorial integrity to great and small states alike.

In regard to these essential rectifications of wrong and assertions of right we feel ourselves to be intimate partners of all the governments and peoples associated together against the Imperialists. We cannot be separated in interest or divided in purpose. We stand together until the end.

Further Readings. See Document 27.

DOCUMENT 27

The Covenant of the League of Nations

At the Versailles peace conference Woodrow Wilson transformed his fourteenth point into the League of Nations. The United States Senate, however, under the leadership of Henry Cabot Lodge, closely scrutinized the Treaty of Versailles and in particular the Covenant of the League of Nations, which represented a new departure for U.S. foreign relations.[27] After heated debate the Senate failed to ratify the Versailles Treaty and the U.S. never joined the League.

శశశ

28 April 1919

THE PREAMBLE

The High Contracting Parties

In order to promote international co-operation and to achieve international peace and security
 by the acceptance of obligations not to resort to war,
 by the prescription of open, just and honourable relations between nations,
 by the firm establishment of the understandings of international law as the
  actual rule of conduct among Governments, and
 by the maintenance of justice and a scrupulous respect for all treaty
  obligations in the dealings of organized peoples with one another,
Agree to this Covenant of the League of Nations. . . .

---

[27]H.W.V. Temperly, editor, *A History of the Peace Conference* (London: H. Frowde, and Hodder & Stoughton, 1920-24), 6:583–93, passim.

Article 2 (Executive Machinery)

The action of the League under this Covenant shall be effected through the instrumentality of an Assembly and of a Council, with a permanent Secretariat. . . .

Article 4 (Council)

The Council shall consist of Representatives of the Principal Allied and Associated Powers, together with Representatives of four other Members of the League. These four Members of the League shall be selected by the Assembly from time to time in its discretion. . . .

Article 8 (Reduction of Armaments)

The Members of the League recognize that the maintenance of peace requires the reduction of national armaments to the lowest point consistent with national safety and the enforcement by common action of international obligations.

The Council, taking account of the geographical situation and circumstances of each State, shall formulate plans for such reduction for the consideration and action of the several Governments.

Such plans shall be subject to reconsideration and revision at least every ten years.

After these plans shall have been adopted by the several Governments, the limits of armaments therein fixed shall not be exceeded without the concurrence of the Council. . . .

Article 10 (Guarantees Against Aggression)

The Members of the League undertake to respect and preserve as against external aggression the territorial integrity and existing political independence of all Members of the League. In case of any such aggression or in case of any threat or danger of such aggression the Council shall advise upon the means by which this obligation shall be fulfilled.

Article 11 (Action in Case of War or Danger of War)

Any war or threat of war, whether immediately affecting any of the Members of the League or not, is hereby declared a matter of concern to the whole League, and the League shall take any action that may be deemed wise and effectual to safeguard the peace of nations. . . .

Article 16 ('Sanctions' of the League)

Should any Member of the League resort to war in disregard of its covenants under Article 12, 13, or 15, it shall *ipso facto* be deemed to have committed an act of war against all other Members of the League, which hereby undertake immediately to subject it to the severance of all trade or financial relations, the prohibition of all intercourse between their nationals and the nationals of the Covenant-breaking State, and the prevention of all financial, commercial, or personal intercourse between the nationals of the Covenant-breaking State and the nationals of any other State, whether a Member of the League or not.

It shall be the duty of the Council in such case to recommend to the several Governments concerned what effective military, naval or air force the Members of the League shall severally contribute to the armed forces to be used to protect the covenants of the League.

The Members of the League agree, further, that they will mutually support one another in the financial and economic measures which are taken under this Article, in order to minimize the loss and inconveniences resulting from the above measures, and that they will mutually support one another in resisting any special measures aimed at one of their number by the Convenant-breaking State, and that they will take the necessary steps to afford passage through their territory to the forces of any of the Members of the League which are co-operating to protect the covenants of the League.

FURTHER READINGS FOR DOCUMENTS 25-26

Ambrosius, Lloyd E., *Woodrow Wilson and the American Diplomatic Tradition: The League Fight in Perspective* (New York: Cambridge University Press, 1987).

Ferrell, Robert H., *Woodrow Wilson and World War I* (New York: Harper & Row, 1985).

Heckscher, August, *Woodrow Wilson: A Biography* (New York: Scribner, 1991).

Maddox, Robert James, *William Borah and American Foreign Policy* (Baton Rouge: Louisiana State University Press, 1969).

Meyer, Arno, *Politics and Diplomacy of Peacemaking* (New York: Knopf, 1967).

Schwabe, Klaus, *Woodrow Wilson, Revolutionary Germany, and Peacemaking, 1918-1919* (Chapel Hill: University of North Carolina Press, 1985).

Stone, Ralph A., *The Irreconcilables* (Lexington: University of Kentucky Press, 1970).

Walworth, Arthur, *Wilson and the Peacemakers* (New York: Norton, 1986).

William C. Widenor, *Henry Cabot Lodge and the Search for an American Foreign Policy* (Berkeley: University of California Press, 1980).

DOCUMENT 28

Normalcy

Warren G. Harding, the Republican nominee for the presidency in 1920, capitalized on the disenchantment with Wilson's leadership and easily defeated James Cox in the general election. In a campaign speech titled "Back to Normal" on 14 May 1920 candidate Harding offered his vision of America's present needs.[28]

There isn't anything the matter with world civilization, except that humanity is viewing it through a vision impaired in a cataclysmal war. Poise has been disturbed and nerves have been racked, and fever has rendered men irrational; sometimes there have been draughts upon the dangerous cup of barbarity and men have wandered far from safe paths, but the human procession still marches in the right direction.

Here, in the United States, we feel the reflex, rather than the hurting wound, but we still think straight, and we mean to act straight, and mean to hold firmly to all that was ours when war involved us, and seek the higher attainments which are the only compensations that so supreme a tragedy may give mankind.

NORMAL CONDITIONS GREAT NEED

America's present need is not heroics, but healing; not nostrums but normalcy; not revolution, but restoration; not agitation, but adjustment; not surgery, but serenity; not the dramatic, but the dispassionate; not experiment, but equipoise; not submergence in internationality, but sustainment in triumphant nationality.

It is one thing to battle successfully against world domination by military autocracy, because the infinite God never intended such a program, but it is quite another thing to revise human nature and suspend the fundamental laws of life and all of life's acquirements.

---

[28]Frederick E. Schortemeier, *Rededicating America: Life and Recent Speeches of Warren G. Harding* (Indianapolis: Frederick E. Schortemeier, 1920), 223–24.

FORMAL PEACE SOUGHT

The world called for peace, and has its precarious variety. America demands peace, formal as well as actual, and means to have it, regardless of political exigencies and campaign issues. If it must be a campaign issue, we shall have peace and discuss it afterward, because the actuality is imperative, and the theory is only illusive. Then we may set our own house in order. We challenged the proposal that an armed autocrat should dominate the world; it ill becomes us to assume that a rhetorical autocrat shall direct all humanity.

This republic has its ample tasks. If we put an end to false economics which lure humanity to utter chaos, ours will be the commanding example of world leadership to-day. If we can prove a representative popular government under which a citizenship seeks what it may do for the government rather than what the government may do for individuals, we shall do more to make democracy safe for the world than all armed conflict ever recorded. The world needs to be reminded that all human ills are not curable by legislation, and that quantity of statutory enactment and excess of government offer no substitute for quality of citizenship.

FURTHER READINGS

Castigliola, Frank, *Awkward Dominion: American Political, Economic, and Cultural Relations with Europe, 1919–1933* (Ithaca, N.Y.: Cornell University Press, 1984).

Cohen, Warren I., *Empire without Tears: American Foreign Relations, 1921–1933* (Philadelphia: Temple University Press, 1987).

Ellis, L. Ethan, *Republican Foreign Policy, 1921–1933* (New Brunswick, N.J.: Rutgers University Press, 1968).

Grieb, Kenneth J., *The Latin American Policy of Warren G. Harding* (Fort Worth: Texas Christian University Press, 1976).

Murray, Robert K., *The Harding Era* (Minneapolis: University of Minnesota Press, 1969).

DOCUMENT 29

The Washington Conference Treaties

At the request of Secretary of State Charles Evans Hughes, many of the countries concerned with the affairs of the Pacific met in Washington from November 1921 through February 1922. The resulting three treaties temporarily lessened international tensions by guaranteeing the current status quo, ending an ominous naval race in capital ships, and reinforcing both the Open Door policy as well as the territorial integrity of China.[29]

ᗡᗡᗡ

THE 4-POWER TREATY

The United States of America, the British Empire, France and Japan,

With a view to the preservation of the general peace and the maintenance of their rights in relation to their insular possessions and insular dominions in the region of the Pacific Ocean,

Have determined to conclude a Treaty to this effect. . . .

I

The High Contracting Parties agree as between themselves to respect their rights in relation to their insular possessions and insular dominions in the region of the Pacific Ocean.

If there should develop between any of the High Contracting Parties a controversy arising out of any Pacific question and involving their said rights which is not satisfactorily settled by diplomacy and is likely to affect the harmonious accord now happily subsisting between them, they shall invite the other High Contracting Parties to a joint conference to which the whole subject will be referred for consideration and adjustment.

II

If the said rights are threatened by the aggressive action of any other Power, the High Contracting Parties shall communicate with one another fully and frankly in order to arrive at an understanding as to the most efficient measures to be taken, jointly or separately, to meet the exigencies of the particular situation.

---

[29]*Papers Relating to the Foreign Relations of the United States, 1922* (Washington, D.C.: U.S. Government Printing Office, 1938), 1:33–35, 247–53, 438–41.

III

This Treaty shall remain in force for ten years from the time it shall take effect, and after the expiration of said period it shall continue to be in force subject to the right of any of the High Contracting Parties to terminate it upon twelve months' notice.

IV

This Treaty shall be ratified as soon as possible in accordance with the constitutional methods of the High Contracting Parties and shall take effect on the deposit of ratifications, which shall take place at Washington, and thereupon the agreement between Great Britain and Japan, which was concluded at London on July 13, 1911, shall terminate. . . .

THE 5-POWER TREATY

The United States of America, the British Empire, France, Italy, and Japan;

Desiring to contribute to the maintenance of the general peace, and to reduce the burdens of competition in armament;

Have resolved, with a view to accomplishing these purposes, to conclude a treaty to limit their respective naval armament. . . .

Article I

The Contracting Powers agree to limit their respective naval armament as provided in the present Treaty. . . .

Article III

Subject to the provisions of Article II, the Contracting Powers shall abandon their respective capital ship building programs, and no new capital ships shall be constructed or acquired by any of the Contracting Powers except replacement tonnage which may be constructed or acquired as specified in Chapter II, Part 3. . . .

Article IV

The total capital ship replacement tonnage of each of the Contracting Powers shall not exceed in standard displacement, for the United States 525,000 tons (533,400 metric tons); for the British Empire 525,000 tons (533,400 metric tons); for France 175,000 tons (177,800 metric tons); for Italy 175,000 tons (177,800 metric tons); for Japan 315,000 tons (320,040 metric tons).

Article V

No capital ship exceeding 35,000 tons (35,560 metric tons) standard displacement shall be acquired by, or constructed by, for, or within the jurisdiction of, any of the Contracting Powers.

Article VI

No capital ship of any of the Contracting Powers shall carry a gun with a calibre in excess of 16 inches (406 millimetres).

Article VII

The total tonnage for aircraft carriers of each of the Contracting Powers shall not exceed in standard displacement, for the United States 135,000 tons (137,160 metric tons); for the British Empire 135,000 tons (137,160 metric tons); for France 60,000 tons (60,960 metric tons); for Italy 60,000 tons (60,960 metric tons); for Japan 81,000 tons (82,296 metric tons). . . .

Article XI

No vessel of war exceeding 10,000 tons (10,160 metric tons) standard displacement, other than a capital ship or aircraft carrier, shall be acquired by, or constructed by, for, or within the jurisdiction of, any of the Contracting Powers. Vessels not specifically built as fighting ships nor taken in time of peace under government control for fighting purposes, which are employed on fleet duties or as troop transports or in some other way for the purpose of assisting in the prosecution of hostilities otherwise than as fighting ships, shall not be within the limitations of this Article.

Article XII

No vessel of war of any of the Contracting Powers, hereafter laid down, other than a capital ship, shall carry a gun with a calibre in excess of 8 inches (203 millimetres). . . .

Article XIX

The United States, the British Empire and Japan agree that the *status quo* at the time of the signing of the present Treaty, with regard to fortifications and naval bases, shall be maintained in their respective territories and possessions. . . .

The maintenance of the *status quo* under the foregoing provisions implies that no new fortifications or naval bases shall be established in the territories and possessions specified; that no measures shall be taken to increase the existing naval facilities for the repair and maintenance of naval forces, and that no increase shall be made in the coast defences of the territories and possessions above specified. This restriction, however, does not preclude such repair and replacement of worn-out weapons and equipment as is customary in naval and military establishments in time of peace.

THE 9-POWER TREATY

The United States of America, Belgium, the British Empire, China, France, Italy, Japan, the Netherlands and Portugal:

Desiring to adopt a policy designed to stabilize conditions in the Far East, to safeguard the rights and interests of China, and to promote intercourse between China and the other Powers upon the basis of equality of opportunity;

Have resolved to conclude a treaty for that purpose. . . .

Article I

The Contracting Powers, other than China, agree:

(1) To respect the sovereignty, the independence, and the territorial and administrative integrity of China;
(2) To provide the fullest and most unembarrassed opportunity to China to develop and maintain for herself an effective and stable government;
(3) To use their influence for the purpose of effectually establishing and maintaining the principle of equal opportunity for the commerce and industry of all nations throughout the territory of China;
(4) To refrain from taking advantage of conditions in China in order to seek special rights or privileges which would abridge the rights of subjects or citizens of friendly States, and from countenancing action inimical to the security of such States. . . .

Article IV

The Contracting Powers agree not to support any agreements by their respective nationals with each other designed to create Spheres of Influence or to provide for the enjoyment of mutually exclusive opportunities in designated parts of Chinese territory.

FURTHER READINGS

Adler, Selig, *The Uncertain Giant* (New York: Macmillan, 1965).

Buckley, Thomas, *The United States and the Washington Conference, 1921–1922* (Knoxville: University of Tennesee Press, 1970).

Cohen, Warren I., *Empire without Tears: American Foreign Relations, 1921–1933* (Philadelphia: Temple University Press, 1987).

Dingman, Roger, *Power in the Pacific: The Origins of Naval Arms Limitations, 1914-1922* (Chicago: University of Chicago Press, 1976).

Glad, Betty, *Charles Evans Hughes and the Illusions of Innocence* (Urbana: University of Illinois Press, 1966).

Marks, Sally, *The Illusion of Peace: International Relations in Europe, 1918–1933* (New York: St. Martin's Press, 1976).

Valone, Stephen J., *'A Policy Calculated to Aid China': The United States and the China Arms Embargo, 1919-1929* (New York: Greenwood Press, 1991).

DOCUMENT 30

The Kellogg-Briand Pact

On 27 August 1927 Secretary of State Frank Kellogg and French Foreign Minister Astiride Briand signed the Pact of Paris, or Kellogg-Briand Pact, by which ultimately some 62 nations renounced war "as an instrument of national policy in their relations with one another."[30]

𝔴𝔴

ARTICLE I

The High Contracting Parties solemnly declare in the names of their respective peoples that they condemn recourse to war for the solution of international controversies, and renounce it as an instrument of national policy in their relations with one another.

ARTICLE II

The High Contracting Parties agree that the settlement or solution of all disputes or conflicts of whatever nature or of whatever origin they may be, which may arise among them, shall never be sought except by pacific means.

FURTHER READINGS

Cohen, Warren I., *Empire without Tears: America's Foreign Relations, 1921–1933* (Philadelphia: Temple University Press, 1987).

Ellis, L. Ethan, *Frank B. Kellogg and American Foreign Relations, 1925–1929* (New Brunswick, N.J.: Rutgers University Press, 1961).

Ferrell, Robert H., *Frank B. Kellogg and Henry L. Stimson* (New York: Cooper Square Publishers, 1963).

———, *Peace in Their Time: The Origins of the Kellogg-Briand Pact* (New Haven, Conn.: Yale University Press, 1952).

Marks, Sally, *The Illusion of Peace: International Relations in Europe, 1918–1933* (New York: St. Martin's Press, 1976).

---

[30]*Papers Relating to the Foreign Relations of the United States, 1928* (Washington, D.C.: U.S. Government Printing Office, 1942), 1:153–55.

DOCUMENT 31

The Stimson Doctrine

In order to expand Japanese possessions in China, elements of the Japanese army fabricated an explosion on the Japanese-owned South Manchurian Railway and used this "Mukden Incident" as a pretext to occupy all of Manchuria. President Herbert Hoover and Secretary of State Henry Stimson responded to Japanese aggression on 7 January 1932 with a policy of nonrecognition known as the Stimson Doctrine.[31]

The American Government continues confident that the work of the neutral commission recently authorized by the Council of the League of Nations will facilitate an ultimate solution of the difficulties now existing between China and Japan. But in view of the present situation and of its own rights and obligations therein, the American Government deems it to be its duty to notify both the Imperial Japanese Government and the Government of the Chinese Republic that it cannot admit the legality of any situation *de facto* nor does it intend to recognize any treaty or agreement entered into between those Governments, or agents thereof, which may impair the treaty rights of the United States or its citizens in China, including those which relate to the sovereignty, the independence, or the territorial and administrative integrity of the Republic of China, or to the international policy relative to China, commonly known as the open door policy; and that it does not intend to recognize any situation, treaty or agreement which may be brought about by means contrary to the covenants and obligations of the Pact of Paris of August 27, 1928, to which Treaty both China and Japan, as well as the United States, are parties.

FURTHER READINGS

Barnhart, Michael, *Japan Prepares for Total War: The Quest for Economic Security, 1919–1941* (Ithaca, N.Y.: Cornell University Press, 1987).

Doenecke, Justus D., *When the Wicked Rise: American Opinion-Makers and the Manchurian Crisis of 1931–1933* (Lewisburg, Pa.: Bucknell University Press, 1984).

Dudden, Arthur Power, *The American Pacific: From the Old China Trade to the Present* (New York: Oxford University Press, 1992).

---

[31]*The China White Paper* (Stanford, CA.: Stanford University Press, 1967), Annexes, 446–47.

Ferrell, Robert H., *Frank B. Kellogg and Henry L. Stimson* (New York: Cooper Square Publishers, 1963).

Iriye, Akira, *Across the Pacific* (New York: Harcourt, Brace and World, 1967).

Rappaport, Armin, *Henry L. Stimson and Japan, 1931–1933* (Chicago: University of Chicago Press, 1963).

Thorne, Christopher, *The Limits of Foreign Policy: The West, The League and The Far Eastern Crisis of 1931–1933* (New York: Putnam, 1973).

DOCUMENT 32

The Good Neighbor Policy

In his Inaugural Address on 4 March 1933 President Franklin D. Roosevelt dedicated the United States to "the policy of the good neighbor."[32] For Latin American nations this meant an end to U.S. military intervention with the abrogation of the Platt Amendment as well as U.S. acceptance of nonintervention resolutions of the Seventh Pan-American Conference (1931) and the Inter-American Conference (1936).

卐卐

Our international trade relations, though vastly important, are in point of time and necessity secondary to the establishment of a sound national economy. I favor as a practical policy the putting of first things first. I shall spare no effort to restore world trade by international economic readjustment, but the emergency at home cannot wait on that accomplishment.

The basic thought that guides these specific means of national recovery is not narrowly nationalistic. It is the insistence, as a first consideration, upon the interdependence of the various elements in and parts of the United States—a recognition of the old and permanently important manifestation of the American spirit of the pioneer. It is the way to recovery. It is the immediate way. It is the strongest assurance that the recovery will endure.

In the field of world policy I would dedicate this Nation to the policy of the good neighbor—the neighbor who resolutely respects himself and, because he does so, respects the rights of others—the neighbor who respects his obligations and respects the sanctity of his agreements in and with a world of neighbors.

If I read the temper of our people correctly, we now realize as we have never realized before our interdependence on each other; that we cannot merely take

---

[32]Samuel I. Rosenman, editor, *The Public Papers and Addresses of Franklin D. Roosevelt* (N.Y.: Random House, 1938), 2:14.

but we must give as well; that if we are to go forward, we must move as a trained and loyal army willing to sacrifice for the good of a common discipline, because without such discipline no progress is made, no leadership becomes effective. We are, I know, ready and willing to submit our lives and property to such discipline, because it makes possible a leadership which aims at a larger good. This I propose to offer, pledging that the larger purposes will bind upon us all as a sacred obligation with a unity of duty hitherto evoked only in time of armed strife.

With this pledge taken, I assume unhesitatingly the leadership of this great army of our people dedicated to a disciplined attack upon our common problems.

FURTHER READINGS

Gellman, Irwin F., *Good Neighbor Diplomacy: United States Policy in Latin America, 1933–1945* (Baltimore: Johns Hopkins University Press, 1979).

Green, David, *The Containment of Latin America* (Chicago: Quadrangle Books, 1971).

Langley, Lester D., *The United States and the Caribbean, 1900–1970* (Athens: University of Georgia Press, 1980).

Munro, Dana, *United States and the Caribbean Republics, 1921–1933* (Princeton, N.J.: Princeton University Press, 1974).

Wood, Bryce, *The Making of the Good Neighbor Policy* (New York: Columbia University Press, 1961).

DOCUMENT 33

The Neutrality Acts

By the 1930s many Americans believed that U.S. participation in World War I had been a mistake and that in particular the "Merchants of Death"—munitions manufacturers—had heavily influenced the decision for war. In order to prevent a replay of the events of 1914–1917, isolationists in Congress passed a series of Neutrality Acts between 1935 and 1939.[33]

---

[33]*U.S. Statutes at Large* (Washington, D.C.: U.S. Government Printing Office, 1936, 1937, 1941), 49, part 1:1081, 1153; 50, part 1:121–22, 127; 54, part 1:4.

31 August 1935

Resolved by the Senate and House of Representatives of the United States of America in Congress assembled, That upon the outbreak or during the progress of war between, or among, two or more foreign states, the President shall proclaim such fact, and it shall thereafter be unlawful to export arms, ammunition, or implements of war from any place in the United States, or possessions of the United States, to any port of such belligerent states, or to any neutral port for transshipment to, or for the use of, a belligerent country.

The President, by proclamation, shall definitely enumerate the arms, ammunition, or implements of war, the export of which is prohibited by this Act.

The President may, from time to time, by proclamation, extend such embargo upon the export of arms, ammunition, or implements of war to other states as and when they may become involved in such war. . . .

29 February 1936

Sec. 1a. Whenever the President shall have issued his proclamation as provided for in section 1 of this Act, it shall thereafter during the period of the war be unlawful for any person within the United States to purchase, sell, or exchange bonds, securities, or other obligations of the government of any belligerent country, or of any political subdivision thereof, or of any person acting for or on behalf of such government, issued after the date of such proclamation, or to make any loan or extend any credit to any such government or person: *Provided*, That if the President shall find that such action will serve to protect the commercial or other interests of the United States or its nationals, he may, in his discretion, and to such extent and under such regulation as he may prescribe, except from the operation of this section ordinary commercial credits and short-time obligations in aid of legal transactions and of a character customarily used in normal peace-time commercial transactions.

The provisions of this section shall not apply to a renewal or adjustment of such indebtedness as may exist on the date of the President's pro-clamation. . . .

1 May 1937

SECTION 1. a. Whenever the President shall find that there exists a state of war between, or among, two or more foreign states, the President shall proclaim such fact, and it shall thereafter be unlawful to export, or attempt to export, or cause to be exported, arms, ammunition, or implements of war from any place in the United States to any belligerent state named in such proclamation, or to any neutral state for transshipment to, or for the use of, any such belligerent state.

b. The President shall, from time to time, by proclamation, extend such embargo upon the export of arms, ammunition, or implements of war to other states as and when they may become involved in such war.

c. Whenever the President shall find that a state of civil strife exists in a foreign state and that such civil strife is of a magnitude or is being conducted under such conditions that the export of arms, ammunition, or implements of war from the United States to such foreign state would threaten or endanger the peace of the United States, the President shall proclaim such fact, and it shall thereafter be unlawful to export, or attempt to export, or cause to be exported, arms, ammunition, or implements of war from any place in the United States to such foreign state, or to any neutral state for transshipment to, or for the use of, such foreign state. . . .

SECTION 9. Whenever the President shall have issued a proclamation under the authority of section 1 of this Act it shall thereafter be unlawful for any citizen of the United States to travel on any vessel of the state or states named in such proclamation, except in accordance with such rules and regulations as the President shall prescribe. . . .

4 November 1939

Sec. 2. a. Whenever the President shall have issued a proclamation under the authority of section 1 a. it shall thereafter be unlawful for any American vessel to carry any passengers or any articles or materials to any state named in such proclamation. . . .

c. Whenever the President shall have issued a proclamation under the authority of section 1 a. it shall thereafter be unlawful to export or transport, or attempt to export or transport, or cause to be exported or transported, from the United States to any state named in such proclamation, any articles or materials except copyrighted articles or materials. until all right, title, and interest therein shall have been transferred to some foreign government, agency, institution, association, partnership, corporation, or national.

Further Readings. See Document 34.

DOCUMENT 34

The Ludlow Amendment

Representative Louis Ludlow sought to isolate the United States still further from foreign wars by introducing legislation for a 22nd Amendment to the Constitution.[34] The Ludlow Amendment would have, in most cases, required a national referendum before the United States could go to war. After intense lobbying by President Roosevelt, a motion to discharge Ludlow's resolution from committee failed by a vote of 209–188.

ooooooooooooooooooooooooooooooooooooooooooooooooooooooooooooooooooooo

SECTION 1. Except in case of attack by armed forces, actual or immediately threatened, upon the United States or its Territorial possessions, or by any non-American nation against any country in the Western Hemisphere, the people shall have the sole power by a national referendum to declare war or to engage in warfare overseas. Congress, when it deems a national crisis to exist in conformance with this article, shall by concurrent resolution refer the question to the people.

FURTHER READINGS FOR DOCUMENTS 33-34

Adler, Selig, *The Isolationist Impulse* (New York: Abelard-Schuman, 1957).

Anderson, Irvine H., *The Standard-Vacuum Oil Company and United States East Asian Policy* (Princeton, N.J.: Princeton University Press, 1975).

Cole, Wayne S., *Roosevelt and the Isolationists* (Lincoln: University of Nebraska Press, 1983).

———, *Senator Gerald P. Nye and American Foreign Relations* (Minneapolis: University of Minnesota Press, 1962).

Divine, Robert A., *The Illusion of Neutrality* (Chicago: University of Chicago Press, 1962).

Guinsburg, Thomas N., *The Pursuit of Isolationism in the United States Senate from Versailles to Pearl Harbor* (New York: Garland, 1982).

Jonas, Manfred, *Isolationism in America* (Ithaca, N.Y.: Cornell University Press, 1966).

Koginos, Manny T., *The Panay Incident* (Lafayette, Ind.: Purdue University Studies, 1967).

Wiltz, John, *From Isolation to War, 1919–1939* (Arlington Heights, Ill.: Harlan Davidson, 1971).

---

[34]*Congressional Record* (Washington, D.C.: U.S. Government Printing Office), 83, part 9: Appendix, 207.

DOCUMENT 35

Roosevelt's "Quarantine" Speech

Roosevelt vigorously condemned renewed Japanese aggression in China in an address on 5 October 1937.[35] *Isolationists, however, sharply criticized the president's suggestion that the epidemic of aggression be in some way quarantined.*

❦❦

The political situation in the world, which of late has been growing progressively worse, is such as to cause grave concern and anxiety to all the peoples and nations who wish to live in peace and amity with their neighbors. . . . Without a declaration of war and without warning or justification of any kind, civilians, including vast numbers of women and children, are being ruthlessly murdered with bombs from the air. In times of so-called peace, ships are being attacked and sunk by submarines without cause or notice. Nations are fomenting and taking sides in civil warfare in nations that have never done them any harm. Nations claiming freedom for themselves deny it to others.

Innocent peoples, innocent nations, are being cruelly sacrificed to a greed for power and supremacy which is devoid of all sense of justice and humane considerations. . . .

The peace-loving nations must make a concerted effort in opposition to those violations of treaties and those ignorings of humane instincts which today are creating a state of international anarchy and instability from which there is no escape through mere isolation or neutrality.

Those who cherish their freedom and recognize and respect the equal right of their neighbors to be free and live in peace, must work together for the triumph of law and moral principles in order that peace, justice and confidence may prevail in the world. There must be a return to a belief in the pledged word, in the value of a signed treaty. There must be recognition of the fact that national morality is as vital as private morality. . . .

It seems to be unfortunately true that the epidemic of world lawlessness is spreading.

---

[35]Samuel I. Rosenman, editor, *The Public Papers and Addresses of Franklin D. Roosevelt* (N.Y.: Random House, 1938), 407–11.

When an epidemic of physical disease starts to spread, the community approves and joins in a quarantine of the patients in order to protect the health of the community against the spread of the disease.

It is my determination to pursue a policy of peace. It is my determination to adopt every practicable measure to avoid involvement in war. It ought to be inconceivable that in this modern era, and in the face of experience, any nation could be so foolish and ruthless as to run the risk of plunging the whole world into war by invading and violating, in contravention of solemn treaties, the territory of other nations that have done them no real harm and are too weak to protect themselves adequately. Yet the peace of the world and the welfare and security of every nation, including our own, is today being threatened by that very thing.

No nation which refuses to exercise forbearance and to respect the freedom and rights of others can long remain strong and retain the confidence and respect of other nations. No nation ever loses its dignity or its good standing by conciliating its differences, and by exercising great patience with, and consideration for, the rights of other nations.

War is a contagion, whether it be declared or undeclared. It can engulf states and peoples remote from the original scene of hostilities. We are determined to keep out of war, yet we cannot insure ourselves against the disastrous effects of war and the dangers of involvement. We are adopting such measures as will minimize our risk of involvement, but we cannot have complete protection in a world of disorder in which confidence and security have broken down.

If civilization is to survive the principles of the Prince of Peace must be restored. Trust between nations must be revived.

Most important of all, the will for peace on the part of peace-loving nations must express itself to the end that nations that may be tempted to violate their agreements and the rights of others will desist from such a course. There must be positive endeavors to preserve peace.

America hates war. America hopes for peace. Therefore, America actively engages in the search for peace.

Further Readings. See Document 39.

DOCUMENT 36

Roosevelt and U.S. Neutrality

Roosevelt explained the neutral posture of the United States toward the war in Europe during a radio address on 3 September 1939.[36] Given the circumstances surrounding the start of the war, however, Roosevelt could not ask, as Wilson had 25 years before, that "every American remain neutral in thought as well."

ⁿⁿ

Tonight my single duty is to speak to the whole of America.

Until four-thirty this morning I had hoped against hope that some miracle would prevent a devastating war in Europe and bring to an end the invasion of Poland by Germany.

For four long years a succession of actual wars and constant crises have shaken the entire world and have threatened in each case to bring on the gigantic conflict which is today unhappily a fact.

It is right that I should recall to your minds the consistent and at times successful efforts of your Government in these crises to throw the full weight of the United States into the cause of peace. In spite of spreading wars I think that we have every right and every reason to maintain as a national policy the fundamental moralities, the teachings of religion and the continuation of efforts to restore peace—for some day, though the time may be distant, we can be of even greater help to a crippled humanity. . . .

You must master at the outset a simple but unalterable fact in modern foreign relations between nations. When peace has been broken anywhere, the peace of all countries everywhere is in danger.

It is easy for you and for me to shrug our shoulders and to say that conflicts taking place thousands of miles from the continental United States, and, indeed, thousands of miles from the whole American Hemisphere, do not seriously affect the Americas—and that all the United States has to do is to ignore them and go about its own business. Passionately though we may desire detachment, we are forced to realize that every word that comes through the air, every ship that sails the sea, every battle that is fought, does affect the American future.

Let no man or woman thoughtlessly or falsely talk of America sending its armies to European fields. At this moment there is being prepared a proclamation of American neutrality. This would have been done even if there

---

[36]B. D. Zevin, editor, *Nothing to Fear: The Selected Addresses of Franklin Delano Roosevelt* (Boston: Houghton Mifflin, Co., 1946), 180–82.

had been no neutrality statute on the books, for this proclamation is in accordance with international law and in accordance with American policy.

This will be followed by a Proclamation required by the existing Neutrality Act. And I trust that in the days to come our neutrality can be made a true neutrality. . . .

This Nation will remain a neutral Nation, but I cannot ask that every American remain neutral in thought as well. Even a neutral has a right to take account of facts. Even a neutral cannot be asked to close his mind or his conscience.

I have said not once, but many times, that I have seen war and that I hate war. I say that again and again.

I hope the United States will keep out of this war. I believe that it will. And I give you assurance and reassurance that every effort of your Government will be directed toward that end.

As long as it remains within my power to prevent, there will be no black-out of peace in the United States.

Further Readings. See Document 39.

DOCUMENT 37

Roosevelt's Fireside Chat on National Security

In a radio address of 29 December 1940 Roosevelt explained to the American people that by becoming the "great arsenal of democracy" the United States could reduce its chances of entering the war.[37]

This is not a fireside chat on war. It is a talk on national security; because the nub of the whole purpose of your President is to keep you now, and your children later, and your grandchildren much later, out of a last-ditch war for the preservation of American independence and all the things that American independence means to you and to me and to ours.

Tonight, in the presence of a world crisis, my mind goes back eight years to a night in the midst of a domestic crisis. It was a time when the wheels of American industry were grinding to a full stop, when the whole banking system of our country had ceased to function.

---

[37]B.D. Zevin, editor, *Nothing to Fear: The Selected Addresses of Franklin Delano Roosevelt* (Boston: Houghton Mifflin, Co., 1946), 248–57, passim.

I well remember that while I sat in my study in the White House, preparing to talk with the people of the United States, I had before my eyes the picture of all those Americans with whom I was talking. I saw the workmen in the mills, the mines, the factories; the girl behind the counter; the small shopkeeper; the farmer doing his spring plowing; the widows and the old men wondering about their life's savings.

I tried to convey to the great mass of American people what the banking crisis meant to them in their daily lives.

Tonight, I want to do the same thing, with the same people, in this new crisis which faces America.

We met the issue of 1933 with courage and realism. We face this new crisis—this new threat to the security of our Nation—with the same courage and realism.

Never before since Jamestown and Plymouth Rock has our American civilization been in such danger as now.

For, on September 27, 1940, by an agreement signed in Berlin, three powerful nations, two in Europe and one in Asia, joined themselves together in the threat that if the United States of America interfered with or blocked the expansion program of these three nations—a program aimed at world control—they would unite in ultimate action against the United States.

The Nazi masters of Germany have made it clear that they intend not only to dominate all life and thought in their own country, but also to enslave the whole of Europe, and then to use the resources of Europe to dominate the rest of the world. . . .

At this moment, the forces of the states that are leagued against all peoples who live in freedom, are being held away from our shores. The Germans and the Italians are being blocked on the other side of the Atlantic by the British, and by the Greeks, and by thousands of soldiers and sailors who were able to escape from subjugated countries. In Asia, the Japanese are being engaged by the Chinese nation in another great defense.

In the Pacific Ocean is our fleet.

Some of our people like to believe that wars in Europe and in Asia are of no concern to us. But it is a matter of most vital concern to us that European and Asiatic war-makers should not gain control of the oceans which lead to this hemisphere. . . .

Does anyone seriously believe that we need to fear attack anywhere in the Americas while a free Britain remains our most powerful naval neighbor in the Atlantic? Does anyone seriously believe, on the other hand, that we could rest easy if the Axis powers were our neighbors there?

If Great Britain goes down, the Axis powers will control the continents of Europe, Asia, Africa, Australasia, and the high seas—and they will be in a position to bring enormous military and naval resources against this hemisphere. It is no exaggeration to say that all of us, in all the Americas, would be living at the point of a gun—a gun loaded with explosive bullets, economic as well as military.

We should enter upon a new and terrible era in which the whole world, our Hemisphere included, would be run by threats of brute force. To survive in such a world, we would have to convert ourselves permanently into a militaristic power on the basis of war economy.

Some of us like to believe that even if Great Britain falls, we are still safe, because of the broad expanse of the Atlantic and of the Pacific.

But the width of those oceans is not what it was in the days of clipper ships. At one point between Africa and Brazil the distance is less than from Washington to Denver, Colorado—five hours for the latest type of bomber. And at the North end of the Pacific Ocean America and Asia almost touch each other.

Even today we have planes that could fly from the British Isles to New England and back again without refueling. And remember that the range of the modern bomber is ever being increased. . . .

There are those who say that the Axis powers would never have any desire to attack the Western Hemisphere. That is the same dangerous form of wishful thinking which has destroyed the powers of resistance of so many conquered peoples. The plain facts are that the Nazis have proclaimed, time and again, that all other races are their inferiors and therefore subject to their orders. And most important of all, the vast resources and wealth of this American Hemisphere constitute the most tempting loot in all the round world.

Let us no longer blind ourselves to the undeniable fact that the evil forces which have crushed and undermined and corrupted so many others are already within our own gates. Your Government knows much about them and every day is ferreting them out.

Their secret emissaries are active in our own and in neighboring countries. They seek to stir up suspicion and dissension to cause internal strife. They try to turn capital against labor, and vice versa. They try to reawaken long slumbering racial and religious enmities which should have no place in this country. They are active in every group that promotes intolerance. They exploit for their own ends our natural abhorrence of war. These trouble-breeders have but one purpose. It is to divide our people into hostile groups and to destroy our unity and shatter our will to defend ourselves.

There are also American citizens, many of them in high places, who, unwittingly in most cases, are aiding and abetting the work of these agents. I do not charge these American citizens with being foreign agents. But I do charge them with doing exactly the kind of work that the dictators want done in the United States.

These people not only believe that we can save our own skins by shutting our eyes to the fate of other nations. Some of them go much further than that. They say that we can and should become the friends and even the partners of the Axis powers. Some of them even suggest that we should imitate the methods of the dictatorships. Americans never can and never will do that. . . .

The British people and their allies today are conducting an active war against this unholy alliance. Our own future security is greatly dependent on the outcome of that fight. Our ability to "keep out of war" is going to be affected by that outcome.

Thinking in terms of today and tomorrow, I make the direct statement to the American people that there is far less chance of the United States getting into war, if we do all we can now to support the nations defending themselves against attack by the Axis than if we acquiesce in their defeat, submit tamely to an Axis victory, and wait our turn to be the object of attack in another war later on.

If we are to be completely honest with ourselves, we must admit that there is risk in any course we may take. But I deeply believe that the great majority of our people agree that the course that I advocate involves the least risk now and the greatest hope for world peace in the future.

The people of Europe who are defending themselves do not ask us to do their fighting. They ask us for the implements of war, the planes, the tanks, the guns, the freighters which will enable them to fight for their liberty and for our security. Emphatically we must get these weapons to them in sufficient volume and quickly enough, so that we and our children will be saved the agony and suffering of war which others have had to endure. . . .

There is no demand for sending an American Expeditionary Force outside our own borders. There is no intention by any member of your Government to send such a force. You can, therefore, nail any talk about sending armies to Europe as deliberate untruth.

Our national policy is not directed towards war. Its sole purpose is to keep war away from our country and our people.

Democracy's fight against world conquest is being greatly aided, and must be more greatly aided, by the rearmament of the United States and by sending every ounce and every ton of munitions and supplies that we can possibly spare to help the defenders who are in the front lines. It is no more unneutral for us to do that than it is for Sweden, Russia and other nations near Germany, to send steel and ore and oil and other war materials into Germany every day in the week.

We are planning our own defense with the utmost urgency; and in its vast scale we must integrate the war needs of Britain and other free nations which are resisting aggression.

This is not a matter of sentiment or of controversial personal opinion. It is a matter of realistic, practical military policy, based on the advice of our military experts who are in close touch with existing warfare. These military and naval experts and the members of the Congress and the Administration have a single-minded purpose—the defense of the United States.

This Nation is making a great effort to produce everything that is necessary in this emergency—and with all possible speed. This great effort requires great sacrifice. . . .

As planes and ships and guns and shells are produced, your Government, with its defense experts, can then determine how best to use them to defend this Hemisphere. The decision as to how much shall be sent abroad and how much shall remain at home must be made on the basis of our over-all military necessities.

We must be the great arsenal of democracy. For us this is an emergency as serious as war itself. We must apply ourselves to our task with the same resolution, the same sense of urgency, the same spirit of patriotism and sacrifice as we would show were we at war. . . .

As President of the United States I call for that national effort. I call for it in the name of this Nation which we love and honor and which we are privileged and proud to serve. I call upon our people with absolute confidence that our common cause will greatly succeed.

Further Readings.   See Document 39.

DOCUMENT 38

The Lend-Lease Act

Congress responded favorably to Roosevelt's request and, in spite of vigorous opposition from isolationists, on 11 March 1941 passed the Lend-Lease Act.[38]

AN ACT

Further to promote the defense of the United States, and for other purposes.

Be it enacted by the Senate and House of Representatives of the United States of America in Congress assembled, That this Act may be cited as "An Act to Promote the Defense of the United States. . . ."

SEC. 3. a. . . . the President may, from time to time, when he deems it in the interest of national defense, authorize the Secretary of War, the Secretary of

---

[38]*U.S. Statutes at Large* (Washington, D.C.: U.S. Government Printing Office, 1942), 55, part 1:31–32.

the Navy, or the head of any other department or agency of the Government—

1. To manufacture in arsenals, factories, and shipyards under their jurisdiction, or otherwise procure, to the extent to which funds are made available therefor, or contracts are authorized from time to time by the Congress, or both, any defense article for the government of any country whose defense the President deems vital to the defense of the United States.

2. To sell, transfer title to, exchange, lease, lend, or otherwise dispose of, to any such government any defense article, but no defense article not manufactured or procured under paragraph 1. shall in any way be disposed of under this paragraph, except after consultation with the Chief of Staff of the Army or the Chief of Naval Operations of the Navy, or both. . . .

3. To test, inspect, prove, repair, outfit, recondition, or otherwise to place in good working order, to the extent to which funds are made available therefor, or contracts are authorized from time to time by the Congress, or both, any defense article for any such government, or to procure any or all such services by private contract.

4. To communicate to any such government any defense information, pertaining to any defense article furnished to such government under paragraph 2. of this subsection. . . .

[SEC. 3.]b. The terms and conditions upon which any such foreign government receives any aid authorized under subsection a. shall be those which the President deems satisfactory, and the benefit to the United States may be payment or repayment in kind or property, or any other direct or indirect benefit which the President deems satisfactory. . . .

[SEC. 3.]d. Nothing in this Act shall be construed to authorize or to permit the authorization of convoying vessels by naval vessels of the United States.

[SEC. 3.]e. Nothing in this Act shall be construed to authorize or to permit the authorization of the entry of any American vessel into a combat area in violation of section 3 of the Neutrality Act of 1939.

Further Readings. See Document 39.

DOCUMENT 39

The Atlantic Charter

*Roosevelt met Prime Minister Winston Churchill off the coast of Newfoundland
and on 14 August 1941 issued the Atlantic Charter, which encompassed eight
"common principles in the national policies of their respective countries."*[39]

The President of the United States of America and the Prime Minister, Mr.
Churchill, representing His Majesty's Government in the United Kingdom,
being met together, deem it right to make known certain common principles in
the national policies of their respective countries on which they base their hopes
for a better future for the world.

First, their countries seek no aggrandizement, territorial or other;

Second, they desire to see no territorial changes that do not accord with the
freely expressed wishes of the peoples concerned;

Third, they respect the right of all peoples to choose the form of government
under which they will live; and they wish to see sovereign rights and self-
government restored to those who have been forcibly deprived of them;

Fourth, they will endeavor, with due respect for their existing obligations, to
further the enjoyment by all states, great or small, victor or vanquished, of
access, on equal terms, to the trade and to the raw materials of the world which
are needed for their economic prosperity;

Fifth, they desire to bring about the fullest collaboration between all Nations
in the economic field with the object of securing, for all, improved labor
standards, economic advancement, and social security;

Sixth, after the final destruction of the Nazi tyranny, they hope to see
established a peace which will afford to all Nations the means of dwelling in
safety within their own boundaries, and which will afford assurance that all the
men in all the lands may live out their lives in freedom from fear and want;

Seventh, such a peace should enable all men to traverse the high seas and
oceans without hindrance;

Eighth, they believe that all of the Nations of the world, for realistic as well
as spiritual reasons, must come to the abandonment of the use of force. Since
no future peace can be maintained if land, sea, or air armaments continue to be
employed by Nations which threaten, or may threaten, aggression outside of
their frontiers, they believe, pending the establishment of a wider and

---

[39]Samuel I. Rosenman, editor, *The Public Papers and Addresses of Franklin D.
Roosevelt* (N.Y.: Random House, 1938), 314–15.

permanent system of general security, that the disarmament of such Nations is essential. They will likewise aid and encourage all other practicable measures which will lighten for peace-loving peoples the crushing burden of armaments.

FURTHER READINGS FOR DOCUMENTS 35-39

Cole, Wayne S., *Roosevelt and the Isolationists* (Lincoln: University of Nebraska Press, 1983).

Dallek, Robert, *Franklin D. Roosevelt and American Foreign Policy, 1933–1945* (New York: Oxford University Press, 1981).

Divine, Robert A., *The Illusion of Neutrality* (Chicago: University of Chicago Press, 1962).

Guinsburg, Thomas N., *The Pursuit of Isolationism in the United States Senate from Versailles to Pearl Harbor* (New York: Garland, 1982).

Herring, George, *Aid to Russia, 1941–1946* (New York: Columbia University Press, 1973).

Kimball, Warren F., *The Most Unsordid Act: Lend-Lease, 1939–1941* (Baltimore: Johns Hopkins University Press, 1969).

————, *The Juggler: Franklin Roosevelt as Wartime Statesman* (Princeton, N.J.: Princeton University Press, 1991).

Thorne, Christopher, *Allies of a Kind* (London: Hamilton, 1978).

Woods, Randall Bennett, *A Changing of the Guard: Anglo-American Relations, 1941–1946* (Chapel Hill: University of North Carolina Press, 1990).

DOCUMENT 40

Roosevelt's Request for a Declaration of War against Japan

The Japanese attack at Pearl Harbor on 7 December 1941 ended the efforts by isolationists to keep the United States out of World War II. The next day President Roosevelt asked Congress for a declaration of war; after thirty-three minutes of debate Congress passed a joint resolution declaring that a state of war existed between the United States and Japan by a vote of 82–0 in the Senate and 388–1 in the House of Representatives.[40]

---

[40]Samuel I. Rosenman, editor, *The Public Papers and Addresses of Franklin D. Roosevelt* (N.Y.: Random House, 1938), 514–15.

**MR. VICE PRESIDENT, AND MR. SPEAKER, AND MEMBERS OF
THE SENATE AND HOUSE OF REPRESENTATIVES:**

YESTERDAY, December 7, 1941—a date which will live in infamy—the
United States of America was suddenly and deliberately attacked by naval and
air forces of the Empire of Japan.

The United States was at peace with that Nation and, at the solicitation of
Japan, was still in conversation with its Government and its Emperor looking
toward the maintenance of peace in the Pacific.   Indeed, one hour after
Japanese air squadrons had commenced bombing in the American Island of
Oahu, the Japanese Ambassador to the United States and his colleague
delivered to our Secretary of State a formal reply to a recent American message.
And while this reply stated that it seemed useless to continue the existing
diplomatic negotiations, it contained no threat or hint of war or of armed
attack.

It will be recorded that the distance of Hawaii from Japan makes it obvious
that the attack was deliberately planned many days or even weeks ago.   During
the intervening time the Japanese Government has deliberately sought to
deceive the United States by false statements and expressions of hope for
continued peace.

The attack yesterday on the Hawaiian Islands has caused severe damage to
American naval and military forces.   I regret to tell you that very many
American lives have been lost.   In addition American ships have been reported
torpedoed on the high seas between San Francisco and Honolulu.

Yesterday the Japanese Government also launched an attack against
Malaya.

Last night Japanese forces attacked Hong Kong.

Last night Japanese forces attacked Guam.

Last night Japanese forces attacked the Philippine Islands.

Last night the Japanese attacked Wake Island.

And this morning the Japanese attacked Midway Island.

Japan has, therefore, undertaken a surprise offensive extending throughout
the Pacific area.   The facts of yesterday and today speak for themselves.   The
people of the United States have already formed their opinions and well
understand the implications to the very life and safety of our Nation.

As Commander in Chief of the Army and Navy I have directed that all
measures be taken for our defense.   But always will our whole Nation
remember the character of the onslaught against us.

No matter how long it may take us to overcome this premeditated invasion,
the American people in their righteous might will win through to absolute
victory.

I believe that I interpret the will of the Congress and of the people when I
assert that we will not only defend ourselves to the uttermost but will make it
very certain that this form of treachery shall never again endanger us.

Hostilities exist. There is no blinking at the fact that our people, our territory, and our interests are in grave danger.

With confidence in our armed forces—with the unbounding determination of our people—we will gain the inevitable triumph—so help us God.

I ask that the Congress declare that since the unprovoked and dastardly attack by Japan on Sunday, December 7, 1941, a state of war has existed between the United States and the Japanese Empire.

FURTHER READINGS

Barnhart, Michael, *Japan Prepares for Total War: The Quest for Economic Security, 1919–1941* (Ithaca, N.Y: Cornell University Press, 1987).

Heinrichs, Waldo H., *Threshold of War: Franklin D. Roosevelt and American Entry into World War II* (New York: Oxford University Press, 1988).

Iriye, Akira, *The Origins of the Second World War in the Pacific* (New York: Longman, 1987).

Marks, Frederick W., *Wind over Sand: The Diplomacy of Franklin Delano Roosevelt* (Athens: University of Georgia Press, 1988).

Prange, Gordon, *At Dawn We Slept: The Untold Story of Pearl Harbor* (New York: McGraw-Hill, 1981).

Toland, John, *Infamy: Pearl Harbor and Its Aftermath* (Garden City, N.Y.: Doubleday, 1982).

Wohlstetter, Roberta, *Pearl Harbor: Warning and Decision* (Stanford, Calif.: Stanford University Press, 1962).

DOCUMENT 41

Declaration of Four Nations on General Security

After a meeting of foreign ministers in Moscow on 1 November 1943, the United States, Great Britain, the Soviet Union and China agreed to act together not only to win the war, but to create a "general international organization" that would "maintain international peace and security." Significantly, four days later the Senate passed by a vote of 85 to 5 a resolution introduced by Senator Tom Connally, the chairman of the Senate Foreign Relations Committee, that included Point 4 of the Declaration of Four Nations on General Security. [41]

---

[41]*Papers Relating to the Foreign Relations of the United States, 1943* (Washington, D.C.: U.S. Government Printing Office, 1963), 1:755–56.

DECLARATION OF FOUR NATIONS ON GENERAL SECURITY

The Governments of the United States of America, the United Kingdom, the Soviet Union and China;

united in their determination, in accordance with the Declaration by the United Nations of January 1, 1942, and subsequent declarations, to continue hostilities against those Axis powers with which they respectively are at war until such powers have laid down their arms on the basis of unconditional surrender;

conscious of their responsibility to secure the liberation of themselves and the peoples allied with them from the menace of aggression;

recognizing the necessity of ensuring a rapid and orderly transition from war to peace and of establishing and maintaining international peace and security with the least diversion of the world's human and economic resources for armaments;

jointly declare:

1. That their united action, pledged for the prosecution of the war against their respective enemies, will be continued for the organization and maintenance of peace and security.
2. That those of them at war with a common enemy will act together in all matters relating to the surrender and disarmament of that enemy.
3. That they will take all measures deemed by them to be necessary to provide against any violation of the terms imposed upon the enemy.
4. That they recognize the necessity of establishing at the earliest practicable date a general international organization, based on the principle of the sovereign equality of all peace-loving states, and open to membership by all such states, large and small, for the maintenance of international peace and security.
5. That for the purposes of maintaining international peace and security pending the reestablishment of law and order and the inauguration of a system of general security, they will consult with one another and as occasion requires with other members of the United Nations with a view to joint action on behalf of the community of nations.
6. That after the termination of hostilities they will not employ their military forces within the territories of other states except for the purposes envisaged in this declaration and after joint consultation.
7. That they will confer and cooperate with one another and with other members of the United Nations to bring about a practicable general agreement with respect to the regulation of armaments in the post-war period.

FURTHER READINGS

Ambrose, Stephen E., *Rise to Globalism* (New York: Penguin Books, 1983).

Campbell, Thomas M., *Masquerade Peace: America's UN Policy, 1944–1945* (Tallahassee: Florida State University Press, 1973).

Divine, Robert A., *Second Chance: The Triumph of Internationalism in America during World War II* (New York: Atheneum, 1967).

Luard, Evan, *A History of the United Nations* (New York: St. Martin's Press, 1982).

Marks, Frederick W., *Wind over Sand: The Diplomacy of Franklin D. Roosevelt* (Athens: University of Georgia Press, 1988).

Mastny, Vojtech, *Russia's Road to the Cold War* (New York: Columbia University Press, 1979).

Sainsbury, Keith, *The Turning Point: Roosevelt, Stalin, Churchill, and Chiang Kai-shek, 1943* (Oxford: Oxford University Press, 1985).

DOCUMENT 42

The Yalta Agreements

Roosevelt, Churchill, and Stalin met in the Crimea during the first weeks of 1945 to finalize wartime military strategy and plan for the postwar world. Ultimately the 11 February 1945 agreements would become very controversial and critics would argue that Roosevelt had failed to protect the interests of the Free World at the Yalta Conference.[42]

తత

PROTOCOL OF THE PROCEEDINGS OF THE CRIMEA CONFERENCE

The Crimea Conference of the Heads of the Governments of the United States of America, the United Kingdom, and the Union of Soviet Socialist Republics which took place from February 4th to 11th came to the following conclusions.

I. World Organization

It was decided:

1. that a United Nations Conference on the proposed world organization should be summoned for Wednesday, 25th April, 1945, and should be held in the United States of America.
2. the Nations to be invited to this Conference should be:

---

[42]*Papers Relating to the Foreign Relations of the United States, 1945* (Washington, D.C.: U.S. Government Printing Office, 1955), *The Conferences of Malta and Yalta*, 975–84, passim.

    a. the United Nations as they existed on the 8th February, 1945 and

    b. such of the Associated Nations as have declared war on the common enemy by 1st March, 1945. (For this purpose by the term "Associated Nations" was meant the eight Associated Nations and Turkey.) When the Conference on World Organization is held, the delegates of the United Kingdom and United States of America will support a proposal to admit to original membership two Soviet Socialist Republics, i.e. the Ukraine and White Russia.

3. that the United States Government on behalf of the Three Powers should consult the Government of China and the French Provisional Government in regard to the decisions taken at the present Conference concerning the proposed World Organization. . . .

II. Declaration on Liberated Europe

The following declaration has been approved:

The Premier of the Union of Soviet Socialist Republics, the Prime Minister of the United Kingdom and the President of the United States of America have consulted with each other in the common interests of the peoples of their countries and those of liberated Europe. They jointly declare their mutual agreement to concert during the temporary period of instability in liberated Europe the policies of their three governments in assisting the peoples liberated from the domination of Nazi Germany and the peoples of the former Axis satellite states of Europe to solve by democratic means their pressing political and economic problems.

The establishment of order in Europe and the re-building of national economic life must be achieved by processes which will enable the liberated peoples to destroy the last vestiges of Nazism and Fascism and to create democratic institutions of their own choice. This is a principle of the Atlantic Charter—the right of all peoples to choose the form of government under which they will live—the restoration of sovereign rights and self-government to those peoples who have been forcibly deprived of them by the aggressor nations.

To foster the conditions in which the liberated peoples may exercise these rights, the three governments will jointly assist the people in any European liberated state or former Axis satellite state in Europe where in their judgment conditions require a. to establish conditions of internal peace; b. to carry out emergency measures for the relief of distressed peoples; c. to form interim governmental authorities broadly representative of all democratic elements in the population and pledged to the earliest possible establishment through free elections of governments responsive to the will of the people; and d. to facilitate where necessary the holding of such elections.

The three governments will consult the other United Nations and provisional authorities or other governments in Europe when matters of direct interest to them are under consideration.

When, in the opinion of the three governments, conditions in any European liberated state or any former Axis satellite state in Europe make such action necessary, they will immediately consult together on the measures necessary to discharge the joint responsibilities set forth in this declaration.

By this declaration we reaffirm our faith in the principles of the Atlantic Charter, our pledge in the Declaration by the United Nations, and our determination to build in co-operation with other peace-loving nations world order under law, dedicated to peace, security, freedom and general well-being of all mankind.

In issuing this declaration, the Three Powers express the hope that the Provisional Government of the French Republic may be associated with them in the procedure suggested.

III. Dismemberment of Germany

It was agreed that Article 12a. of the Surrender Terms for Germany should be amended to read as follows:

The United Kingdom, the United States of America and the Union of Soviet Socialist Republics shall possess supreme authority with respect to Germany. In the exercise of such authority they will take such steps, including the complete disarmament, demilitarization and dismemberment of Germany as they deem requisite for future peace and security.

The study of the procedure for the dismemberment of Germany was referred to a Committee, consisting of Mr. [Anthony] Eden (Chairman), Mr. [John G.] Winant and Mr. [Fedor T.] Gousev. This body would consider the desirability of associating with it a French representative.

IV. Zone of Occupation for the French and Control Council for Germany

It was agreed that a zone in Germany, to be occupied by the French Forces, should be allocated to France. This zone would be formed out of the British and American zones and its extent would be settled by the British and Americans in consultation with the French Provisional Government.

It was also agreed that the French Provisional Government should be invited to become a member of the Allied Control Council for Germany.

V. Reparation

The following protocol has been approved:

1. Germany must pay in kind for the losses caused by her to the Allied nations in the course of the war. Reparations are to be received in the first instance by those countries which have borne the main burden of the war, have suffered the heaviest losses and have organized victory over the enemy.
2. Reparation in kind is to be exacted from Germany in three following forms:
   a. Removals within 2 years from the surrender of Germany or the cessation of organized resistance from the national wealth of Germany located on the territory of Germany herself as well as outside her territory (equipment, machine-tools, ships, rolling stock, German investments abroad, shares of industrial, transport and other enterprises in Germany etc.), these removals to be carried out chiefly for [the] purpose of destroying the war potential of Germany.
   b. Annual deliveries of goods from current production for a period to be fixed.
   c. Use of German labor.
3. For the working out on the above principles of a detailed plan for exaction of reparation from Germany an Allied Reparation Commission will be set up in Moscow. It will consist of three representatives—one from the Union of Soviet Socialist Republics, one from the United Kingdom and one from the United States of America.
4. With regard to the fixing of the total sum of the reparation as well as the distribution of it among the countries which suffered from the German aggression the Soviet and American delegations agreed as follows:

The Moscow Reparation Commission should take in its initial studies as a basis for discussion the suggestion of the Soviet Government that the total sum of the reparation in accordance with the points a. and b. of the paragraph 2 should be 20 billion dollars and that 50% of it should go to the Union of Soviet Socialist Republics.

The British delegation was of the opinion that pending consideration of the reparation question by the Moscow Reparation Commission no figures of reparation should be mentioned. The above Soviet-American proposal has been passed to the Moscow Reparation Commission as one of the proposals to be considered by the Commission. . . . .

VII. Poland

The following Declaration on Poland was agreed by the Conference:

A new situation has been created in Poland as a result of her complete liberation by the Red Army. This calls for the establishment of a Polish Provisional Government which can be more broadly based than was possible before the recent liberation of the Western part of Poland. The Provisional Government which is now functioning in Poland should therefore be reorganized on a broader democratic basis with the inclusion of democratic leaders from Poland itself and from Poles abroad. This new Government should then be called the Polish Provisional Government of National Unity.

Mr. Molotov, Mr. Harriman and Sir A. Clark Kerr are authorized as a commission to consult in the first instance in Moscow with members of the present Provisional Government and with other Polish democratic leaders from within Poland and from abroad, with a view to the reorganization of the present Government along the above lines. This Polish Provisional Government of National Unity shall be pledged to the holding of free and unfettered elections as soon as possible on the basis of universal suffrage and secret ballot. In these elections all democratic and anti-Nazi parties shall have the right to take part and to put forward candidates.

When a Polish Provisional Government of National Unity has been properly formed in conformity with the above, the Government of the U.S.S.R., which now maintains diplomatic relations with the present Provisional Government of Poland, and the Government of the United Kingdom and the Government of the U.S.A. will establish diplomatic relations with the new Polish Provisional Government of National Unity, and will exchange Ambassadors by whose reports the respective Governments will be kept informed about the situation in Poland.

The three Heads of Government consider that the Eastern frontier of Poland should follow the Curzon Line with digressions from it in some regions of five to eight kilometers in favor of Poland. They recognized that Poland must receive substantial accessions of territory in the North and West. They feel that the opinion of the new Polish Provisional Government of National Unity should be sought in due course on the extent of these accessions and that the final delimitation of the Western frontier of Poland should thereafter await the Peace Conference.

VIII. Yugoslavia

It was agreed to recommend to Marshal Tito and to Dr. Subasic:
a. that the Tito-Subasic Agreement should immediately be put into effect and a new Government formed on the basis of the Agreement.

b. that as soon as the new Government has been formed it should declare:

    i. that the Anti-Fascist Assembly of National Liberation (AUNOJ) will be extended to include members of the last Yugoslav Skupstina who have not compromised themselves by collaboration with the enemy, thus forming a body to be known as a temporary Parliament; and

    ii. that legislative acts passed by the Anti-Fascist Assembly of National Liberation (AUNOJ) will be subject to subsequent ratification by a Constituent Assembly. . . .

XIII. Meetings of the Three Foreign Secretaries

The Conference agreed that permanent machinery should be set up for consultation between the three Foreign Secretaries; they should meet as often as necessary, probably about every three or four months.

These meetings will be held in rotation in the three capitals, the first meeting being held in London. . . .

AGREEMENT REGARDING ENTRY OF THE SOVIET UNION INTO THE WAR AGAINST JAPAN

Top Secret

AGREEMENT

The leaders of the three Great Powers—the Soviet Union, the United States of America and Great Britain—have agreed that in two or three months after Germany has surrendered and the war in Europe has terminated the Soviet Union shall enter into the war against Japan on the side of the Allies on condition that:

1. The *status quo* in Outer-Mongolia (The Mongolian People's Republic) shall be preserved;

2. The former rights of Russia violated by the treacherous attack of Japan in 1904 shall be restored, viz:

    a. the southern part of Sakhalin as well as all the islands adjacent to it shall be returned to the Soviet Union,

    b. the commercial port of Darien shall be internationalized, the preeminent interests of the Soviet Union in this port being safeguarded and the lease of Port Arthur as a naval base of the USSR restored,

    c. the Chinese-Eastern Railroad and the South-Manchurian Railroad which provides an outlet to Darien shall be jointly operated by the establishment of a joint Soviet-Chinese Company it being understood that the preeminent interests of the Soviet Union shall be safeguarded and that China shall retain full sovereignty in Manchuria;

3. The Kuril islands shall be handed over to the Soviet Union.

It is understood, that the agreement concerning Outer-Mongolia and the ports and railroads referred to above will require concurrence of Generalissimo Chiang Kai-Shek. The President will take measures in order to obtain this concurrence on advice from Marshal Stalin.

The Heads of the three Great Powers have agreed that these claims of the Soviet Union shall be unquestionably fulfilled after Japan has been defeated.

For its part the Soviet Union expresses its readiness to conclude with the National Government of China a pact of friendship and alliance between the USSR and China in order to render assistance to China with its armed forces for the purpose of liberating China from the Japanese yoke.

Signed:

J. Stalin
Franklin D. Roosevelt
Winston S. Churchill

FURTHER READINGS

Buhite, Russell, *Decisions at Yalta* (Wilmington, Del.: Scholarly Resources, 1986).

Clemens, Diane Shaver, *Yalta* (New York: Oxford University Press, 1970).

Dallek, Robert, *Franklin D. Roosevelt and American Foreign Policy, 1933–1945* (New York: Oxford University Press, 1981).

Harbutt, Fraser J., *The Iron Curtain: Churchill, America, and the Origins of the Cold War* (New York: Oxford University Press, 1986).

Mastny, Vojtech, *Russia's Road to the Cold War* (New York: Columbia University Press, 1979).

Theoharis, Athan G., *The Yalta Myths* (Columbia: University of Missouri Press, 1970).

Watt, Donald Cameron, "Britain and the Historiography of the Yalta Conference and the Cold War," *Diplomatic History*, 13, no. 1 (Winter 1989): 67-98.

DOCUMENT 43

The Potsdam Agreements

At the Potsdam Conference, the victorious Allied Powers determined how they would treat defeated Germany and also attempted to resolve a number of other pressing issues.[43]

☙☙☙

PROTOCOL OF THE PROCEEDINGS OF THE BERLIN CONFERENCE

The Berlin Conference of the Three Heads of Government of the U.S.S.R., U.S.A., and U.K., which took place from July 17 to August 1, 1945, came to the following conclusions:

I. Establishment of a Council of Foreign Ministers

The Conference reached the following agreement for the establishment of a Council of Foreign Ministers to do the necessary preparatory work for the peace settlements:

1. There shall be established a Council composed of the Foreign Ministers of the United Kingdom, the Union of Soviet Socialist Republics, China, France and the United States.

2.   i. The Council shall normally meet in London, which shall be the permanent seat of the joint Secretariat which the Council will form. Each of the Foreign Ministers will be accompanied by a high-ranking Deputy, duly authorized to carry on the work of the Council in the absence of his Foreign Minister, and by a small staff of technical advi[s]ers.

    ii. The first meeting of the Council shall be held in London not later than September 1st 1945. Meetings may be held by common agreement in other capitals as may be agreed from time to time. . . .

---

[43]*Papers Relating to the Foreign Relations of the United States, 1945* (Washington, D.C.: U.S. Government Printing Office, 1960), *Conference at Berlin (Potsdam)*, II: 1478–97, passim.

II. The Principle to Govern the Treatment of Germany in the Initial Control Period

A. Political Principles

1. In accordance with the Agreement on Control Machinery in Germany, supreme authority in Germany is exercised, on instructions from their respective Governments, by the Commanders-in-Chief of the armed forces of the United States of America, the United Kingdom, the Union of Soviet Socialist Republics, and the French Republic, each in his own zone of occupation, and also jointly, in matters affecting Germany as a whole, in their capacity as members of the Control Council.

2. So far as is practicable, there shall be uniformity of treatment of the German population throughout Germany.

3. The purposes of the occupation of Germany by which the Control Council shall be guided are:

   i. The complete disarmament and demilitarization of Germany and the elimination or control of all German industry that could be used for military production. . . .

   ii. To convince the German people that they have suffered a total military defeat and that they cannot escape responsibility for what they have brought upon themselves, since their own ruthless warfare and the fanatical Nazi resistance have destroyed German economy and made chaos and suffering inevitable.

   iii. To destroy the National Socialist Party and its affiliated and supervised organizations, to dissolve all Nazi institutions, to ensure that they are not revived in any form, and to prevent all Nazi and militarist activity or propaganda.

   iv. To prepare for the eventual reconstruction of German political life on a democratic basis and for eventual peaceful cooperation in international life by Germany.

4. All Nazi laws which provided the basis of the Hitler regime or established discrimination on grounds of race, creed, or political opinion shall be abolished. No such discriminations, whether legal, administrative or otherwise, shall be tolerated.

5. War criminals and those who have participated in planning or carrying out Nazi enterprises involving or resulting in atrocities or war crimes shall be arrested and brought to judgment. Nazi leaders, influential Nazi supporters and high officials of Nazi organizations and institutions and any other persons dangerous to the occupation or its objectives shall be arrested and interned.

6. All members of the Nazi Party who have been more than nominal participants in its activities and all other persons hostile to Allied purposes shall be removed from public and semi-public office, and from positions of responsibility in important private undertakings. Such persons shall be replaced by persons who, by their political and moral qualities, are deemed capable of assisting in developing genuine democratic institutions in Germany. . . .

B. Economic Principles

11. In order to eliminate Germany's war potential, the production of arms, ammunition and implements of war as well as all types of aircraft and sea-going ships shall be prohibited and prevented. Production of metals, chemicals, machinery and other items that are directly necessary to a war economy shall be rigidly controlled and restricted to Germany's approved post-war peacetime needs to meet the objectives stated in Paragraph 15. Productive capacity not needed for permitted production shall be removed in accordance with the reparations plan recommended by the Allied Commission on Reparations and approved by the Governments concerned or if not removed shall be destroyed.

12. At the earliest practicable date, the German economy shall be decentralized for the purpose of eliminating the present excessive concentration of economic power as exemplified in particular by cartels, syndicates, trusts and other monopolistic arrangements. Notwithstanding this, however, and for the purpose of achieving the objectives set forth herein, certain forms of central administrative machinery, particularly in the fields of Finance, Transportation and Communications, shall be maintained or restored.

13. In organizing the German Economy, primary emphasis shall be given to the development of agriculture and peaceful domestic industries.

14. During the period of occupation Germany shall be treated as a single economic unit. To this end common policies shall be established in regard to:

a. mining and industrial production and allocation;
b. agriculture, forestry and fishing;
c. wages, prices and rationing;
d. import and export programs for Germany as a whole;
e. currency and banking, central taxation and customs;
f. reparation and removal of industrial war potential;
g. transportation and communications. . . .

III. Reparations from Germany

1. Reparation claims of the U.S.S.R., shall be met by removals from the zone of Germany occupied by the U.S.S.R., and from appropriate German external assets.

2. The U.S.S.R. undertakes to settle the reparation claims of Poland from its own share of reparations.

3. The reparation claims of the United States, the United Kingdom and other countries entitled to reparations shall be met from the Western Zones and from appropriate German external assets.

4. In addition to the reparations to be taken by the U.S.S.R. from its own zone of occupation, the U.S.S.R. shall receive additionally from the Western Zones:
    a. 15 per cent of such usable and complete industrial capital equipment, in the first place from the metallurgical, chemical and machine manufacturing industries as is unnecessary for the German peace economy and should be removed from the Western Zones of Germany, in exchange for an equivalent value of food, coal, potash, zinc, timber, clay products, petroleum products, and such other commodities as may be agreed upon.

    b. 10 per cent of such industrial capital equipment as is unnecessary for the German peace economy and should be removed from the Western Zones, to be transferred to the Soviet Government on reparations account without payment or exchange of any kind in return.

    Removals of equipment as provided in (a) and (b) above shall be made simultaneously.

5. The amount of equipment to be removed from the Western Zones on account of reparations must be determined within six months from now at the latest. . . .

VIII. Poland

A. Declaration

We have taken note with pleasure of the agreement reached among representative Poles from Poland and abroad which has made possible the formation, in accordance with the decisions reached at the Crimea Conference, of a Polish Provisional Government of National Unity recognised by the Three Powers. The establishment by the British and United States Governments of diplomatic relations with the Polish Provisional Government has resulted in the withdrawal of their recognition from the former Polish Government in London, which no longer exists.

The British and U.S. Governments have taken measures to protect the interests of the Polish Provisional Government, as the recognised Government of the Polish State, in the property belonging to the Polish State located in their territories and under their control whatever the form of this property may be. They have further taken measures to prevent alienation to third parties of such property. All proper facilities will be given to the Polish Provisional Government for the exercise of the ordinary legal remedies for the recovery of any property belonging to the Polish State which may have been wrongfully alienated. . . .

The Three Powers note that the Polish Provisional Government in accordance with the decisions of the Crimea Conference has agreed to the holding of free and unfettered elections as soon as possible on the basis of universal suffrage and secret ballot in which all democratic and anti-Nazi parties shall have the right to take part and to put forward candidates; and that representatives of the Allied Press shall enjoy full freedom to report to the world upon developments in Poland before and during the elections. . . .

XIV. Iran

It was agreed that Allied troops should be withdrawn immediately from Tehran, and that further stages of the withdrawal of troops from Iran should be considered at the meeting of the Council of Foreign Ministers to be held in London in September, 1945. . . .

XVI. The Black Sea Straits

The Three Governments recognized that the Convention on the Straits concluded at Montreux should be revised as failing to meet present-day conditions.

It was agreed that as the next step the matter should be the subject of direct conversations between each of the three Governments and the Turkish Government.

FURTHER READINGS

Feis, Herbert, *Between War and Peace: The Potsdam Conference* (Princeton, N.J.: Princeton University Press, 1960).

Gaddis, John Lewis, *The United States and the Origins of the Cold War* (New York: Columbia University Press, 1972).

Gormly, James L., *From Potsdam to the Cold War: Big Three Diplomacy, 1945–1947* (Wilmington, Del.: SR Books, 1990).

LaFeber, Walter, *America, Russia and the Cold War* (New York: McGraw-Hill, 1985).

Leffler, Melvyn P., *A Preponderance of Power: National Security, the Truman Administration, and the Cold War* (Stanford, Calif.: Stanford University Press, 1992).

Patterson, Thomas, *On Every Front: The Making and Unmaking of the Cold War* (New York: Norton, 1979).

DOCUMENT 44

The Long Telegram

George Kennan, the U.S. chargé d'affaires at Moscow, sent his famous "Long Telegram" to the State Department on 22 February 1946.[44] Kennan's analysis of Soviet conduct and his recommendations to U.S. policymakers were widely read in official Washington circles, and profoundly affected the future course of U.S. foreign affairs.

ΨΨΨΨΨΨΨΨΨΨΨΨΨΨΨΨΨΨΨΨΨΨΨΨΨΨΨΨΨΨΨΨΨΨΨΨΨΨΨΨΨΨΨΨΨΨΨΨΨΨΨΨΨΨΨΨ

PART 1: BASIC FEATURES OF POST WAR SOVIET OUTLOOK, AS PUT FORWARD BY OFFICIAL PROPAGANDA MACHINE, ARE AS FOLLOWS:

a. USSR still lives in antagonistic "capitalist encirclement" with which in the long run there can be no permanent peaceful coexistence. As stated by Stalin in 1927 to a delegation of American workers: In course of further development of international revolution there will emerge two centers of

---

[44]*Papers Relating to the Foreign Relations of the United States, 1946* (Washington, D.C.: U.S. Government Printing Office, 1969), 6:697–709, passim.

world significance: a socialist center, drawing to itself the countries which tend toward socialism, and a capitalist center, drawing to itself the countries that incline toward capitalism. Battle between these two centers for command of world economy will decide fate of capitalism and of communism in entire world.

b. Capitalist world is beset with internal conflicts, inherent in nature of capitalist society. These conflicts are insoluble by means of peaceful compromise. Greatest of them is that between England and US.

c. Internal conflicts of capitalism inevitably generate wars. Wars thus generated may be of two kinds: intra-capitalist wars between two capitalist states, and wars of intervention against socialist world. Smart capitalists, vainly seeking escape from inner conflicts of capitalism, incline toward latter.

d. Intervention against USSR, while it would be disastrous to those who undertook it, would cause renewed delay in progress of Soviet socialism and must therefore be forestalled at all costs.

e. Conflicts between capitalist states, though likewise fraught with danger for USSR, nevertheless hold out great possibilities for advancement of socialist cause, particularly if USSR remains militarily powerful, ideologically monolithic and faithful to its present brilliant leadership.

f. It must be borne in mind that capitalist world is not all bad. In addition to hopelessly reactionary and bourgeois elements, it includes 1. certain wholly enlightened and positive elements united in acceptable communistic parties and 2. certain other elements now described for tactical reasons as progressive or democratic. whose reactions, aspirations and activities happen to be "objectively" favorable to interests of USSR. These last must be encouraged and utilized for Soviet purposes.

g. Among negative elements of bourgeois-capitalist society, most dangerous of all are those whom Lenin called false friends of the people, namely the moderate-socialist or social-democratic leaders in other words, non-Communist left-wing. These are more dangerous than out-and-out reactionaries, for latter at least march under their true colors, whereas moderate left-wing leaders confuse people by employing devices of socialism to serve interests of reactionary capital.

So much for premises. To what deductions do they lead from standpoint of Soviet policy? To following:

a. Everything must be done to advance relative strength of USSR as factor in international society. Conversely, no opportunity must be missed to reduce strength and influence, collectively as well as individually, of capitalist powers.

b. Soviet efforts, and those of Russia's friends abroad, must be directed toward deepening and exploiting of differences and conflicts between capitalist powers. If these eventually deepen into an "imperialist" war, this war must be turned into revolutionary upheavals within the various capitalist countries.

c. "Democratic-progressive" elements abroad are to be utilized to maximum to bring pressure to bear on capitalist governments along lines agreeable to Soviet interests.

d. Relentless battle must be waged against socialist and social-democratic leaders abroad.

PART 2: BACKGROUND OF OUTLOOK

Before examining ramifications of this party line in practice there are certain aspects of it to which I wish to draw attention.

First, it does not represent natural outlook of Russian people. Latter are, by and large, friendly to outside world, eager for experience of it, eager to measure against it talents they are conscious of possessing, eager above all to live in peace and enjoy fruits of their own labor. Party line only represents thesis which official propaganda machine puts forward with great skill and persistence to a public often remarkably resistant in the stronghold of its innermost thoughts. But party line is binding for outlook and conduct of people who make up apparatus of power—party, secret police and Government—and it is exclusively with these that we have to deal. . . .

At bottom of Kremlin's neurotic view of world affairs is traditional and instinctive Russian sense of insecurity. Originally, this was insecurity of a peaceful agricultural people trying to live on vast exposed plain in neighborhood of fierce nomadic peoples. To this was added, as Russia came into contact with economically advanced West, fear of more competent, more powerful, more highly organized societies in that area. But this latter type of insecurity was one which afflicted rather Russian rulers than Russian people; for Russian rulers have invariably sensed that their rule was relatively archaic in form, fragile and artificial in its psychological foundation, unable to stand comparison or contact with political systems of Western countries. For this reason they have always feared foreign penetration, feared direct contact between Western world and their own, feared what would happen if Russians learned truth about world without or if foreigners learned truth about world within. And they have learned to seek security only in patient but deadly struggle for total destruction of rival power, never in compacts and compromises with it.

It was no coincidence that Marxism, which had smouldered ineffectively for half a century in Western Europe, caught hold and blazed for first time in Russia. Only in this land which had never known a friendly neighbor or indeed any tolerant equilibrium of separate powers, either internal or international, could a doctrine thrive which viewed economic conflicts of society as insoluble by peaceful means. After establishment of Bolshevist regime, Marxist dogma, rendered even more truculent and intolerant by Lenin's interpretation, became a perfect vehicle for sense of insecurity with which Bolsheviks, even more than previous Russian rulers, were afflicted. In this dogma, with its basic altruism of purpose, they found justification for their instinctive fear of outside world, for the dictatorship without which they did not know how to rule, for cruelties they did not dare not to inflict, for sacrifices they felt bound to demand. In the name of Marxism they sacrificed every single ethical value in their methods and tactics. Today they cannot dispense with it. It is fig leaf of their moral and intellectual respectability. Without it they would stand before history, at best, as only the last of that long succession of cruel and wasteful Russian rulers who have relentlessly forced country on to ever new heights of military power in order to guarantee external security of their internally weak regimes. This is why Soviet purposes must always be solemnly clothed in trappings of Marxism, and why no one should underrate importance of dogma in Soviet affairs. Thus Soviet leaders are driven [by?] necessities of their own past and present position to put forward a dogma which [apparent omission] outside world as evil, hostile and menacing, but as bearing within itself germs of creeping disease and destined to be wracked with growing internal convulsions until it is given final *coup de grace* by rising power of socialism and yields to new and better world. This thesis provides justification for that increase of military and police power of Russian state, for that isolation of Russian population from outside world, and for that fluid and constant pressure to extend limits of Russian police power which are together the natural and instinctive urges of Russian rulers. Basically this is only the steady advance of uneasy Russian nationalism, a centuries old movement in which conceptions of offense and defense are inextricably confused. But in new guise of international Marxism, with its honeyed promises to a desperate and war torn outside world, it is more dangerous and insidious than ever before. . . .

PART 3: PROJECTION OF SOVIET OUTLOOK IN PRACTICAL POLICY ON OFFICIAL LEVEL

We have now seen nature and background of Soviet program. What may we expect by way of its practical implementation?

Soviet policy, as Department implies in its query under reference, is conducted on two planes: 1. official plane represented by actions undertaken officially in name of Soviet Government; and 2. subterranean plane of actions undertaken by agencies for which Soviet Government does not admit responsibility.

Policy promulgated on both planes will be calculated to serve basic policies a. to d. outlined in part 1. Actions taken on different planes will differ considerably, but will dovetail into each other in purpose, timing and effect.

On official plane we must look for following:

a. Internal policy devoted to increasing in every way strength and prestige of Soviet state: intensive military-industrialization; maximum development of armed forces; great displays to impress outsiders; continued secretiveness about internal matters, designed to conceal weaknesses and to keep opponents in dark.

b. Wherever it is considered timely and promising, efforts will be made to advance official limits of Soviet power. For the moment, these efforts are restricted to certain neighboring points conceived of here as being of immediate strategic necessity, such as Northern Iran, Turkey, possibly Bornholm. However, other points may at any time come into question, if and as concealed Soviet political power is extended to new areas. Thus a "friendly" Persian Government might be asked to grant Russia a port on Persian Gulf. Should Spain fall under Communist control, question of Soviet base at Gibraltar Strait might be activated. But such claims will appear on official level only when unofficial preparation is complete.

c. Russians will participate officially in international organizations where they see opportunity of extending Soviet power or of inhibiting or diluting power of others. Moscow sees in UNO not the mechanism for a permanent and stable world society founded on mutual interest and aims of all nations, but an arena in which aims just mentioned can be favorably pursued. As long as UNO is considered here to serve this purpose, Soviets will remain with it. But if at any time they come to conclusion that it is serving to embarrass or frustrate their aims for power expansion and if they see better prospects for pursuit of these aims along other lines, they will not hesitate to abandon UNO. . . .

d. Toward colonial areas and backward or dependent peoples, Soviet policy, even on official plane, will be directed toward weakening of power and influence and contacts of advanced Western nations, on theory that in so far as this policy is successful, there will be created a vacuum which will favor Communist-Soviet penetration. . . .

PART 4: FOLLOWING MAY BE SAID AS TO WHAT WE MAY EXPECT BY WAY OF IMPLEMENTATION OF BASIC SOVIET POLICIES ON UNOFFICIAL, OR SUBTERRANEAN PLANE, I.E. ON PLANE FOR WHICH SOVIET GOVERNMENT ACCEPTS NO RESPONSIBILITY

Agencies utilized for promulgation of policies on this plane are following:

1. Inner central core of Communist Parties in other countries. While many of persons who compose this category may also appear and act in unrelated public capacities, they are in reality working closely together as an underground operating directorate of world communism, a concealed Comintern tightly coordinated and directed by Moscow. It is important to

remember that this inner core is actually working on underground lines, despite legality of parties with which it is associated.

2. Rank and file of Communist Parties. Note distinction is drawn between these and persons defined in paragraph 1. This distinction has become much sharper in recent years. Whereas formerly foreign Communist Parties represented a curious and from Moscow's standpoint often inconvenient. mixture of conspiracy and legitimate activity, now the conspiratorial element has been neatly concentrated in inner circle and ordered underground, while rank and file—no longer even taken into confidence about realities of movement—are thrust forward as bona fide internal partisans of certain political tendencies within their respective countries, genuinely innocent of conspiratorial connection with foreign states. Only in certain countries where communists are numerically strong do they now regularly appear and act as a body. . . .

3. A wide variety of national associations or bodies which can be dominated or influenced by such penetration. These include: labor unions, youth leagues, women's organizations, racial societies, religious societies, social organizations, cultural groups, liberal magazines, publishing houses, etc.

4. International organizations which can be similarly penetrated through influence over various national components. Labor, youth and women's organizations are prominent among them. Particular, almost vital, importance is attached in this connection to international labor movement. In this, Moscow sees possibility of sidetracking western governments in world affairs and building up international lobby capable of compelling governments to take actions favorable to Soviet interests in various countries and of paralyzing actions disagreeable to USSR. . . .

It may be expected that component parts of this far-flung apparatus will be utilized, in accordance with their individual suitability, as follows:

a. To undermine general political and strategic potential of major western powers. Efforts will be made in such countries to disrupt national self confidence, to hamstring measures of national defense, to increase social and industrial unrest, to stimulate all forms of disunity. All persons with grievances, whether economic or racial, will be urged to seek redress not in mediation and compromise, but in defiant violent struggle for destruction of other elements of society. Here poor will be set against rich, black against white, young against old, newcomers against established residents, etc.

b. On unofficial plane particularly violent efforts will be made to weaken power and influence of Western Powers of [on] colonial backward, or dependent peoples. On this level, no holds will be barred. Mistakes and weaknesses of western colonial administration will be mercilessly exposed and exploited. Liberal opinion in Western countries will be mobilized to weaken colonial policies. Resentment among dependent peoples will be stimulated. And while latter are being encouraged to seek independence of Western Powers, Soviet dominated puppet political machines will be undergoing preparation to take over domestic power in respective colonial areas when independence is achieved.

c. Where individual governments stand in path of Soviet purposes pressure will be brought for their removal from office. This can happen where governments directly oppose Soviet foreign policy aims Turkey, Iran., where they seal their territories off against Communist penetration Switzerland, Portugal., or where they compete too strongly, like Labor Government in England, for moral domination among elements which it is important for Communists to dominate. . . .

d. In foreign countries Communists will, as a rule, work toward destruction of all forms of personal independence, economic, political or moral. Their system can handle only individuals who have been brought into complete dependence on higher power. Thus, persons who are financially independent—such as individual businessmen, estate owners, successful farmers, artisans and all those who exercise local leadership or have local prestige, such as popular local clergymen or political figures, are anathema. . . .

e. Everything possible will be done to set major Western Powers against each other. Anti-British talk will be plugged among Americans, anti-American talk among British. Continentals, including Germans, will be taught to abhor both Anglo-Saxon powers. Where suspicions exist, they will be fanned; where not, ignited. . . .

f. In general, all Soviet efforts on unofficial international plane will be negative and destructive in character, designed to tear down sources of strength beyond reach of Soviet control. This is only in line with basic Soviet instinct that there can be no compromise with rival power and that constructive work can start only when Communist power is dominant. But behind all this will be applied insistent, unceasing pressure for penetration and command of key positions in administration and especially in police apparatus of foreign countries. The Soviet regime is a police regime par excellence, reared in the dim half world of Tsarist police intrigue, accustomed to think primarily in terms of police power. This should never be lost sight of in gauging Soviet motives.

PART 5: [PRACTICAL DEDUCTIONS FROM STANDPOINT OF US POLICY]

In summary, we have here a political force committed fanatically to the belief that with US there can be no permanent *modus vivendi*, that it is desirable and necessary that the internal harmony of our society be disrupted, our traditional way of life be destroyed, the international authority of our state be broken, if Soviet power is to be secure. This political force has complete power of disposition over energies of one of the world's greatest peoples and resources of world's richest national territory, and is borne along by deep and powerful currents of Russian nationalism. . . . This is admittedly not a pleasant picture. Problem of how to cope with this force in [is] undoubtedly greatest task our diplomacy has ever faced and probably greatest it will ever have to face. It should be point of departure from which our political general staff work at present juncture should proceed. It should be approached with same thoroughness and care as solution of major strategic problem in war, and if necessary, with no smaller outlay in planning effort. I cannot attempt to suggest all answers here. But I would like to record my conviction that problem is within our power to solve—and that without recourse to any general military conflict. And in support of this conviction there are certain observations of a more encouraging nature I should like to make:

1. Soviet power, unlike that of Hitlerite Germany, is neither schematic nor adventuristic. It does not work by fixed plans. It does not take unnecessary risks. Impervious to logic of reason, and it is highly sensitive to logic of force. For this reason it can easily withdraw—and usually does—when strong resistance is encountered at any point. Thus, if the adversary has sufficient force and makes clear his readiness to use it, he rarely has to do so. If situations are properly handled there need be no prestige-engaging showdowns.

2. Gauged against Western World as a whole, Soviets are still by far the weaker force. Thus, their success will really depend on degree of cohesion, firmness and vigor which Western World can muster. And this is factor which it is within our power to influence.

3. Success of Soviet system, as form of international power, is not yet finally proven. . . .

For these reasons I think we may approach calmly and with good heart problem of how to deal with Russia. As to how this approach should be made, I only wish to advance, by way of conclusion, following comments:

1. Our first step must be to apprehend, and recognize for what it is, the nature of the movement with which we are dealing. We must study it with same courage, detachment, objectivity, and same determination not to be emotionally provoked or unseated by it, with which doctor studies unruly and unreasonable individual.

2. We must see that our public is educated to realities of Russian situation. I cannot over-emphasize importance of this. Press cannot do this alone. It must be done mainly by Government, which is necessarily more experienced and better informed on practical problems involved. In this we need not be deterred by [ugliness?] of picture. I am convinced that there would be far less hysterical anti-Sovietism in our country today if realities of this situation were better understood by our people. There is nothing as dangerous or as terrifying as the unknown. It may also be argued that to

reveal more information on our difficulties with Russia would reflect unfavorably on Russian-American relations. I feel that if there is any real risk here involved, it is one which we should have courage to face, and sooner the better. But I cannot see what we would be risking. Our stake in this country, even coming on heels of tremendous demonstrations of our friendship for Russian people, is remarkably small. We have here no investments to guard, no actual trade to lose, virtually no citizens to protect, few cultural contacts to preserve. Our only stake lies in what we hope rather than what we have; and I am convinced we have better chance of realizing those hopes if our public is enlightened and if our dealings with Russians are placed entirely on realistic and matter-of-fact basis.

3. Much depends on health and vigor of our own society. World communism is like malignant parasite which feeds only on diseased tissue. This is point at which domestic and foreign policies meet. Every courageous and incisive measure to solve internal problems of our own society, to improve self-confidence, discipline, morale and community spirit of our own people, is a diplomatic victory over Moscow worth a thousand diplomatic notes and joint communiqués. If we cannot abandon fatalism and indifference in face of deficiencies of our own society, Moscow will profit—Moscow cannot help profiting by them in its foreign policies.

4. We must formulate and put forward for other nations a much more positive and constructive picture of sort of world we would like to see than we have put forward in past. It is not enough to urge people to develop political processes similar to our own. Many foreign peoples, in Europe at least, are tired and frightened by experiences of past, and are less interested in abstract freedom than in security. They are seeking guidance rather than responsibilities. We should be better able than Russians to give them this. And unless we do, Russians certainly will.

5. Finally we must have courage and self-confidence to cling to our own methods and conceptions of human society. After all, the greatest danger that can befall us in coping with this problem of Soviet communism, is that we shall allow ourselves to become like those with whom we are coping.

Kennan

FURTHER READINGS

Gaddis, John Lewis, *The United States and the Origins of the Cold War* (New York: Columbia University Press, 1972).

Harbutt, Fraser J., *The Iron Curtain: Churchill, America, and the Origins of the Cold War* (New York: Oxford University Press, 1986).

Hixson, Walter, *George F. Kennan: Cold War Iconoclast* (New York: Columbia University Press, 1989).

Kennan, George F., *Memoirs*, 2 volumes (Boston: Little, Brown, 1967–72).

LaFeber, Walter, *America, Russia and the Cold War* (New York: McGraw-Hill, 1991).

Larson, Deborah, *Origins of Containment* (Princeton, N.J.: Princeton University Press, 1985).

Leffler, Melvin P., *A Preponderance of Power: National Security, the Truman Administration, and the Cold War* (Stanford, Calif.: Stanford University Press, 1992).

McCoy, Donald, *The Presidency of Harry S. Truman* (Lawrence: University Press of Kansas, 1984).

Paterson, Thomas G., *On Every Front: The Making and Unmaking of the Cold War* (New York: Norton, 1992).

Stephenson, Anders, *Kennan and the Art of Foreign Policy* (Cambridge, Mass.: Harvard University Press, 1989).

DOCUMENT 45

The Truman Doctrine

On 21 February 1947 the British government informed the United States that it could no longer support the Greek government in its battle against Communist rebels. On 12 March 1947 President Harry S. Truman told Congress that "it must be the policy of the United States to support free peoples who are resisting attempted subjugation by armed minorities or by outside pressure" and asked for $400 million to aid Greece and Turkey.[45]

MR. PRESIDENT, MR. SPEAKER, MEMBERS OF THE CONGRESS OF THE UNITED STATES:

The gravity of the situation which confronts the world today necessitates my appearance before a joint session of the Congress.

The foreign policy and the national security of this country are involved.

One aspect of the present situation, which I present to you at this time for your consideration and decision, concerns Greece and Turkey.

The United States has received from the Greek Government an urgent appeal for financial and economic assistance. Preliminary reports from the American Economic Mission now in Greece and reports from the American Ambassador in Greece corroborate the statement of the Greek Government that assistance is imperative if Greece is to survive as a free nation.

---

[45]*Public Papers of the Presidents: Harry Truman, 1947* (Washington, D.C.: U.S. Government Printing Office, 1963), 176–80.

I do not believe that the American people and the Congress wish to turn a deaf ear to the appeal of the Greek Government.

Greece is not a rich country. Lack of sufficient natural resources has always forced the Greek people to work hard to make both ends meet. Since 1940, this industrious, peace loving country has suffered invasion, four years of cruel enemy occupation, and bitter internal strife.

When forces of liberation entered Greece they found that the retreating Germans had destroyed virtually all the railways, roads, port facilities, communications, and merchant marine. More than a thousand villages had been burned. Eighty-five percent of the children were tubercular. Livestock, poultry, and draft animals had almost disappeared. Inflation had wiped out practically all savings.

As a result of these tragic conditions, a militant minority, exploiting human want and misery, was able to create political chaos which, until now, has made economic recovery impossible.

Greece is today without funds to finance the importation of those goods which are essential to bare subsistence. Under these circumstances the people of Greece cannot make progress in solving their problems of reconstruction. Greece is in desperate need of financial and economic assistance to enable it to resume purchases of food, clothing, fuel and seeds. These are indispensable for the subsistence of its people and are obtainable only from abroad. Greece must have help to import the goods necessary to restore internal order and security so essential for economic and political recovery.

The Greek Government has also asked for the assistance of experienced American administrators, economists and technicians to insure that the financial and other aid given to Greece shall be used effectively in creating a stable and self-sustaining economy and in improving its public administration.

The very existence of the Greek state is today threatened by the terrorist activities of several thousand armed men, led by Communists, who defy the government's authority at a number of points, particularly along the northern boundaries. A Commission appointed by the United Nations Security Council is at present investigating disturbed conditions in northern Greece and alleged border violations along the frontier between Greece on the one hand and Albania, Bulgaria, and Yugoslavia on the other.

Meanwhile, the Greek Government is unable to cope with the situation. The Greek army is small and poorly equipped. It needs supplies and equipment if it is to restore authority to the government throughout Greek territory.

Greece must have assistance if it is to become a self-supporting and self-respection democracy.

The United States must supply this assistance. We have already extended to Greece certain types of relief and economic aid but these are inadequate.

There is no other country to which democratic Greece can turn. No other nation is willing and able to provide the necessary support for a democratic Greek government.

The British Government, which has been helping Greece, can give no further financial or economic aid after March 31. Great Britain finds itself under the necessity of reducing or liquidating its commitments in several parts of the world, including Greece.

We have considered how the United Nations might assist in this crisis. But the situation is an urgent one requiring immediate action, and the United Nations and its related organizations are not in a position to extend help of the kind that is required.

It is important to note that the Greek Government has asked for our aid in utilizing effectively the financial and other assistance we may give to Greece, and in improving its public administration. It is of the utmost importance that we supervise the use of any funds made available to Greece, in such a manner that each dollar spent will count toward making Greece self-supporting, and will help to build an economy in which a healthy democracy can flourish.

No government is perfect. One of the chief virtues of a democracy, however, is that its defects are always visible and under democratic processes can be pointed out and corrected. The government of Greece is not perfect. Nevertheless it represents 85 percent of the members of the Greek Parliament who were chosen in an election last year. Foreign observers, including 692 Americans, considered this election to be a fair expression of the views of the Greek people.

The Greek Government has been operating in an atmosphere of chaos and extremism. It has made mistakes. The extension of aid by this country does not mean that the United States condones everything that the Greek Government has done or will do. We have condemned in the past, and we condemn now, extremist measures of the right or the left. We have in the past advised tolerance, and we advise tolerance now.

Greece's neighbor, Turkey, also deserves our attention.

The future of Turkey as an independent and economically sound state is clearly no less important to the freedom-loving peoples of the world than the future of Greece. The circumstances in which Turkey finds itself today are considerably different from those of Greece. Turkey has been spared the disasters that have beset Greece. And during the war, the United States and Great Britain furnished Turkey with material aid.

Nevertheless, Turkey now needs our support.

Since the war Turkey has sought additional financial assistance from Great Britain and the United States for the purpose of effecting that modernization necessary for the maintenance of its national integrity.

That integrity is essential to the preservation of order in the Middle East.

The British Government has informed us that, owing to its own difficulties, it can no longer extend financial or economic aid to Turkey.

As in the case of Greece, if Turkey is to have the assistance it needs, the United States must supply it. We are the only country able to provide that help.

I am fully aware of the broad implications involved if the United States extends assistance to Greece and Turkey, and I shall discuss these implications with you at this time.

One of the primary objectives of the foreign policy of the United States is the creation of conditions in which we and other nations will be able to work out a way of life free from coercion. This was a fundamental issue in the war with Germany and Japan. Our victory was won over countries which sought to impose their will, and their way of life, upon other nations.

To ensure the peaceful development of nations, free from coercion, the United States has taken a leading part in establishing the United Nations. The United Nations is designed to make possible lasting freedom and independence for all its members. We shall not realize our objectives, however, unless we are willing to help free peoples to maintain their free institutions and their national integrity against aggressive movements that seek to impose upon them totalitarian regimes. This is no more than a frank recognition that totalitarian regimes imposed upon free peoples, by direct or indirect aggression, undermine the foundations of international peace and hence the security of the United States.

The peoples of a number of countries of the world have recently had totalitarian regimes forced upon them against their will. The Government of the United States has made frequent protests against coercion and intimidation, in violation of the Yalta agreement, in Poland, Rumania, and Bulgaria. I must also state that in a number of other countries there have been similar developments.

At the present moment in world history nearly every nation must choose between alternative ways of life. The choice is too often not a free one.

One way of life is based upon the will of the majority, and is distinguished by free institutions, representative government, free elections, guarantees of individual liberty, freedom of speech and religion, and freedom from political oppression.

The second way of life is based upon the will of a minority forcibly imposed upon the majority. It relies upon terror and oppression, a controlled press and radio, fixed elections, and the suppression of personal freedoms.

I believe that it must be the policy of the United States to support free peoples who are resisting attempted subjugation by armed minorities or by outside pressures.

I believe that we must assist free peoples to work our their own destinies in their own way. I believe that our help should be primarily through economic and financial aid which is essential to economic stability and orderly political processes.

The world is not static, and the *status quo* is not sacred. But we cannot allow changes in the *status quo* in violation of the Charter of the United Nations by such methods as coercion, or by such subterfuges as political infiltration. In helping free and independent nations to maintain their freedom, the United States will be giving effect to the principles of the Charter of the United Nations.

It is necessary only to glance at a map to realize that the survival and integrity of the Greek nation are of grave importance in a much wider situation. If Greece should fall under the control of an armed minority, the effect upon its neighbor, Turkey, would be immediate and serious. Confusion and disorder might well spread throughout the entire Middle East.

Moreover, the disappearance of Greece as an independent state would have a profound effect upon those countries in Europe whose peoples are struggling against great difficulties to maintain their freedoms and their independence while they repair the damages of war.

It would be an unspeakable tragedy if these countries, which have struggled so long against overwhelming odds, should lose that victory for which they sacrificed so much. Collapse of free institutions and loss of independence would be disastrous not only for them but for the world. Discouragement and possibly failure would quickly be the lot of neighboring peoples striving to maintain their freedom and independence.

Should we fail to aid Greece and Turkey in this fateful hour, the effect will be far reaching to the West as well as to the East.

We must take immediate and resolute action.

I therefore ask the Congress to provide authority for assistance to Greece and Turkey in the amount of $400,000,000 for the period ending June 30, 1948. In requesting these funds, I have taken into consideration the maximum amount of relief assistance which would be furnished to Greece out of the $350,000,000 which I recently requested that the Congress authorize for the prevention of starvation and suffering in countries devastated by the war.

In addition to funds, I ask the Congress to authorize the detail of American civilian and military personnel to Greece and Turkey, at the request of those countries, to assist in the tasks of reconstruction, and for the purpose of supervising the use of such financial and material assistance as may be furnished. I recommend that authority also be provided for the instruction and training of selected Greek and Turkish personnel. . . .

This is a serious course upon which we embark.

I would not recommend it except that the alternative is much more serious.

The United States contributed $341,000,000,000 toward winning World War II. This is an investment in world freedom and world peace.

The assistance that I am recommending for Greece and Turkey amounts to little more than 1/10 of 1 percent of this investment. It is only common sense that we should safeguard this investment and make sure that it was not in vain.

The seeds of totalitarian regimes are nurtured by misery and want. They spread and grow in the evil soil of poverty and strife. They reach their full growth when the hope of a people for a better life has died.

We must keep that hope alive.

The free peoples of the world look to us for support in maintaining their freedoms. If we falter in our leadership, we may endanger the peace of the world—and we shall surely endanger the welfare of this Nation.

Great responsibilities have been placed upon us by the swift movement of events.

I am confident that the Congress will face these responsibilities squarely.

FURTHER READINGS

Alvarez, David J., *Bureaucracy and Cold War Ideology* (Thessaloniki: Institute for Balkan Studies, 1980).

Freeland, Richard, *The Truman Doctrine and the Origins of McCarthyism* (New York: Knopf, 1971).

Gaddis, John L., *Strategies of Containment* (New York: Oxford University Press, 1982).

Iatrides, John O., *Revolt in Athens* (Princeton, N.J.: Princeton University Press, 1972).

————, editor, *Greece in the 1940s* (Hanover, N.H.: University Press of New England, 1981).

Jones, Howard, *"A New Kind of War": America's Global Strategy and the Truman Doctrine in Greece* (New York: Oxford University Press, 1989).

Kuniholm, Bruce, *The Origins of the Cold War in the Near East* (Princeton, N.J.: Princeton University Press, 1980).

Pach, Jr., Chester J., *Arming the Free World: The Origins of the United States Military Assistance Program, 1945–1950* (Chapel Hill: University of North Carolina Press, 1991).

Wittner, Lawrence S., *American Intervention in Greece, 1943–1949* (New York: Columbia University Press, 1982).

DOCUMENT 46

The Marshall Plan

In an address at the commencement exercises at Harvard University on 5 June 1947, Secretary of State George Marshall suggested that the United

States should extend financial assistance to war-ravaged European nations.[46]
*Congress responded to Marshall's declaration that "our policy is directed not
against any country or doctrine but against hunger, poverty, desperation, and
chaos" by passing the Economic Cooperation Act on 3 April 1948.*

ᵹᵹᵹ

I need not tell you gentlemen that the world situation is very serious. That
must be apparent to all intelligent people. I think one difficulty is that the
problem is one of such enormous complexity that the very mass of facts
presented to the public by press and radio make it exceedingly difficult for the
man in the street to reach a clear appraisement of the situation. Furthermore,
the people of this country are distant from the troubled areas of the earth and it
is hard for them to comprehend the plight and consequent reactions of the
long–suffering peoples, and the effect of those reactions on their governments
in connection with our efforts to promote peace in the world.

In considering the requirements for the rehabilitation of Europe[,] the
physical loss of life, the visible destruction of cities, factories, mines and
railroads was correctly estimated, but it has become obvious during recent
months that this visible destruction was probably less serious than the
dislocation of the entire fabric of European economy. For the past 10 years
conditions have been highly abnormal. The feverish preparation for war and
the more feverish maintenance of the war effort engulfed all aspects of national
economies. Machinery has fallen into disrepair or is entirely obsolete. Under
the arbitrary and destructive Nazi rule, virtually every possible enterprise was
geared into the German war machine. Long-standing commercial ties, private
institutions, banks, insurance companies and shipping companies disappeared,
through loss of capital, absorption through nationalization[,] or by simple
destruction.   In many countries, confidence in the local currency has been
severely shaken. The breakdown of the business structure of Europe during the
war was complete. Recovery has been seriously retarded by the fact that two
years after the close of hostilities a peace settlement with Germany and Austria
has not been agreed upon. But even given a more prompt solution of these
difficult problems, the rehabilitation of the economic structure of Europe quite
evidently will require a much longer time and greater effort than had been
foreseen.

There is a phase of this matter which is both interesting and serious. The
farmer has always produced the foodstuffs to exchange with the city dweller for
the other necessities of life. This division of labor is the basis of modern

---

[46]*Papers Relating to the Foreign Relations of the United States, 1947* (Washington,
D.C.: U.S. Government Printing Office, 1972), 3:237–39.

civilization. At the present time it is threatened with breakdown. The town and city industries are not producing adequate goods to exchange with the food-producing farmer. Raw materials and fuel are in short supply. Machinery is lacking or worn out. The farmer or the peasant cannot find the goods for sale which he desires to purchase. So the sale of his farm produce for money which he cannot use seems to him an unprofitable transaction. He, therefore, has withdrawn many fields from crop cultivation and is using them for grazing. He feeds more grain to stock and finds for himself and his family an ample supply of food, however short he may be on clothing and the other ordinary gadgets of civilization. Meanwhile people in the cities are short of food and fuel. So the governments are forced to use their foreign money and credits to procure these necessities abroad. This process exhausts funds which are urgently needed for reconstruction. Thus a very serious situation is rapidly developing which bodes no good for the world. The modern system of the division of labor upon which the exchange of products is based is in danger of breaking down.

The truth of the matter is that Europe's requirements for the next three or four years of foreign food and other essential products—principally from America—are so much greater than her present ability to pay that she must have substantial additional help or face economic, social and political deterioration of a very grave character.

The remedy lies in breaking the vicious circle and restoring the confidence of the European people in the economic future of their own countries and of Europe as a whole. The manufacturer and the farmer throughout wide areas must be able and willing to exchange their products for currencies the continuing value of which is not open to question.

Aside from the demoralizing effect on the world at large and the possibilities of disturbances arising as a result of the desperation of the people concerned, the consequences to the economy of the United States should be apparent to all. It is logical that the United States should do whatever it is able to do to assist in the return of normal economic health in the world, without which there can be no political stability and no assured peace. Our policy is directed not against any country or doctrine but against hunger, poverty, desperation and chaos. Its purpose should be the revival of a working economy in the world so as to permit the emergence of political and social conditions in which free institutions can exist. Such assistance, I am convinced, must not be on a piecemeal basis as various crises develop. Any assistance that this Government may render in the future should provide a cure rather than a mere palliative. Any government that is willing to assist in the task of recovery will find full cooperation, I am sure, on the part of the United States Government. Any government which maneuvers to block the recovery of other countries cannot expect help from us. Furthermore, governments, political parties, or groups which seek to perpetuate human misery in order to profit therefrom politically or otherwise will encounter the opposition of the United States.

It is already evident that, before the United States Government can proceed much further in its efforts to alleviate the situation and help start the European world on its way to recovery, there must be some agreement among the countries of Europe as to the requirements of the situation and the part those countries themselves will take in order to give proper effect to whatever action might be undertaken by this Government. It would be neither fitting nor efficacious for this Government to undertake to draw up unilaterally a program designed to place Europe on its feet economically. This is the business of the Europeans. The initiative, I think, must come from Europe. The role of this country should consist of friendly aid in the drafting of a European program and of later support of such a program so far as it may be practical for us to do so. The program should be a joint one, agreed to by a number, if not all European nations.

An essential part of any successful action on the part of the United States is an understanding on the part of the people of America of the character of the problem and the remedies to be applied. Political passion and prejudice should have no part. With foresight, and a willingness on the part of our people to face up to the vast responsibility which history has clearly placed upon our country, the difficulties I have outlined can and will be overcome.

FURTHER READINGS

Gimbel, John, *The Origins of the Marshall Plan* (Stanford, Calif.: Stanford University Press, 1976).

Hogan, Michael J., *The Marshall Plan: America, Britain, and the Reconstruction of Western Europe, 1947–1952* (New York: Columbia University Press, 1987).

Mayne, Richard, *Recovery of Europe* (New York: Harper & Row, 1970).

Milward, Alan, *The Reconstruction of Western Europe, 1945–51* (Berkeley: University of California Press, 1984).

Pollard, Robert A., *Economic Security and the Origins of the Cold War* (New York: Columbia University Press, 1985).

Wexler, Imanuel, *The Marshall Plan Revisited* (Westport, Conn.: Greenwood Press, 1983).

DOCUMENT 47

The North Atlantic Treaty Organization

By signing the North Atlantic Treaty on 4 April 1949 the United States indicated its willingness to revolutionize its foreign policy and enter into an "entangling alliance." On 21 July 1949 the Senate ratified the NATO treaty by a vote of 82 to 13.[47]

ᴥᴥ

BY THE PRESIDENT OF THE UNITED STATES OF AMERICA

A PROCLAMATION

WHEREAS the North Atlantic Treaty was signed at Washington on April 4, 1949 by the respective Plenipotentiaries of the United States of America, the Kingdom of Belgium, Canada, the Kingdom of Denmark, France, Iceland, Italy, the Grand Duchy of Luxembourg, the Kingdom of the Netherlands, the Kingdom of Norway, Portugal, and the United Kingdom of Great Britain and Northern Ireland;

WHEREAS the text of the said Treaty, in English and French languages, is word for word as follows:

NORTH ATLANTIC TREATY

The Parties to this Treaty reaffirm their faith in the purposes and principles of the Charter of the United Nations and their desire to live in peace with all peoples and all governments.

They are determined to safeguard the freedom, common heritage and civilization of their peoples, founded on the principles of democracy, individual liberty and the rule of law. They seek to promote stability and well-being in the North Atlantic area.

They are resolved to unite their efforts for collective defense and for the preservation of peace and security.

They therefore agree to this North Atlantic Treaty:

Article 1

The Parties undertake, as set forth in the Charter of the United Nations, to settle any international disputes in which they may be involved by peaceful means in such a manner that international peace and security, and justice, are not endangered, and to refrain in their international relations from the threat or use of force in any manner inconsistent with the purposes of the United Nations.

---

[47]*U.S. Statutes at Large* (Washington, D.C.: U.S. Government Printing Office, 1950), 63, part 2:2241–44.

Article 2

The Parties will contribute toward the further development of peaceful and friendly international relations by strengthening their free institutions, by bringing about a better understanding of the principles upon which these institutions are founded, and by promoting conditions of stability and well–being. They will seek to eliminate conflict in their international economic policies and will encourage economic collaboration between any or all of them.

Article 3

In order more effectively to achieve the objectives of this Treaty, the Parties, separately and jointly, by means of continuous and effective self-help and mutual aid, will maintain and develop their individual and collective capacity to resist armed attack.

Article 4

The Parties will consult together whenever, in the opinion of any of them, the territorial integrity, political independence or security of any of the Parties is threatened.

Article 5

The Parties agree that an armed attack against one or more of them in Europe or North America shall be considered an attack against them all; and consequently they agree that, if such an armed attack occurs, each of them, in exercise of the right of individual or collective self-defense recognized by Article 51 of the Charter of the United Nations, will assist the Party or Parties so attacked by taking forthwith, individually and in concert with the other Parties, such action as it deems necessary, including the use of armed force, to restore and maintain the security of the North Atlantic area.

Any such armed attack and all measures taken as a result thereof shall immediately be reported to the Security Council. Such measures shall be terminated when the Security Council has taken the measures necessary to restore and maintain international peace and security.

Article 6

For the purpose of Article 5 an armed attack on one or more of the Parties is deemed to include an armed attack on the territory of any of the Parties in Europe or North America, on the Algerian departments of France, on the occupation forces of any Party in Europe, on the islands under the jurisdiction of any Party in the North Atlantic area north of the Tropic of Cancer or on the vessels or aircraft in this area of any of the Parties. . . .

Article 10

The Parties may, by unanimous agreement, invite any other European state in a position to further the principles of this Treaty and to contribute to the security of the North Atlantic area to accede to this Treaty. Any state so invited may become a party to the Treaty by depositing its instrument of accession with the Government of the United States of America. The Government of the United States of America will inform each of the Parties of the deposit of each such instrument of accession.

FURTHER READINGS

Ireland, Timothy P., *Creating the Entangling Alliance* (Westport, Conn.: Greenwood Press, 1981).

Kaplan, Lawrence S., *The United States and NATO* (Lexington: University of Kentucky Press, 1984).

Osgood, Robert, *NATO: The Entangling Alliance* (Chicago: University of Chicago Press, 1962).

Pach, Jr., Chester J., *Arming the Free World: The Origins of the United States Military Assistance Program, 1945–1950* (Chapel Hill, University of North Carolina Press, 1991).

Reid, Escott, *Time of Fear and Hope: The Making of the North Atlantic Treaty* (Toronto: McClelland and Stewart, 1977).

DOCUMENT 48

The China White Paper

Secretary of State Dean Acheson attempted to explain how Communist forces under Mao Zedong (Mao Tse-tung) had defeated the Nationalist Government of China headed by Jiang Jieshi (Chiang Kai-shek) in a compilation of documents entitled The China White Paper.[48] *In spite of Acheson's declaration that "the unfortunate but inescapable fact is that the ominous result of the civil war in China was beyond the control of the government of the United States," critics would cotinue to charge that the Truman administration had "lost" China to communism.*

ﾟﾟ

---

[48]*The China White Paper* (Stanford, Calif.: Stanford University Press, 1967), iii–xvii, passim.

LETTER OF TRANSMITTAL

Department of State
Washington, July 30, 1949

THE PRESIDENT: In accordance with your wish, I have had compiled a record of our relations with China, special emphasis being placed on the last five years. This record is being published and will therefore be available to the Congress and to the people of the United States. . . .

The interest of the people and the Government of the United States in China goes far back into our history. Despite the distance and broad differences in background which separate China and the United States, our friendship for that country has always been intensified by the religious, philanthropic and cultural ties which have united the two peoples, and has been attested by many acts of good will over a period of many years, including the use of the Boxer indemnity for the education of Chinese students, the abolition of extraterritoriality during the Second World War, and our extensive aid to China during and since the close of the war. The record shows that the United States has consistently maintained and still maintains those fundamental principles of our foreign policy toward China which include the doctrine of the Open Door, respect for the administrative and territorial integrity of China, and opposition to any foreign domination of China. . . .

From the wartime cooperation with the Soviet Union and from the costly campaigns against the Japanese came the Yalta Agreement. The American Government and people awaited with intense anxiety the assault on the main islands of Japan which it was feared would cost up to a million American casualties before Japan was conquered. The atomic bomb was not then a reality and it seemed impossible that the war in the Far East could be ended without this assault. It thus became a primary concern of the American Government to see to it that the Soviet Union enter the war against Japan at the earliest possible date in order that the Japanese Army in Manchuria might not be returned to the homeland at the critical moment. It was considered vital not only that the Soviet Union enter the war but that she do so before our invasion of Japan, which already had been set for the autumn of 1945.

At Yalta, Marshal Stalin not only agreed to attack Japan within two or three months after V-E Day but limited his "price" with reference to Manchuria substantially to the position which Russia had occupied there prior to 1904. We for our part, in order to obtain this commitment and thus to bring the war to a close with a consequent saving of American, Chinese and other Allied lives, were prepared to and did pay the requisite price. Two facts must not, however, be lost sight of in this connection. First, the Soviet Union when she finally did enter the war against Japan, could in any case have seized all the territories in question and considerably more regardless of what our attitude might have been.   Second, the Soviets on their side in the Sino-Soviet Treaty arising from the Yalta Agreement, agreed to give the National Government of China moral and material support and moreover formalized their assurances of noninterference in China's internal affairs.   Although the unexpectedly early collapse of Japanese resistance later made some of the provisions of the Yalta Agreement seem unnecessary, in the light of the predicted course of the war at that time they were considered to be not only justified but clearly advantageous. Although dictated by military necessity, the Agreement and the subsequent Sino-Soviet Treaty in fact imposed limitations on the action which Russia would, in any case, have been in a position to take. . . .

When peace came the United States was confronted with three possible alternatives in China: 1. it could have pulled out lock, stock and barrel; 2. it could have intervened militarily on a major scale to assist the Nationalists to destroy the Communists; 3. it could, while assisting the Nationalists to assert their authority over as much of China as possible, endeavor to avoid a civil war by working for a compromise between the two sides.

The first alternative would, and I believe American public opinion at the time so felt, have represented an abandonment of our international responsibilities and of our traditional policy of friendship for China before we had made a determined effort to be of assistance.   The second alternative policy, while it may look attractive theoretically and in retrospect, was wholly impracticable.   The Nationalists had been unable to destroy the Communists during the 10 years before the war.   Now after the war the Nationalists were, as indicated above, weakened, demoralized, and unpopular.   They had quickly dissipated their popular support and prestige in the areas liberated from the Japanese by the conduct of their civil and military officials.   The Communists on the other hand were much stronger than they had ever been and were in control of most of North China.   Because of the ineffectiveness of the Nationalist forces which was later to be tragically demonstrated, the Communists probably could have been dislodged only by American arms.   It is obvious that the American people would not have sanctioned such a colossal commitment of our armies in 1945 or later.   We therefore came to the third alternative policy whereunder we faced the facts of the situation and attempted to assist in working out a *modus vivendi* which would avert civil war but nevertheless preserve and even increase the influence of the National Government. . . .

The reasons for the failures of the Chinese National Government appear in some detail in the attached record.   They do not stem from any inadequacy of American aid.   Our military observers on the spot have reported that the Nationalist armies did not lose a single battle during the crucial year of 1948 through lack of arms or ammunition.   The fact was that the decay which our observers had detected in Chungking early in the war had fatally sapped the powers of resistance of the Kuomintang.   Its leaders had proved incapable of meeting the crisis confronting them, its troops had lost the will to fight, and its Government had lost popular support. The Communists, on the other hand, through a ruthless discipline and fanatical zeal, attempted to sell themselves as guardians and liberators of the people. The Nationalist armies did not have to be defeated; they disintegrated. History has proved again and again that a regime without faith in itself and an army without morale cannot survive the test of battle. . . .

The historic policy of the United States of friendship and aid toward the people of China was, however, maintained in both peace and war. Since V-J Day, the United States Government has authorized aid to Nationalist China in the form of grants and credits totaling approximately 2 billion dollars, an amount equivalent in value to more than 50 percent of the monetary expenditures of the Chinese Government and of proportionately greater magnitude in relation to the budget of that Government than the United States has provided to any nation of Western Europe since the end of the war. In addition to these grants and credits, the United States Government has sold the Chinese Government large quantities of military and civilian war surplus property with a total procurement cost of over 1 billion dollars, for which the agreed realization to the United States was 232 million dollars. A large proportion of the military supplies furnished the Chinese armies by the United States since V-J Day has, however, fallen into the hands of the Chinese Communists through the military ineptitude of the Nationalist leaders, their defections and surrenders, and the absence among their forces of the will to fight.

It has been urged that relatively small amounts of additional aid—military and economic—to the National Government would have enabled it to destroy communism in China. The most trustworthy military, economic, and political information available to our Government does not bear out this view.

A realistic appraisal of conditions in China, past and present, leads to the conclusion that the only alternative open to the United States was full-scale intervention in behalf of a Government which had lost the confidence of its own troops and its own people. Such intervention would have required the expenditure of even greater sums than have been fruitlessly spent thus far, the command of Nationalist armies by American officers, and the probable participation of American armed forces—land, sea, and air—in the resulting war. Intervention of such a scope and magnitude would have been resented by the mass of the Chinese people, would have diametrically reversed our historic policy, and would have been condemned by the American people.

It must be admitted frankly that the American policy of assisting the Chinese people in resisting domination by any foreign power or powers is now confronted with the gravest difficulties. The heart of China is in Communist hands. The Communist leaders have foresworn their Chinese heritage and have publicly announced their subservence to a foreign power, Russia, which during the last 50 years, under czars and Communists alike, has been most assiduous in its efforts to extend its control in the Far East. In the recent past, attempts at foreign domination have appeared quite clearly to the Chinese people as external aggression and as such have been bitterly and in the long run successfully resisted. Our aid and encouragement have helped them to resist. In this case, however, the foreign domination has been masked behind the façade of a vast crusading movement which apparently has seemed to many Chinese to be wholly indigenous and national. Under these circumstances, our aid has been unavailing.

The unfortunate but inescapable fact is that the ominous result of the civil war in China was beyond the control of the government of the United States. Nothing that this country did or could have done within the reasonable limits of its capabilities could have changed that result; nothing that was left undone by this country has contributed to it. It was the product of internal Chinese forces, forces which this country tried to influence but could not. A decision was arrived at within China, if only a decision by default.

And now it is abundantly clear that we must face the situation as it exists in fact. We will not help the Chinese or ourselves by basing our policy on wishful thinking. We continue to believe that, however tragic may be the immediate future of China and however ruthlessly a major portion of this great people may be exploited by a party in the interest of a foreign imperialism, ultimately the profound civilization and the democratic individualism of China will reassert themselves and she will throw off the foreign yoke. I consider that we should encourage all developments in China which now and in the future work toward this end.

In the immediate future, however, the implementation of our historic policy of friendship for China must be profoundly affected by current developments. It will necessarily be influenced by the degree to which the Chinese people come to recognize that the Communist regime serves not their interests but those of Soviet Russia and the manner in which, having become aware of the facts, they react to this foreign domination. One point, however, is clear. Should the Communist regime lend itself to the aims of Soviet Russian imperialism and attempt to engage in aggression against China's neighbors, we and the other members of the United Nations would be confronted by a situation violative of the principles of the United Nations Charter and threatening international peace and security.

Meanwhile our policy will continue to be based upon our own respect for the Charter, our friendship for China, and our traditional support for the Open Door and for China's independence and administrative and territorial integrity.

Respectfully yours,

Dean Acheson

FURTHER READINGS

Buhite, Russell, *Soviet-American Relations in Asia, 1945–1954* (Norman: University of Oklahoma Press, 1981).

Cohen, Warren I., *America's Response to China* (New York: Columbia University Press, 1990).

Dudden, Arthur Power, *The American Pacific: From the Old China Trade to the Present* (New York: Oxford University Press, 1992).

Fairbank, John K., *The United States and China* (Cambridge, Mass.: Harvard University Press, 1979).

Iriye, Akira, *The Cold War in Asia* (Englewood Cliffs, N.J.: Prentice-Hall, 1974).

Kahn, E. J., *The China Hands* (New York: Viking, 1972).

Martin, Edwin, *Divided Counsel: The Anglo-American Response to Communist Victory in China* (Lexington: University Press of Kentucky, 1986).

Newman, Robert P., *Owen Lattimore and the "Loss" of China* (Berkeley: University of California Press, 1992).

Schaller, Michael, *The United States and China in the Twentieth Century* (New York: Oxford University Press, 1979).

DOCUMENT 49

NSC–68

In January 1950 President Harry Truman initiated a review of U.S. defense policy. Paul Nitze, director of the State Department's Policy Planning Staff, wrote most of the resulting analysis, which was called National Security Council Paper Number 68 (NSC–68).[49] *In the report Nitze argued that only a ramatic increase in military spending could allow the United States to counter the threat posed by Communism. Truman would initiate such a policy after the start of the conflict in Korea.*

ᎦᎦ

---

[49]*Papers Relating to the Foreign Relations of the United States, 1950* (Washington, D.C.: U.S. Government Printing Office, 1977), 1:235–92, passim.

ANALYSIS

I. BACKGROUND OF THE PRESENT CRISIS

Within the past thirty-five years the world has experienced two global wars of tremendous violence. It has witnessed two revolutions—the Russian and the Chinese—of extreme scope and intensity. It has also seen the collapse of five empires—the Ottoman, the Austro-Hungarian, German, Italian and Japanese—and the drastic decline of two major imperial systems, the British and the French. During the span of one generation, the international distribution of power has been fundamentally altered. For several centuries it had proved impossible for any one nation to gain such preponderant strength that a coalition of other nations could not in time face it with greater strength. The international scene was marked by recurring periods of violence and war, but a system of sovereign and independent states was maintained, over which no state was able to achieve hegemony.

Two complex sets of factors have now basically altered this historical distribution of power. First, the defeat of Germany and Japan and the decline of the British and French Empires have interacted with the development of the United States and the Soviet Union in such a way that power has increasingly gravitated to these two centers. Second, the Soviet Union, unlike previous aspirants to hegemony, is animated by a new fanatic faith, antithetical to our own, and seeks to impose its absolute authority over the rest of the world. Conflict has, therefore, become endemic and is waged, on the part of the Soviet Union, by violent or non-violent methods in accordance with the dictates of expediency. With the development of increasingly terrifying weapons of mass destruction, every individual faces the ever-present possibility of annihilation should the conflict enter the phase of total war.

On the one hand, the people of the world yearn for relief from the anxiety arising from the risk of atomic war. On the other hand, any substantial further extension of the area under the domination of the Kremlin would raise the possibility that no coalition adequate to confront the Kremlin with greater strength could be assembled. It is in this context that this Republic and its citizens in the ascendancy of their strength stand in their deepest peril. The issues that face us are momentous, involving the fulfillment or destruction not only of this Republic but of civilization itself. They are issues which will not await our deliberations. With conscience and resolution this Government and the people it represents must now take new and fateful decisions.

II. FUNDAMENTAL PURPOSE OF THE UNITED STATES

The fundamental purpose of the United States is laid down in the Preamble to the Constitution: ". . . to form a more perfect Union, establish Justice, insure domestic Tranquility, provide for the common defence, promote the general Welfare, and secure the Blessings of Liberty to ourselves and our Posterity." In essence, the fundamental purpose is to assure the integrity and vitality of our free society, which is founded upon the dignity and worth of the individual.

Three realities emerge as a consequence of this purpose: Our determination to maintain the essential elements of individual freedom, as set forth in the Constitution and Bill of Rights; our determination to create conditions under which our free and democratic system can live and prosper; and our determination to fight if necessary to defend our way of life, for which as in the Declaration of Independence, "with a firm reliance on the protection of Divine Providence, we mutually pledge to each other our lives, our Fortunes and our sacred Honor."

III. FUNDAMENTAL DESIGN OF THE KREMLIN

The fundamental design of those who control the Soviet Union and the international communist movement is to retain and solidify their absolute power, first in the Soviet Union and second in the areas now under their control. In the minds of the Soviet leaders, however, achievement of this design requires the dynamic extension of their authority and the ultimate elimination of any effective opposition to their authority.

The design, therefore, calls for the complete subversion or forcible destruction of the machinery of government and structure of society in the countries of the non-Soviet world and their replacement by an apparatus and structure subservient to and controlled from the Kremlin. To that end Soviet efforts are now directed toward the domination of the Eurasian land mass. The United States, as the principal center of power in the non-Soviet world and the bulwark of opposition to Soviet expansion, is the principal enemy whose integrity and vitality must be subverted or destroyed by one means of another if the Kremlin is to achieve its fundamental design. . . .

V. SOVIET INTENTIONS AND CAPABILITIES

A. Political and Psychological

The Kremlin's design for world domination begins at home. The first concern of a despotic oligarchy is that the local base of its power and authority be secure. The massive fact of the iron curtain isolating the Soviet peoples from the outside world, the repeated political purges within the U.S.S.R. and the institutionalized crimes of the MVD are evidence that the Kremlin does not feel secure at home and that "the entire coercive force of the socialist state" is more than ever one of seeking to impose its absolute authority over "the economy, manner of life, and consciousness of people" (Vyshinski, "The Law of the Soviet State", [sic] p. 74). Similar evidence in the satellite states of Eastern Europe leads to the conclusion that this same policy, in less advanced phases, is being applied to the Kremlin's colonial areas.

Being a totalitarian dictatorship, the Kremlin's objectives in these policies, is the total subjective submission of the peoples now under its control. The concentration camp is the prototype of the society which these policies are designed to achieve, a society in which the personality of the individual is so broken and perverted that he participates affirmatively in his own degradation.

The Kremlin's policy toward areas not under its control is the elimination of resistance to its will and the extension of its influence and control. It is driven to follow this policy because it cannot, for the reasons set forth in Chapter IV, tolerate the existence of free societies; to the Kremlin the most mild and inoffensive free society is an affront, a challenge and a subversive influence. Given the nature of the Kremlin, and the evidence at hand, it seems clear that the ends toward which this policy is directed are the same as those where its control has already been established.

The means employed by the Kremlin in pursuit of this policy are limited only by considerations of expediency. Doctrine is not a limiting factor; rather it dictates the employment of violence, subversion and deceit, and rejects moral considerations. In any event, the Kremlin's conviction of its own infallibility has made its devotion to theory so subjective that past or present pronouncements as to doctrine offer no reliable guide to future actions. The only apparent restraints on resort to war are, therefore, calculations of practicality.

With particular reference to the United States, the Kremlin's strategic and tactical policy is affected by its estimate that we are not only the greatest immediate obstacle which stands between it and world domination, we are also the only power which could release forces in the free and Soviet worlds which could destroy it. The Kremlin's policy toward us is consequently animated by a peculiarly virulent blend of hatred and fear. Its strategy has been one of attempting to undermine the complex of forces, in this country and in the rest of the free world, on which our power is based. In this it has both adhered to doctrine and followed the sound principle of seeking maximum results with minimum risks and commitments. The present application of this strategy is a new form of expression for traditional Russian caution. However, there is no justification in Soviet theory or practice for predicting that, should the Kremlin become convinced that it could cause our downfall by one conclusive blow, it would not seek that solution. . . .

B. Economic

The Kremlin has no economic intentions unrelated to its overall policies. Economics in the Soviet world is not an end in itself. The Kremlin's policy, in so far as it has to do with economics, is to utilize economic processes to contribute to the overall strength, particularly the war-making capacity of the Soviet system. The material welfare of the totalitariat is severely subordinated to the interest of the system. . . .

C. Military

The Soviet Union is developing the military capacity to support its design for world domination. The Soviet Union actually possesses armed forces far in excess of those necessary to defend its national territory. These armed forces are probably not yet considered by the Soviet Union to be sufficient to initiate a war which would involve the United States. This excessive strength, coupled now with an atomic capability, provides the Soviet Union with great coercive power for use in time of peace in furtherance of its objectives and serves as a deterrent to the victims of its aggression from taking any action in opposition to its tactics which would risk war.

Should a major war occur in 1950 the Soviet Union and its satellites are considered by the Joint Chiefs of Staff to be in a sufficiently advanced state of preparation immediately to undertake and carry out the following campaigns.

a. To overrun Western Europe, with the possible exception of the Iberian and Scandinavian Peninsulas; to drive toward the oil-bearing areas of the Near and Middle East; and to consolidate Communist gains in the Far East;
b. To launch air attacks against the British Isles and air and sea attacks against the lines of communications of the Western Powers in the Atlantic and Pacific;
c. To attack selected targets with atomic weapons, now including the likelihood of such attacks against targets in Alaska, Canada, and the United States. Alternatively, this capability, coupled with other actions open to the Soviet Union, might deny the United Kingdom as an effective base of operations for allied forces. It also should be possible for the Soviet Union to prevent any allied "Normandy" type amphibious operations intended to force a reentry into the continent of Europe.

After the Soviet Union completed its initial campaigns and consolidated its positions in the Western European area, it could simultaneously conduct:

a. Full-scale air and limited sea operations against the British Isles;
b. Invasions of the Iberian and Scandinavian Peninsulas;

c. Further operations in the Near and Middle East, continued air operations against the North American continent, and air and sea operations against Atlantic and Pacific lines of communication; and

d. Diversionary attacks in other areas.

During the course of the offensive operations listed in the second and third paragraphs above, the Soviet Union will have an air defense capability with respect to the vital areas of its own and its satellites' territories which can oppose but cannot prevent allied air operations against these areas.

It is not known whether the Soviet Union possesses war reserves and arsenal capabilities sufficient to supply its satellite armies or even its own forces throughout a long war. It might not be in the interest of the Soviet Union to equip fully its satellite armies, since the possibility of defections would exist.

It is not possible at this time to assess accurately the finite disadvantages to the Soviet Union which may accrue through the implementation of the Economic Cooperation Act of 1948, as amended, and the Mutual Defense Assistance Act of 1949. It should be expected that, as this implementation progresses, the internal security situation of the recipient nations should improve concurrently. In addition, a strong United States military position, plus increases in the armaments of the nations of Western Europe, should strengthen the determination of the recipient nations to counter Soviet moves and in event of war could be considered as likely to delay operations and increase the time required for the Soviet Union to overrun Western Europe. In all probability, although United States backing will stiffen their determination, the armaments increase under the present aid programs will not be of any major consequence prior to 1952. Unless the military strength of the Western European nations is increased on a much larger scale than under current programs and at an accelerated rate, it is more than likely that those nations will not be able to oppose even by 1960 the Soviet armed forces in war with any degree of effectiveness. Considering the Soviet Union military capability, the long-range allied military objective in Western Europe must envisage an increased military strength in that area sufficient possibly to deter the Soviet Union from a major war or, in any event, to delay materially the overrunning of Western Europe and, if feasible, to hold a bridgehead on the continent against Soviet Union offensives. . . .

VI. U.S. INTENTIONS AND CAPABILITIES—ACTUAL AND POTENTIAL

A. Political and Psychological

Our overall policy at the present time may be described as one designed to foster a world environment in which the American system can survive and flourish. It therefore rejects the concept of isolation and affirms the necessity of our positive participation in the world community.

This broad intention embraces two subsidiary policies. One is a policy which we would probably pursue even if there were no Soviet threat. It is a policy of attempting to develop a healthy international community. The other is the policy of "containing" the Soviet system. These two policies are closely interrelated and interact on one another. Nevertheless, the distinction between them is basically valid and contributes to a clearer understanding of what we are trying to do.

The policy of striving to develop a healthy international community is the long-term constructive effort which we are engaged in. It was this policy which gave rise to our vigorous sponsorship of the United Nations. It is of course the principal reason for our long continuing endeavors to create and now develop the Inter-American system. It, as much as containment, underlay our efforts to rehabilitate Western Europe. Most of our international economic activities can likewise be explained in terms of this policy.

In a world of polarized power, the policies designed to develop a healthy international community are more than ever necessary to our own strength.

As for the policy of "containment," it is one which seeks by all means short of war to 1. block further expansion of Soviet power, 2. expose the falsities of Soviet pretensions, 3. induce a retraction of the Kremlin's control and influence and 4. in general, so foster the seeds of destruction within the Soviet system that the Kremlin is brought at least to the point of modifying its behavior to conform to generally accepted international standards.

It was and continues to be cardinal in this policy that we possess superior overall power in ourselves or in dependable combination with other like-minded nations. One of the most important ingredients of power is military strength. In the concept of "containment," the maintenance of a strong military posture is deemed to be essential for two reasons: 1. as an ultimate guarantee of our national security and 2. as an indispensable backdrop to the conduct of the policy of "containment." Without superior aggregate military strength, in being and readily mobilizable, a policy of "containment"—which is in effect a policy of calculated and gradual coercion—is no more than a policy of bluff.

At the same time, it is essential to the successful conduct of a policy of "containment" that we always leave open the possibility of negotiation with the U.S.S.R. A diplomatic freeze—and we are in one now—tends to defeat the very purposes of "containment" because it raises tensions at the same time that it makes Soviet retractions and adjustments in the direction of moderated behavior more difficult. It also tends to inhibit our initiative and deprives us of opportunities for maintaining a moral ascendancy in our struggle with the Soviet system.

In "containment" it is desirable to exert pressure in a fashion which will avoid so far as possible directly challenging Soviet prestige, to keep open the possiblity for the U.S.S.R. to retreat before pressure with a minimum loss of face and to secure political advantage from the failure of the Kremlin to yield or take advantage of the openings we leave it.

We have failed to implement adequately these two fundamental aspects of "containment." In the face of obviously mounting Soviet military strength ours has declined relatively. Partly as a byproduct of this, but also for other reasons, we now find ourselves at a diplomatic impasse with the Soviet Union, with the Kremlin growing bolder, with both of us holding on grimly to what we have and with ourselves facing difficult decisions. . . .

C. Military

The United States now possesses the greatest military potential of any single nation in the world. The military weaknesses of the United States vis-à-vis the Soviet Union, however, include its numerical inferiority in forces in being and in total manpower. Coupled with the inferiority of forces in being, the United States also lacks tenable positions from which to employ its forces in event of war and munitions power in being and readily available.

It is true that the United States armed forces are now stronger than ever before in other times of apparent peace; it is also true that there exists a sharp disparity between our actual military strength and our commitments. The relationship of our strength to our present commitments, however, is not alone the governing factor. The world situation, as well as commitments, should govern; hence, our military strength more properly should be related to the world situation confronting us. When our military strength is related to the world situation and balanced against the likely exigencies of such a situation, it is clear that our military strength is becoming dangerously inadequate.

If war should begin in 1950, the United States and its allies will have the military capability of conducting defensive operations to provide a reasonable measure of protection to the Western Hemisphere, bases in the Western Pacific, and essential military lines of communication; and an inadequate measure of protection to vital military bases in the United Kingdom and in the Near and Middle East. We will have the capability of conducting powerful offensive air operations against vital elements of the Soviet war-making capacity.

The scale of the operations listed in the preceding paragraph is limited by the effective forces and material in being of the United States and its allies vis-à-vis the Soviet Union. Consistent with the aggressive threat facing us and in consonance with overall strategic plans, the United States must provide to its allies on a continuing basis as large amounts of military assistance as possible without serious detriment to the United States operational requirements.

If the potential military capabilities of the United States and its allies were rapidly and effectively developed, sufficient forces could be produced probably to deter war, or if the Soviet Union chooses war, to withstand the initial Soviet attacks, to stabilize supporting attacks, and to retaliate in turn with even greater impact on the Soviet capabilities. From the military point of view alone, however, this would require not only the generation of the necessary military forces but also the development and stockpiling of improved weapons of all types.

Under existing peacetime conditions, a period of from two to three years is required to produce a material increase in military power. Such increased power could be provided in a somewhat shorter period in a declared period of emergency or in wartime through a full-out national effort. . . .

IX. POSSIBLE COURSES OF ACTION

Introduction. Four possible courses of action by the United States in the present situation can be distinguished. They are:

a Continuation of current policies, with current and currently projected programs for carrying out these policies;

b. Isolation;

c. War; and

d. A more rapid building up of the political, economic, and military strength of the free world than provided under *a*, with the purpose of reaching, if possible, a tolerable state of order among nations without war and of preparing to defend ourselves in the event that the free world is attacked. . . .

A. The First Course—Continuation of Current Policies, with Current and Currently Projected Programs for Carrying out These Policies

1. *Military aspects.* On the basis of current programs, the United States has a large potential military capability but an actual capability which, though improving, is declining relative to the U.S.S.R., particularly in light of its probable fission bomb capability and possible thermonuclear bomb capability. The same holds true for the free world as a whole relative to the Soviet world as a whole. If war breaks out in 1950 or in the next few years, the United States and its allies, apart from a powerful atomic blow, will be compelled to conduct delaying actions, while building up their strength for a general offensive. A frank evaluation of the requirements, to defend the United States and its vital interests and to support a vigorous initiative in

the cold war, on the one hand, and of present capabilities, on the other, indicates that there is a sharp and growing disparity between them. . . .

B. The Second Course—Isolation

Continuation of present trends, it has been shown above, will lead progressively to the withdrawal of the United States from most of its present commitments in Europe and Asia and to our isolation in the Western Hemisphere and its approaches. This would result not from a conscious decision but from a failure to take the actions necessary to bring our capabilities into line with our commitments and thus to a withdrawal under pressure. This pressure might come from our present Allies, who will tend to seek other "solutions" unless they have confidence in our determination to accelerate our efforts to build a successfully functioning political and economic system in the free world.

There are some who advocate a deliberate decision to isolate ourselves. Superficially, this has some attractiveness as a course of action, for it appears to bring our commitments and capabilities into harmony by reducing the former and by concentrating our present, or perhaps even reduced, military expenditures on the defense of the United States.

This argument overlooks the relativity of capabilities. With the United States in an isolated position, we would have to face the probability that the Soviet Union would quickly dominate most of Eurasia, probably without meeting armed resistance. It would thus acquire a potential far superior to our own, and would promptly proceed to develop this potential with the purpose of eliminating our power, which would, even in isolation, remain as a challenge to it and as an obstacle to the imposition of its kind of order in the world. . . .

C. The Third Course—War

Some Americans favor a deliberate decision to go to war against the Soviet Union in the near future. It goes without saying that the idea of "preventive" war—in the sense of a military attack not provoked by a military attack upon us or our allies—is generally unacceptable to Americans. Its supporters argue that since the Soviet Union is in fact at war with the free world now and that since the failure of the Soviet Union to use all-out military force is explainable on grounds of expediency, we are at war and should conduct ourselves accordingly. Some further argue that the free world is probably unable, except under the crisis of war, to mobilize and direct its resources to the checking and rolling back of the Kremlin's drive for world dominion. This is a powerful argument in the light of history, but the considerations against war are so compelling that the free world must demonstrate that this argument is wrong. The case for war is premised on the assumption that the United States could launch and sustain an attack of sufficient impact to gain a decisive advantage for the free world in a long war and perhaps to win an early decision.

The ability of the United States to launch effective offensive operations is now limited to attack with atomic weapons. A powerful blow could be delivered upon the Soviet Union, but it is estimated that these operations alone would not force or induce the Kremlin to capitulate and that the Kremlin would still be able to use the forces under its control to dominate most or all of Eurasia. This would probably mean a long and difficult struggle during which the free institutions of Western Europe and many freedom-loving people would be destroyed and the regenerative capacity of Western Europe dealt a crippling blow.

Apart from this, however, a surprise attack upon the Soviet Union, despite the provocativeness of recent Soviet behavior, would be repugnant to many Americans. Although the American people would probably rally in support of the war effort, the shock of responsibility for a surprise attack would be morally corrosive. . . .

D. The Remaining Course of Action—a Rapid Build-up of Political, Economic, and Military Strength in the Free World.

A more rapid build-up of political, economic, and military strength and thereby of confidence in the free world than is now contemplated is the only course which is consistent with progress toward achieving our fundamental purpose. The frustration of the Kremlin design requires the free world to develop a successfully functioning political and economic system and a vigorous political offensive against the Soviet Union. These, in turn, require an adequate military shield under which they can develop. It is necessary to have the military power to deter, if possible, Soviet expansion, and to defeat, if necessary, aggressive Soviet or Soviet-directed actions of a limited or total character. The potential strength of the free world is great; its ability to develop these military capabilities and its will to resist Soviet expansion will be determined by the wisdom and will with which it undertakes to meet its political and economic problems. . . .

CONCLUSIONS

A continuation of present trends would result in a serious decline in the strength of the free world relative to the Soviet Union and its satellites. This unfavorable trend arises from the inadequacy of current programs and plans rather than from any error in our objectives and aims. These trends lead in the direction of isolation, not by deliberate decision but by lack of the necessary basis for a vigorous initiative in the conflict with the Soviet Union.

Our position as the center of power in the free world places a heavy responsibility upon the United States for leadership. We must organize and enlist the energies and resources of the free world in a positive program for peace which will frustrate the Kremlin design for world domination by creating a situation in the free world to which the Kremlin will be compelled to adjust. Without such a cooperative effort, led by the United States, we will have to make gradual withdrawals under pressure until we discover one day that we have sacrificed positions of vital interest.

It is imperative that this trend be reversed by a much more rapid and concerted build-up of the actual strength of both the United States and the other nations of the free world. The analysis shows that this will be costly and will involve significant domestic financial and economic adjustments. . . .

In summary, we must, by means of a rapid and sustained build-up of the political, economic, and military strength of the free world, and by means of an affirmative program intended to wrest the initiative from the Soviet Union, confront it with convincing evidence of the determination and ability of the free world to frustrate the Kremlin to the new situation.   Failing that, the unwillingness of the determination and ability of the free world to frustrate the Kremlin design of a world dominated by its will. Such evidence is the only means short of war which eventually may force the Kremlin to abandon its present course of action and to negotiate acceptable agreements on issues of major importance.

The whole success of the proposed program hangs ultimately on recognition by this Government, the American people, and all free peoples, that the cold war is in fact a real war in which the survival of the free world is at stake. Essential prerequisites to success are consultations with Congressional leaders designed to make the program the object of non-partisan legislative support, and a presentation to the public of a full explanation of the facts and implications of the present international situation.   The prosecution of the program will require of us all the ingenuity, sacrifice, and unity demanded by the vital importance of the issue and the tenacity to persevere until our national objectives have been attained.

FURTHER READINGS

Callahan, David, *Dangerous Capabilities: Paul Nitze and the Cold War* (New York: Harper & Row, 1990).

Cumings, Bruce, *The Origins of the Korean War,* volume II, *The Roaring of the Cataract, 1947–1950* (Princeton, N.J.: Princeton University Press, 1990).

Gaddis, John L., *Russia, the Soviet Union, and the United States* (New York: Knopf, 1978).

LaFeber, Walter, *America, Russia, and the Cold War* (New York: McGraw-Hill, 1985).

Reardon, Steven L., *The Evolution of American Strategic Doctrine: Paul H. Nitze and the Soviet Challenge* (Boulder, Colo.: Westview Press, 1984).

Talbott, Strobe, *The Master of the Game: Paul Nitze and the Nuclear Peace* (New York: Knopf, 1988).

DOCUMENT 50

The Korean War

On 25 June 1950 the North Korean army crossed the thirty-eighth parallel to invade South Korea. President Truman responded by ordering U.S. military forces to defend South Korea and asked the United Nations for support in resisting North Korean aggression. Truman announced these and other decisions to the American people on 27 June 1950.[50]

In Korea the Government forces, which were armed to prevent border raids and to preserve internal security, were attacked by invading forces from North Korea. The Security Council of the United Nations called upon the invading troops to cease hostilities and to withdraw to the 38th parallel. This they have not done but on the contrary have pressed the attack. The Security Council called upon all members of the United Nations to render every assistance to the United Nations in the execution of this resolution. In these circumstances I have ordered United States air and sea forces to give the Korean Government troops cover and support.

The attack upon Korea makes it plain beyond all doubt that Communism has passed beyond the use of subversion to conquer independent nations and will now use armed invasion and war. It has defied the orders of the Security Council of the United Nations issued to preserve international peace and security. In these circumstances the occupation of Formosa by Communist forces would be a direct threat to the security of the Pacific area and to the United States forces performing their lawful and necessary functions in that area.

Accordingly I have ordered the Seventh Fleet to prevent any attack upon Formosa. As a corollary of this action I am calling upon the Chinese Government on Formosa to cease all air and sea operations against the mainland. The Seventh Fleet will see that this is done. The determination of

---

[50]Glenn D. Paige, *The Korean Decision* (N.Y.: The Free Press, 1968), 188–89.

the future status of Formosa must await the restoration of security in the Pacific, a peace settlement with Japan, or consideration by the United Nations.

I have also directed that United States Forces in the Philippines be strengthened and that military assistance to the Philippine Government be accelerated.

I have similarly directed acceleration in the furnishing of military assistance to the forces of France and the Associated States in Indochina and the dispatch of a military mission to provide close working relations with those forces.

I know that all members of the United Nations will consider carefully the consequences of this latest aggression in Korea in defiance of the Charter of the United Nations. A return to the rule of force in international affairs would have far-reaching effects. The United States will continue to uphold the rule of law.

I have instructed Ambassador Austin, as the Representative of the United States to the Security Council, to report these steps to the Council.

FURTHER READINGS

Caridi, Ronald, *The Korean War and American Politics* (Philadelphia: University of Pennsylvania Press, 1969).

Cumings, Bruce, *The Origins of the Korean War,* volume II, *The Roaring of the Cataract, 1947–1950* (Princeton, N.J.: Princeton University Press, 1990).

Foot, Rosemary, *A Substitute for Victory: The Politics of Peacemaking at the Korean Armistice Talks* (Ithaca, N.Y.: Cornell University Press, 1990).

———, *The Wrong War* (Ithaca, N.Y.: Cornell University Press, 1985).

Kaufman, Burton I., *The Korean War* (Philadelphia: Temple University Press, 1986).

Merrill, John, *Korea: The Peninsular Origins of the War* (Newark: University of Delaware Press, 1989).

Paige, Glenn D., *The Korea Decision* (New York: Free Press, 1975).

Schaller, Michael, *Douglas MacArthur: The Far Eastern General* (New York: Oxford University Press, 1989).

DOCUMENT 51

Eisenhower and Guatemala

When President Jacobo Arbenz of Guatemala expropriated about 400,000 acres of land owned by the United Fruit Company and appointed communists to government posts, President Dwight D. Eisenhower feared that the Soviet Union was undermining U.S. interests in Latin America. After receiving this report from Ambassador John Peurifoy, Eisenhower authorized the CIA to topple the Arbenz regime in June 1954.[51]

THE AMBASSADOR IN GUATEMALA (PEURIFOY) TO THE DEPARTMENT OF STATE

SECRET   GUATEMALA CITY, December 17, 1953–7 p.m.

154.   President and Mrs. Arbenz entertained my wife and me privately at dinner last night and we had a frank six hour discussion of the Communist problem here lasting until two this morning.   President showed depth of his feeling against United Fruit Company and his admiration for Guatemala's Communist leaders, leaving no doubt he intended to continue to collaborate with them.

I opened conversation by telling President I was interested in seeing what I could do to improve relations and asked if he had any suggestions.   He began by saying problem here is one between United Fruit Company and his government.   He spoke at length and bitterly on Fruit Company's history since 1904, complaining especially that now his Government has a $70 million budget to meet and collects only $150,000 in taxes.

I interrupted here to say I thought we should put first things first, that as long as Communists exerted their present influence in Guatemalan Government I did not see real hope of better relations. . . .

I came away definitely convinced that if President is not a Communist he will certainly do until one comes along, and that normal approaches will not work in Guatemala.   I am now assessing situation in this light and expect to submit recommendations in a few days.

FURTHER READINGS

Ameringer, Charles D., *U.S. Foreign Intelligence: The Secret Side of American History* (Lexington, Mass.: Lexington Books, 1990).

Gleijeses, Piero, *Shattered Hope: The Guatemalan Revolution and the United States, 1944–1954* (Princeton, N.J.: Princeton University Press, 1991).

Immerman, Richard H., *The CIA in Guatemala: The Foreign Policy of Intervention* (Austin: University of Texas Press, 1982).

Jeffreys-Jones, Rhodi, *The CIA and American Democracy* (New Haven, Conn.: Yale University Press, 1989).

---

[51]*Papers Relating to the Foreign Relations of the United States, 1953–1954* (Washington, D.C.: U.S. Government Printing Office, 1983), 4:1091–93.

Rabe, Stephen G., *Eisenhower and Latin America* (Chapel Hill: University of North Carolina Press, 1988).

Schlesinger, Stephen C. and Kinzer, Stephen, *Bitter Fruit: The Untold Story of the American Coup in Guatemala* (Garden City, N.Y.: Doubleday, 1982).

DOCUMENT 52

The Domino Theory

At a press conference on 7 April 1954 Eisenhower explained the importance of French Indochina to the free world by explaining the "falling domino" principle.[52]

Q. Robert Richards, Copley Press: Mr. President, would you mind commenting on the strategic importance of Indochina to the free world? I think there has been, across the country, some lack of understanding on just what it means to us.

THE PRESIDENT. You have, of course, both the specific and the general when you talk about such things.

First of all, you have the specific value of a locality in its production of materials that the world needs.

Then you have the possibility that many human beings pass under a dictatorship that is inimical to the free world.

Finally, you have broader considerations that might follow what you would call the "falling domino" principle. You have a row of dominoes set up, you knock over the first one, and what will happen to the last one is the certainty that it will go over very quickly. So you could have a beginning of a disintegration that would have the most profound influences.

Now, with respect to the first one, two of the items from this particular area that the world uses are tin and tungsten. They are very important. There are others, of course, the rubber plantations and so on.

Then with respect to more people passing under this domination, Asia, after all, has already lost some 450 million of its peoples to the Communist dictatorship, and we simply can't afford greater losses.

But when we come to the possible sequence of events, the loss of Indochina, of Burma, of Thailand, of the Peninsula, and Indonesia following, now you

---

[52]*Public Papers of the Presidents: Dwight D. Eisenhower, 1954* (Washington, D.C.: U.S. Government Printing Office, 1960), 382–83.

begin to talk about areas that not only multiply the disadvantages that you would suffer through loss of materials, sources of materials, but now you are talking really about millions and millions and millions of people.

Finally, the geographical position achieved thereby does many things. It turns the so-called island defensive chain of Japan, Formosa, of the Philippines and to the southward; it moves in to threaten Australia and New Zealand.

It takes away, in its economic aspects, that region that Japan must have as a trading area or Japan, in turn, will have only one place in the world to go—that is, toward the Communist areas in order to live.

So, the possible consequences of the loss are just incalculable to the free world.

FURTHER READINGS

Ambrose, Stephen E., *Eisenhower* (New York: Simon and Schuster, 1984).

Anderson, David L., *Trapped by Success: The Eisenhower Administration and Vietnam, 1953-1961* (New York: Columbia University Press, 1991).

Divine, Robert A , *Eisenhower and the Cold War* (New York: Oxford University Press, 1981).

Greenstein, Fred I., *The Hidden-Hand Presidency: Eisenhower as Leader* (New York: Basic Books, 1982).

Pach, Jr., Chester J. and Richardson, Elmo, *The Presidency of Dwight D. Eisenhower* (Lawrence: University Press of Kansas, 1991).

DOCUMENT 53

The Eisenhower Doctrine

In the aftermath of the 1956 Suez Crisis, President Eisenhower feared communist penetration into the Middle East. On 5 January 1957 the president informed a joint session of Congress of his desire to forestall this possibility, and two months later Congress approved what would be called the Eisenhower Doctrine.[53]

🎏🎏🎏

---

[53]*Public Papers of the Presidents: Dwight D. Eisenhower, 1957* (Washington, D.C.: U.S. Government Printing Office, 1958), 6–16, passim.

TO THE CONGRESS OF THE UNITED STATES:

First may I express to you my deep appreciation of your courtesy in giving me, at some inconvenience to yourselves, this early opportunity of addressing you on a matter I deem to be of grave importance to our country.

In my forthcoming State of the Union Message, I shall review the international situation generally. There are worldwide hopes which we can reasonably entertain, and there are worldwide responsibilities which we must carry to make certain that freedom—including our own—may be secure.

There is, however, a special situation in the Middle East which I feel I should, even now, lay before you. . . .

II.

Russia's rulers have long sought to dominate the Middle East. That was true of the Czars and it is true of the Bolsheviks. The reasons are not hard to find. They do not affect Russia's security, for no one plans to use the Middle East as a base for aggression against Russia. Never for a moment has the United States entertained such a thought.

The Soviet Union has nothing whatsoever to fear from the United States in the Middle East, or anywhere else in the world, so long as its rulers do not themselves first resort to aggression.

That statement I make solemnly and emphatically.

Neither does Russia's desire to dominate the Middle East spring from its own economic interest in the area. Russia does not appreciably use or depend upon the Suez Canal. In 1955 Soviet traffic through the Canal represented only about three fourths of 1% of the total. The Soviets have no need for, and could provide no market for, the petroleum resources which constitute the principal natural wealth of the area. Indeed, the Soviet Union is a substantial exporter of petroleum products.

The reason for Russia's interest in the Middle East is solely that of power politics. Considering her announced purpose of Communizing the world, it is easy to understand her hope of dominating the Middle East.

This region has always been the crossroads of the continents of the Eastern Hemisphere. The Suez Canal enables the nations of Asia and Europe to carry on the commerce that is essential if these countries are to maintain well-rounded and prosperous economies. The Middle East provides a gateway between Eurasia and Africa.

It contains about two thirds of the presently known oil deposits of the world and it normally supplies the petroleum needs of many nations of Europe, Asia and Africa. The nations of Europe are peculiarly dependent upon this supply, and this dependency relates to transportation as well as to production! This has been vividly demonstrated since the closing of the Suez Canal and some of the pipelines. Alternate ways of transportation and, indeed, alternate sources of power can, if necessary, be developed. But these cannot be considered as early prospects.

These things stress the immense importance of the Middle East. If the nations of that area should lose their independence, if they were dominated by alien forces hostile to freedom, that would be both a tragedy for the area and for many other free nations whose economic life would be subject to near strangulation. Western Europe would be endangered just as though there had been no Marshall Plan, no North Atlantic Treaty Organization. The free nations of Asia and Africa, too, would be placed in serious jeopardy. And the countries of the Middle East would lose the markets upon which their economies depend. All this would have the most adverse, if not disastrous, effect upon our own nation's economic life and political prospects. . . .

Thus, we have these simple and indisputable facts:

1. The Middle East, which has always been coveted by Russia, would today be prized more than ever by International Communism.
2. The Soviet rulers continue to show that they do not scruple to use any means to gain their ends.
3. The free nations of the Mid East need, and for the most part want, added strength to assure their continued independence. . . .

VI.

It is nothing new for the President and the Congress to join to recognize that the national integrity of other free nations is directly related to our own security.

We have joined to create and support the security system of the United Nations. We have reinforced the collective security system of the United Nations by a series of collective defense arrangements. Today we have security treaties with 42 other nations which recognize that our peace and security are intertwined. We have joined to take decisive action in relation to Greece and Turkey and in relation to Taiwan.

Thus, the United States through the joint action of the President and the Congress, or, in the case of treaties, the Senate, has manifested in many endangered areas its purpose to support free and independent governments—and peace—against external menace, notably the menace of International Communism. Thereby we have helped to maintain peace and security during a period of great danger. It is now essential that the United States should manifest through joint action of the President and the Congress our determination to assist those nations of the Mid East area, which desire that assistance.

The action which I propose would have the following features.

It would, first of all, authorize the United States to cooperate with and assist any nation or group of nations in the general area of the Middle East in the development of economic strength dedicated to the maintenance of national independence.

It would, in the second place, authorize the Executive to undertake in the same region programs of military assistance and cooperation with any nation or group of nations which desires such aid.

It would, in the third place, authorize such assistance and cooperation to include the employment of the armed forces of the United States to secure and protect the territorial integrity and political independence of such nations, requesting such aid, against overt armed aggression from any nation controlled by International Communism.

These measures would have to be consonant with the treaty obligations of the United States, including the Charter of the United Nations and with any action or recommendations of the United Nations. They would also, if armed attack occurs, be subject to the overriding authority of the United Nations Security Council in accordance with the Charter.

The present proposal would, in the fourth place, authorize the President to employ, for economic and defensive military purposes, sums available under the Mutual Security Act of 1954, as amended, without regard to existing limitation. . . .

VIII.

In the situation now existing, the greatest risk, as is often the case, is that ambitious despots may miscalculate. If power-hungry Communists should either falsely or correctly estimate that the Middle East is inadequately defended, they might be tempted to use open measures of armed attack. If so, that would start a chain of circumstances which would almost surely involve the United States in military action. I am convinced that the best insurance against this dangerous contingency is to make clear now our readiness to cooperate fully and freely with our friends of the Middle East in ways consonant with the purposes and principles of the United Nations. I intend promptly to send a special mission to the Middle East to explain the cooperation we are prepared to give.

FURTHER READINGS

Ambrose, Stephen E., *Eisenhower* (New York: Simon and Schuster, 1984).

Brands, Jr., H. William, *Cold Warriors: Eisenhower's Generation and American Foreign Policy* (New York: Columbia University Press, 1988).

————, *The Specter of Neutralism: The United States and the Emergence of the Third World, 1947–1960* (New York: Columbia University Press, 1989).

Divine, Robert, *Eisenhower and the Cold War* (New York: Oxford University Press, 1981).

Pach, Jr., Chester J. and Richardson, Elmo, *The Presidency of Dwight D. Eisenhower* (Lawrence: University Press of Kansas, 1991).

DOCUMENT 54

The Bay of Pigs

In the wake of the failure to topple Fidel Castro from power with the Bay of Pigs operation, on 20 April 1961 President John F. Kennedy explained to the members of the American Society of Newspaper Editors the lessons to be learned from this episode.[54]

I have decided in the last 24 hours to discuss briefly at this time the recent events in Cuba. On that unhappy island, as in so many other arenas of the contest for freedom, the news has grown worse instead of better. I have emphasized before that this was a struggle of Cuban patriots against a Cuban dictator. While we could not be expected to hide our sympathies, we made it repeatedly clear that the armed forces of this country would not intervene in any way.

Any unilateral American intervention, in the absence of an external attack upon ourselves or an ally, would have been contrary to our traditions and to our international obligations. But let the record show that our restraint is not inexhaustible. Should it ever appear that the inter-American doctrine of non-interference merely conceals or excuses a policy of nonaction—if the nations of this Hemisphere should fail to meet their commitments against outside Communist penetration—then I want it clearly understood that this Government will not hesitate in meeting its primary obligations which are to the security of our Nation! . . .

But there are from this sobering episode useful lessons for us all to learn. Some may be still obscure, and await further information. Some are clear today.

First, it is clear that the forces of communism are not to be underestimated, in Cuba or anywhere else in the world. The advantages of a police state—its use of mass terror and arrests to prevent the spread of free dissent—cannot be overlooked by those who expect the fall of every fanatic tyrant. If the self-discipline of the free cannot match the iron discipline of the mailed fist—in economic, political, scientific and all the other kinds of struggles as well as the military—then the peril to freedom will continue to rise.

Secondly, it is clear that this Nation, in concert with all the free nations of this hemisphere, must take an ever closer and more realistic look at the menace

---

[54]*Public Papers of the Presidents: John F. Kennedy, 1961* (Washington, D.C.: U.S. Government Printing Office, 1962), 304–6.

of external Communist intervention and domination in Cuba. The American people are not complacent about Iron Curtain tanks and planes less than 90 miles from their shore. But a nation of Cuba's size is less a threat to our survival than it is a base for subverting the survival of other free nations throughout the hemisphere. It is not primarily our interest or our security but theirs which is now, today, in the greater peril. It is for their sake as well as our own that we must show our will. . . .

Third, and finally, it is clearer than ever that we face a relentless struggle in every corner of the globe that goes far beyond the clash of armies or even nuclear armaments. The armies are there, and in large number. The nuclear armaments are there. But they serve primarily as the shield behind which subversion, infiltration, and a host of other tactics steadily advance, picking off vulnerable areas one by one in situations which do not permit our own armed intervention.

Power is the hallmark of this offensive—power and discipline and deceit. The legitimate discontent of yearning people is exploited. The legitimate trappings of self-determination are employed. But once in power, all talk of discontent is repressed, all self-determination disappears, and the promise of a revolution of hope is betrayed, as in Cuba, into a reign of terror. . . .

We dare not fail to see the insidious nature of this new and deeper struggle. We dare not fail to grasp the new concepts, the new tools, the new sense of urgency we will need to combat it—whether in Cuba or South Vietnam. And we dare not fail to realize that this struggle is taking place every day, without fanfare, in thousands of villages and markets—day and night—and in classrooms all over the globe.

The message of Cuba, of Laos, of the rising din of Communist voices in Asia and Latin America—these messages are all the same. The complacent, the self-indulgent, the soft societies are about to be swept away with the debris of history. Only the strong, only the industrious, only the determined, only the courageous, only the visionary who determine the real nature of our struggle can possibly survive.

No greater task faces this country or this administration. No other challenge is more deserving of our every effort and energy. Too long we have fixed our eyes on traditional military needs, on armies prepared to cross borders, on missiles poised for flight. Now it should be clear that this is no longer enough—that our security may be lost piece by piece, country by country, without the firing of a single missile or the crossing of a single border.

We intend to profit from this lesson. We intend to reexamine and reorient our forces of all kinds—our tactics and our institutions here in this community. We intend to intensify our efforts for a struggle in many ways more difficult than war, where disappointment will often accompany us.

For I am convinced that we in this country and in the free world possess the necessary resource, and the skill, and the added strength that comes from a belief in the freedom of man. And I am equally convinced that history will record the fact that this bitter struggle reached its climax in the late 1950's and the early 1960's. Let me then make clear as the President of the United States that I am determined upon our system's survival and success, regardless of the cost and regardless of the peril!

FURTHER READINGS

Giglio, James N., *The Presidency of John F. Kennedy* (Lawrence: University Press of Kansas, 1991).

Higgins, Trumbull, *The Perfect Failure: Kennedy, Eisenhower and the Bay of Pigs* (New York: Norton, 1987).

Morley, Morris, *Imperial State and Revolution: The United States and Cuba, 1952–1986* (New York: Cambridge University Press, 1987).

Parmet, Herbert S., *JFK* (New York: Dial Press, 1983).

Smith, Wayne S., *The Closest of Enemies: A Personal and Diplomatic Account of U.S.-Cuban Relations since 1957* (New York: Norton, 1987).

Welch, Richard W., *Response to Revolution: The United States and the Cuban Revolution, 1959–1961* (Chapel Hill: University of North Carolina Press, 1985).

Wyden, Peter, *Bay of Pigs* (New York: Simon and Schuster, 1979).

DOCUMENT 55

The Cuban Missile Crisis

On 22 October 1962 President John Kennedy informed the people of the United States of the presence of nuclear missile sites on Cuba.[55] The United States and Soviet Union remained on the brink of a nuclear confrontation until 28 October, when Nikita Khrushchev promised to withdraw the missiles.

GOOD EVENING, MY FELLOW CITIZENS:

This Government, as promised, has maintained the closest surveillance of the Soviet military buildup on the island of Cuba. Within the past week, unmistakable evidence has established the fact that a series of offensive missile sites is now in preparation on that imprisoned island. The purpose of these

---

[55]*Public Papers of the Presidents: John F. Kennedy, 1962* (Washington, D.C.: U.S. Government Printing Office, 1963), 806–9.

bases can be none other than to provide a nuclear strike capability against the Western Hemisphere. . . .

But this secret, swift, and extraordinary buildup of Communist missiles—in an area well known to have a special and historical relationship to the United States and the nations of the Western Hemisphere, in violation of Soviet assurances, and in defiance of American and hemispheric policy—this sudden, clandestine decision to station strategic weapons for the first time outside of Soviet soil—is a deliberately provocative and unjustified change in the status quo which cannot be accepted by this country, if our courage and our commitments are ever to be trusted again by either friend or foe.

The 1930's taught us a clear lesson: aggressive conduct, if allowed to go unchecked and unchallenged, ultimately leads to war. This nation is opposed to war. We are also true to our word. Our unswerving objective, therefore, must be to prevent the use of these missiles against this or any other country, and to secure their withdrawal or elimination from the Western Hemisphere.

Our policy has been one of patience and restraint, as befits a peaceful and powerful nation, which leads a worldwide alliance. We have been determined not to be diverted from our central concerns by mere irritants and fanatics. But now further action is required—and it is under way; and these actions may only be the beginning. We will not prematurely or unnecessarily risk the costs of worldwide nuclear war in which even the fruits of victory would be ashes in our mouth—but neither will we shrink from that risk at any time it must be faced.

Acting, therefore, in the defense of our own security and of the entire Western Hemisphere, and under the authority entrusted to me by the Constitution as endorsed by the resolution of the Congress, I have directed that the following *initial* steps be taken immediately:

First: To halt this offensive buildup, a strict quarantine on all offensive military equipment under shipment to Cuba is being initiated. All ships of any kind bound for Cuba from whatever nation or port will, if found to contain cargoes of offensive weapons, be turned back. This quarantine will be extended, if needed, to other types of cargo and carriers. We are not at this time, however, denying the necessities of life as the Soviets attempted to do in their Berlin blockade of 1948.

Second: I have directed the continued and increased close surveillance of Cuba and its military buildup. The foreign ministers of the OAS, in their communiqué of October 6, rejected secrecy on such matters in this hemisphere. Should these offensive military preparations continue, thus increasing the threat to the hemisphere, further action will be justified. I have directed the Armed Forces to prepare for any eventualities; and I trust that in the interest of both the Cuban people and the Soviet technicians at the sites, the hazards to all concerned of continuing this threat will be recognized.

Third: It shall be the policy of this Nation to regard any nuclear missile launched from Cuba against any nation in the Western Hemisphere as an attack by the Soviet Union on the United States, requiring a full retaliatory response upon the Soviet Union. . . .

Seventh and finally: I call upon Chairman Khrushchev to halt and eliminate this clandestine, reckless, and provocative threat to world peace and to stable relations between our two nations. I call upon him further to abandon this course of world domination, and to join in an historic effort to end the perilous arms race and to transform the history of man. He has an opportunity now to move the world back from the abyss of destruction—by returning to his government's own words that it had no need to station missiles outside its own territory, and withdrawing these weapons from Cuba—by refraining from any action which will widen or deepen the present crisis—and then by participating in a search for peaceful and permanent solutions. . . .

My fellow citizens: let no one doubt that this is a difficult and dangerous effort on which we have set out. No one can foresee precisely what course it will take or what costs or casualties will be incurred. Many months of sacrifice and self-discipline lie ahead—months in which both our patience and our will will be tested—months in which many threats and denunciations will keep us aware of our dangers. But the greatest danger of all would be to do nothing.

The path we have chosen for the present is full of hazards, as all paths are—but it is the one most consistent with our character and courage as a nation and our commitments around the world. The cost of freedom is always high—but Americans have always paid it. And one path we shall never choose, and that is the path of surrender or submission.

Our goal is not the victory of might, but the vindication of right—not peace at the expense of freedom, but both peace *and* freedom, here in this hemisphere, and, we hope, around the world. God willing, that goal will be achieved.

Thank you and good night.

FURTHER READINGS

Beschloss, Michael, *The Crisis Years: Kennedy and Khrushchev, 1960–1963* (New York: Burlingame Books, 1991).

Blasier, Cole, *The Hovering Giant* (Pittsburgh: University of Pittsburgh Press, 1976).

"The Cuban Missile Crisis Reconsidered," *Diplomatic History*, 14, no. 2 (Spring 1990): 205–56.

Detzer, David, *The Brink* (New York: Crowell, 1979).

Dinerstein, Herbert, *The Making of a Missile Crisis: October 1962* (Baltimore: Johns Hopkins University Press, 1976).

Giglio, James N., *The Presidency of John F. Kennedy* (Lawrence: University Press of Kansas, 1991).

Kern, Montague, Levering, Patrica W., and Levering, Ralph B., *The Kennedy Crisis: The Press, The Presidency, and Foreign Policy* (Chapel Hill: University of North Carolina Press, 1983).

Morley, Morris, *Imperial State and Revolution: The United States and Cuba, 1952–1987* (New York: Cambridge University Press, 1987).

Parmet, Herbert S., *JFK* (New York: Dial Press, 1983).

Paterson, Thomas G., editor, *Kennedy's Quest for Victory: American Foreign Policy, 1961–1963* (New York: Oxford University Press, 1989).

DOCUMENT 56

The Gulf of Tonkin Resolution

President Lyndon Baines Johnson, who alleged that North Vietnamese patrol boats had attacked U.S. naval vessels in international waters, received authorization on 7 August 1964 from Congress "to take all necessary measures to repel any armed attack against the forces of the United States and to prevent further aggression."[56] Johnson would later use the Gulf of Tonkin Resolution to americanize the war in South Vietnam.

TO PROMOTE THE MAINTENANCE OF INTERNATIONAL PEACE AND SECURITY IN SOUTHEAST ASIA

Whereas naval units of the Communist regime in Vietnam, in violation of the principles of the Charter of the United Nations and of international law, have deliberately and repeatedly attacked United States naval vessels lawfully present in international waters, and have thereby created a serious threat to international peace; and

Whereas these attacks are part of a deliberate and systematic campaign of aggression that the Communist regime in North Vietnam has been waging against its neighbors and the nations joined with them in the collective defense of their freedom; and

Whereas the United States is assisting the peoples of southeast Asia to protect their freedom and has no territorial, military or political ambitions in that area, but desires only that these peoples should be left in peace to work out their own destinies in their own way: Now, therefore, be it

Resolved by the Senate and House of Representatives of the United States of America in Congress assembled.

---

[56]Gareth Porter, editor, *Vietnam: A History in Documents* (N.Y.: New American Library, 1981), 286–87.

That the Congress approves and supports the determination of the President, as Commander in Chief, to take all necessary measures to repel any armed attack against the forces of the United States and to prevent further aggression.

SEC. 2. The United States regards as vital to its national interest and to world peace the maintenance of international peace and security in southeast Asia. Consonant with the Constitution of the United States and the Charter of the United Nations and in accordance with its obligations under the Southeast Asia Collective Defense Treaty, the United States is, therefore, prepared, as the President determines, to take all necessary steps, including the use of armed force, to assist any member or protocol state of the Southeast Asia Collective Defense Treaty requesting assistance in defense of its freedom.

SEC. 3. This resolution shall expire when the President shall determine that the peace and security of the area is reasonably assured by international conditions created by the action of the United Nations or otherwise, except that it may be terminated earlier by concurrent resolution of the Congress.

FURTHER READINGS

Berman, Larry, *Planning a Tragedy: The Americanization of the War in Vietnam* (New York: Norton, 1982).

————, *Lyndon Johnson's War* (New York: Norton, 1989).

Herring, George C., *America's Longest War: The United States and Vietnam, 1950-1975* (New York: Wiley, 1979).

Kahin, George, *Intervention: How America Became Involved in Vietnam* (New York: Knopf, 1986).

Karnow, Stanley, *Vietnam: A History* (New York: Viking Press, 1983).

Rotter, Andrew J., *The Path to Vietnam* (Ithaca, N.Y.: Cornell University Press, 1987).

Young, Marilyn B., *The Vietnam Wars* (New York: HarperCollins, 1991).

DOCUMENT 57

Clark Clifford and the Reappraisal of U.S. Policy toward the War in Vietnam

In the wake of the Tet offensive President Johnson asked Secretary of Defense Clark Clifford to chair a task force that would determine how an additional 200,000 troops could be sent to South Vietnam. Instead, as Clifford explained in an article in Foreign Affairs, *he emerged from these discussions not only highly critical of Johnson's military policies, but also "conscious of our obligations and involvements elsewhere in the world."*[57]

✿✿✿

I was also conscious of our obligations and involvements elsewhere in the world. There were certain hopeful signs in our relations with the Soviet Union, but both nations were hampered in moving towards vitally important talks on the limitation of strategic weapons so long as the United States was committed to a military solution in Viet Nam. We could not afford to disregard our interests in the Middle East, South Asia, Africa, Western Europe and elsewhere. Even accepting the validity of our objective in Viet Nam, that objective had to be viewed in the context of our overall national interest, and could not sensibly be pursued at a price so high as to impair our ability to achieve other, and perhaps even more important, foreign policy objectives.

Also, I could not free myself from the continuing nagging doubt left over from that August trip, that if the nations living in the shadow of Viet Nam were not now persuaded by the domino theory, perhaps it was time for us to take another look. Our efforts had given the nations in that area a number of years following independence to organize and build their security. I could see no reason at this time for us to continue to add to our commitment. . . .

And so, after these exhausting days, I was convinced that the military course we were pursuing was not only endless, but hopeless. . . . I was . . . convinced, our primary goal should be to level off our involvement, and to work toward gradual disengagement.

Further Readings. See Document 58.

---

[57]Clark M. Clifford, "A Viet Nam Reappraisal," *Foreign Affairs*, 47, no. 4 (July 1969): 612–13.

DOCUMENT 58

Lyndon Johnson's Post-Tet Address to the Nation

In view of Secretary of Defense Clifford's report and escalating unrest in the United States, on 31 March 1968 President Johnson announced a partial bombing halt in Vietnam, which he hoped would lead to productive peace talks and his decision not to pursue reelection.[58]

Tonight I renew the offer I made last August—to stop the bombardment of North Viet-Nam. We ask that talks begin promptly, that they be serious talks on the substance of peace. We assume that during those talks Hanoi will not take advantage of our restraint.

We are prepared to move immediately toward peace through negotiations.

So tonight, in the hope that this action will lead to early talks, I am taking the first step to deescalate the conflict. We are reducing—substantially reducing—the present level of hostilities. And we are doing so unilaterally and at once.

UNILATERAL DEESCALATION BY UNITED STATES

Tonight I have ordered our aircraft and our naval vessels to make no attacks on North Viet-Nam, except in the area north of the demilitarized zone where the continuing enemy buildup directly threatens Allied forward positions and where the movements of their troops and supplies are clearly related to that threat.

The area in which we are stopping our attacks includes almost 90 percent of North Viet-Nam's population and most of its territory. Thus there will be no attacks around the principal populated areas or in the food-producing areas of North Viet-Nam.

Even this very limited bombing of the North could come to an early end if our restraint is matched by restraint in Hanoi. But I cannot in good conscience stop all bombing so long as to do so would immediately and directly endanger the lives of our men and our allies. Whether a complete bombing halt becomes possible in the future will be determined by events.

Our purpose in this action is to bring about a reduction in the level of violence that now exists.

It is to save the lives of brave men and to save the lives of innocent women and children. It is to permit the contending forces to move closer to a political settlement.

---

[58]Porter, *Vietnam Documents*, 366–69.

And tonight I call upon the United Kingdom and I call upon the Soviet Union, as cochairmen of the Geneva conferences and as permanent members of the United Nations Security Council, to do all they can to move from the unilateral act of deescalation that I have just announced toward genuine peace in Southeast Asia.

Now, as in the past, the United States is ready to send its representatives to any forum, at any time, to discuss the means of bringing this ugly war to an end.

I am designating one of our most distinguished Americans, Ambassador Averell Harriman, as my personal representative for such talks. In addition, I have asked Ambassador Llewellyn Thompson, who returned from Moscow for consultation, to be available to join Ambassador Harriman at Geneva or any other suitable place just as soon as Hanoi agrees to a conference.

I call upon President Ho Chi Minh to respond positively and favorably to this new step toward peace.

But if peace does not come now through negotiations, it will come when Hanoi understands that our common resolve is unshakable and our common strength is invincible.

A CALL FOR NATIONAL UNITY

Finally, my fellow Americans, let me say this:

Of those to whom much is given, much is asked. I cannot say, and no man could say, that no more will be asked of us.

Yet, I believe that now, no less than when the decade began, this generation of Americans is willing to "pay any price, bear any burden, meet any hardship, support any friend, oppose any foe to assure the survival and the success of liberty." Since those words were spoken by John F. Kennedy, the people of America have kept that compact with mankind's noblest cause.

And we shall continue to keep it.

Yet I believe that we must always be mindful of this one thing, whatever the trials and the tests ahead: The ultimate strength of our country and our cause will lie not in powerful weapons or infinite resources or boundless wealth but will lie in the unity of our people.

This I believe very deeply. . . .

Through all time to come, I think America will be a stronger nation, a more just society, and a land of greater opportunity and fulfillment because of what we have all done together in these years of unparalleled achievement.

Our reward will come in the life of freedom, peace, and hope that our children will enjoy through ages ahead.

What we won when all of our people united just must not now be lost in suspicion, distrust, selfishness, and politics among any of our people.

Believing this as I do, I have concluded that I should not permit the Presidency to become involved in the partisan divisions that are developing in this political year.

With America's sons in the fields far away, with America's future under challenge right here at home, with our hopes and the world's hopes for peace in the balance every day, I do not believe that I should devote an hour or a day of my time to any personal partisan causes or to any duties other than the awesome duties of this Office—the Presidency of your country.

Accordingly, I shall not seek, and I will not accept, the nomination of my party for another term as your President.

But let men everywhere know, however, that a strong, a confident, and a vigilant America stands ready tonight to seek an honorable peace—and stands ready tonight to defend an honored cause—whatever the price, whatever the burden, whatever the sacrifices that duty may require. Thank you for listening.

Good night and God bless all of you.

FURTHER READINGS FOR DOCUMENTS 57-58

Berman, Larry, *Lyndon Johnson's War: The Road to Stalemate in Vietnam* (New York: Norton, 1989).

Gardner, Lloyd C., *Approaching Vietnam* (New York: Norton, 1988).

Hellmann, John, *American Myth and the Legacy of Vietnam* (New York: Columbia University Press, 1986).

Herring, George C., *America's Longest War: The United States and Vietnam, 1950-1975* (New York: Wiley, 1979).

Palmer, Jr., Bruce, *The 25-Year War* (Lexington: University Press of Kentucky, 1986).

Podhoretz, Norman, *Why We Were in Vietnam* (New York: Simon and Schuster, 1982).

Rotter, Andrew J., *The Path to Vietnam* (Ithaca, N.Y.: Cornell University Press, 1987).

Schandler, Herbert Y., *The Unmaking of a President* (Princeton, N.J.: Princeton University Press, 1977).

Young, Marilyn B., *The Vietnam Wars, 1945–1990* (New York: HarperCollins, 1991).

DOCUMENT 59

Linkage

On 4 February 1969 President Richard M. Nixon sent a letter to several cabinet officials that was written by National Security Advisor Henry Kissinger.[59] In it they explained their intention to change the manner in which the United States dealt with the Soviet Union by advancing relations "on a front at least as broad to make clear that we see some relationship between political and military issues." With "linkage," progress on curbing the nuclear arms race would be

---

[59]From *White House Years* by Henry Kissinger. Copyright (c) 1979 by Henry A. Kissinger. By permission Little, Brown and Company, 135–36.

related to progress in discussions on other issues, such as the situation in the
Middle East and peace talks in Paris.

I believe that the basis for a viable settlement is a mutual recognition of our
vital interests. We must recognize that the Soviet Union has interests; in the
present circumstances we cannot but take account of them in defining our own.
We should leave the Soviet leadership in no doubt that we expect them to adopt
a similar approach toward us. . . . In the past, we have often attempted to settle
things in a fit of enthusiasm, relying on personal diplomacy. But the "spirit"
that permeated various meetings lacked a solid basis of mutual interest, and
therefore, every summit meeting was followed by a crisis in less than a year.

I am convinced that the great issues are fundamentally interrelated. I do not
mean this to establish artificial linkages between specific elements of one or
another issue or between tactical steps that we may elect to take. But I do
believe that crisis or confrontation in one place and real cooperation in another
cannot long be sustained simultaneously. I recognize that the previous
Administration took the view that when we perceive a mutual interest on an
issue with the USSR, we should pursue agreement and attempt to insulate it as
much as possible from the ups and downs of conflicts elsewhere. This may well
be sound on numerous bilateral and practical matters such as cultural or
scientific exchanges. But, on the crucial issues of our day, I believe we must
seek to advance on a front at least broad enough to make clear that we see some
relationship between political and military issues. I believe that the Soviet
leaders should be brought to understand that they cannot expect to reap the
benefits of cooperation in one area while seeking to take advantage of tension
or confrontation elsewhere. Such a course involves the danger that the Soviets
will use talks on arms as a safety valve on intransigence elsewhere. . . .

I would like to illustrate what I have in mind in one case of immediate and
widespread interest—the proposed talks on strategic weapons. I believe our
decision on when and how to proceed does not depend exclusively on our
review of the purely military and technical issues, although these are of key
importance. This decision should also be taken in the light of the prevailing
political context and, in particular, in light of progress toward stabilizing the
explosive Middle East situation, and in light of the Paris talks [on Vietnam]. I
believe I should retain the freedom to ensure, to the extent that we have control
over it, that the timing of talks with the Soviet Union on strategic weapons is
optimal. This may, in fact, mean delay beyond that required for our review of
the technical issues. Indeed, it means that we should—at least in our public
position—keep open the option that there may be no talks at all.

FURTHER READINGS

Ambrose, Stephen E., *Nixon*, 3 volumes (New York: Simon and Schuster, 1987–1991).

Gaddis, John Lewis, *The United States and the End of the Cold War* (New York: Oxford University Press, 1992).

Garthoff, Raymond L., *Détente and Confrontation: American-Soviet Relations from Nixon to Reagan* (Washington, D.C.: Brookings Institution, 1994).

Isaacson, Walter, *Kissinger* (New York: Simon and Schuster, 1992).

Parmet, Herbert, *Richard Nixon and His America* (Boston: Little, Brown, 1990).

Schulzinger, Robert D., *Henry Kissinger* (New York: Columbia University Press, 1989).

DOCUMENT 60

The Nixon Doctrine

On 25 July 1969 President Nixon presented what would ultimately become known as the "Nixon Doctrine," which reflected not merely the nation's disenchantment with the war in Vietnam, but a disinclination to become involved in future Asian conflicts as well.[60]

⚔⚔

[4.] Q. Mr. President, sir, on the question of U.S. military relationships in Asia, if I may ask a hypothetical question: If a leader of one of the countries with which we have had close military relationships, either through SEATO or in Vietnam, should say, "Well, you are pulling out of Vietnam with your troops, we can read in the newspapers. How can we know that you will remain to play a significant role as you say you wish to do in security arrangements in Asia?" What kind of an approach can you take to that question?

THE PRESIDENT. I have already indicated that the answer to that question is not an easy one—not easy because we will be greatly tempted when that question is put to us to indicate that if any nation desires the assistance of the United States militarily in order to meet an internal or external threat, we will provide it.

However, I believe that the time has come when the United States, in our relations with all of our Asian friends, be quite emphatic on two points: One, that we will keep our treaty commitments, our treaty commitments, for example, with Thailand under SEATO; but, two, that as far as the problems of internal security are concerned, as far as the problems of military defense,

---

[60]*Public Papers of the Presidents: Richard Nixon, 1969* (Washington, D.C.: U.S. Government Printing Office, 1971), 548–49.

except for the threat of a major power involving nuclear weapons, that the United States is going to encourage and has a right to expect that this problem will be increasingly handled by, and the responsibility for it taken by, the Asian nations themselves.

I believe, incidentally, from my preliminary conversations with several Asian leaders over the past few months that they are going to be willing to undertake this responsibility. It will not be easy. But if the United States just continues down the road of responding to requests for assistance, of assuming the primary responsibility for defending these countries when they have internal problems or external problems, they are never going to take care of themselves.

I should add to that, too, that when we talk about collective security for Asia, I realize that at this time that looks like a weak reed. It actually is. But looking down the road—I am speaking now of 5 years from now, 10 years from now—I think collective security, insofar as it deals with internal threats to any one of the countries, or insofar as it deals with a threat other than that posed by a nuclear power, I believe that this is an objective which free Asian nations, independent Asian nations, can seek and which the United States should support.

[5.] Q. Mr. President, when you speak of internal threats, do you include threats internally assisted by a country from the outside, such as we have in Vietnam?

THE PRESIDENT. Generally speaking, that is the kind of internal threat that we do have in the Asian countries. For example, in Thailand the threat is one that is indigenous to a certain extent to the northeast and the north, but that would not be too serious if it were not getting the assistance that it was from the outside. The same is true in several of the other Asian countries.

FURTHER READINGS

Ambrose, Stephen E., *Nixon*, 3 volumes (New York: Simon and Schuster, 1987–1991).

Gaddis, John Lewis, *The United States and the End of the Cold War* (New York: Oxford University Press, 1992).

Garthoff, Raymond L., *Détente and Confrontation: American-Soviet Relations from Nixon to Reagan* (Washington, D.C.: Brookings Institution, 1994).

Isaacson, Walter, *Kissinger* (New York: Simon and Schuster, 1992).

Litwak, Robert, *Détente and the Nixon Doctrine* (New York: Cambridge University Press, 1984).

Parmet, Herbert, *Richard Nixon and His America* (Boston: Little, Brown, 1990).

Schulzinger, Robert D., *Henry Kissinger* (New York: Columbia University Press, 1989).

Stevenson, Richard W., *The Rise and Fall of Détente* (Urbana: University of Illinois Press, 1985).

Thornton, Richard, *The Nixon-Kissinger Years: The Reshaping of American Foreign Policy* (New York: Paragon House, 1989).

DOCUMENT 61

The Strategic Arms Limitation Treaty

President Nixon and Soviet President Leonid Brezhnev signed the Strategic Arms Limitation Treaty [SALT] in Moscow on 26 May 1972.[61] While only a first step, SALT 1 represented an unprecedented move by placing limits on certain types of nuclear weapons.

❧❧❧

ARTICLE I

The Parties undertake not to start construction of additional fixed land-based intercontinental ballistic missile (ICBM launchers after July 1, 1972.

ARTICLE II

The Parties undertake not to convert land-based launchers for light ICBMs, or for ICBMs of older types deployed prior to 1964, into land-based launchers for heavy ICBMs of types deployed after that time.

ARTICLE III

The Parties undertake to limit submarine-launched ballistic missile (SLBM launchers and modern ballistic missile submarines to the numbers operational and under construction on the date of the signature of this Interim Agreement, and in addition to launchers and submarines constructed under procedures established by the Parties as replacements for an equal number of ICBM launchers of older types deployed prior to 1964 or for launchers on older submarines.

ARTICLE IV

Subject to the provisions of this Interim Agreement, modernization and replacement of strategic offensive ballistic missiles and launchers covered by this Interim Agreement may be undertaken. . . .

---

[61]U.S. Department of State, *Bulletin* (Washington, D.C.: U.S. Government Printing Office, 1972), June 26, 1972, 920–21.

ARTICLE VII

The Parties undertake to continue active negotiations for limitations on strategic offensive arms. The obligations provided for in this Interim Agreement shall not prejudice the scope or terms of the limitations on strategic offensive arms which may be worked out in the course of further negotiations. . . .

[Protocol]

The Parties understand that, under Article III of the Interim Agreement, for the period during which that Agreement remains in force:

The U.S. may have no more than 710 ballistic missile launchers on submarines (SLBMs and no more than 44 modern ballistic missile submarines. The Soviet Union may have no more than 950 ballistic missile launchers on submarines and no more than 62 modern ballistic missile submarines.

Additional ballistic missile launchers on submarines up to the above mentioned levels, in the U.S.—over 656 ballistic missile launchers on nuclear-powered submarines, and in the U.S.S.R.—over 740 ballistic missile launchers on nuclear-powered submarines, operational and under construction, may become operational as replacements for equal numbers of ballistic missile launchers of older types deployed prior to 1964 or of ballistic missile launchers on older submarines.

The deployment of modern SLBMs on any submarine, regardless of type, will be counted against the total level of SLBMs permitted for the U.S. and the U.S.S.R.

This Protocol shall be considered an integral part of the Interim Agreement.

FURTHER READINGS

Ambrose, Stephen E., *Nixon*, 3 volumes (New York: Simon and Schuster, 1987–1991).

Bowker, Mike and Williams, Phil, *Superpower Détente: A Reappraisal* (London: Royal Institute of International Affairs, 1988).

Gaddis, John Lewis, *The United States and the End of the Cold War* (New York: Oxford University Press, 1992).

Garthoff, Raymond L., *Détente and Confrontation: American-Soviet Relations from Nixon to Reagan* (Washington, D.C.: Brookings Institution, 1994).

Isaacson, Walter, *Kissinger* (New York: Simon and Schuster, 1992).

Litwak, Robert, *Détente and the Nixon Doctrine* (New York: Cambridge University Press, 1984).

Newhouse, John, *Cold Dawn: The Inside Story of SALT* (New York: Holt, Rinehart and Winston, 1973).

Parmet, Herbert, *Richard Nixon and His America* (Boston: Little, Brown, 1990).

Schulzinger, Robert D., *Henry Kissinger* (New York: Columbia University Press, 1989).

Smith, Gerard, *Doubletalk: The Story of the First Strategic Arms Limitations Talks* (Garden City, N.Y.: Doubleday, 1980).

Stevenson, Richard W., *The Rise and Fall of Détente* (Urbana: University of Illinois Press, 1985).

Thornton, Richard, *The Nixon-Kissinger Years: The Reshaping of American Foreign Policy* (New York: Paragon House, 1989).

DOCUMENT 62

Carter's Human Rights Foreign Policy

In an address at the Commencement Exercises at the University of Notre Dame on 22 May 1977, President Jimmy Carter stated his intention to reaffirm "America's commitment to human rights as a fundamental tenet of our foreign policy."[62]

ᏇᏇᏇ

But I want to speak to you today about the strands that connect our actions overseas with our essential character as a nation. I believe we can have a foreign policy that is democratic, that is based on fundamental values, and that uses power and influence, which we have, for humane purposes. We can also have a foreign policy that the American people both support and, for a change, know about and understand.

I have a quiet confidence in our own political system. Because we know that democracy works, we can reject the arguments of those rulers who deny human rights to their people.

We are confident that democracy's example will be compelling, and so we seek to bring that example closer to those from whom in the past few years we have been separated and who are not yet convinced about the advantages of our kind of life.

We are confident that the democratic methods are the most effective, and so we are not tempted to employ improper tactics here at home or abroad. . . .

For too many years, we've been willing to adopt the flawed and erroneous principles and tactics of our adversaries, sometimes abandoning our own values for theirs. We've fought fire with fire, never thinking that fire is better quenched with water. This approach failed, with Vietnam the best example of its intellectual and moral poverty. But through failure we have now found our

---

[62]*Public Papers of the Presidents: Administration of Jimmy Carter, 1977* (Washington, D.C.: U.S. Government Printing Office, 1977), 955–62.

way back to our own principles and values, and we have regained our lost confidence.

By the measure of history, our Nation's 200 years are very brief, and our rise to world eminence is briefer still. It dates from 1945, when Europe and the old international order lay in ruins. Before then, America was largely on the periphery of world affairs. But since then, we have inescapably been at the center of world affairs.

Our policy during this period was guided by two principles: a belief that Soviet expansion was almost inevitable but that it must be contained, and the corresponding belief in the importance of an almost exclusive alliance among non-Communist nations on both sides of the Atlantic. That system could not last forever unchanged. Historical trends have weakened its foundation. The unifying threat of conflict with the Soviet Union has become less intensive, even though the competition has become more extensive.

The Vietnamese war produced a profound moral crisis, sapping worldwide faith in our own policy and our system of life, a crisis of confidence made even more grave by the covert pessimism of some of our leaders.

In less than a generation, we've seen the world change dramatically. The daily lives and aspirations of most human beings have been transformed. Colonialism is nearly gone. A new sense of national identity now exists in almost 100 new countries that have been formed in the last generation. Knowledge has become more widespread. Aspirations are higher. As more people have been freed from traditional constraints, more have been determined to achieve, for the first time in their lives, social justice.

The world is still divided by ideological disputes, dominated by regional conflicts, and threatened by danger that we will not resolve the differences of race and wealth without violence or without drawing into combat the major military powers. We can no longer separate the traditional issues of war and peace from the new global questions of justice, equity, and human rights. . . .

First, we have reaffirmed America's commitment to human rights as a fundamental tenet of our foreign policy. In ancestry, religion, color, place of origin, and cultural background, we Americans are as diverse a nation as the world has ever seen. No common mystique of blood or soil unites us. What draws us together, perhaps more than anything else, is a belief in human freedom. We want the world to know that our Nation stands for more than financial prosperity.

This does not mean that we can conduct our foreign policy by rigid moral maxims. We live in a world that is imperfect and which will always be imperfect—a world that is complex and confused and which will always be complex and confused.

I understand fully the limits of moral suasion. We have no illusion that changes will come easily or soon. But I also believe that it is a mistake to undervalue the power of words and of the ideas that words embody. In our own history, that power has ranged from Thomas Paine's "Common Sense" to Martin Luther King, Jr.'s "I Have a Dream."

In the life of the human spirit, words *are* action, much more so than many of us may realize who live in countries where freedom of expression is taken for granted. The leaders of totalitarian nations understand this very well. The proof is that words are precisely the action for which dissidents in those countries are being persecuted.

Nonetheless, we can already see dramatic, worldwide advances in the protection of the individual from the arbitrary power of the state. For us to ignore this trend would be to lose influence and moral authority in the world. To lead it will be to regain the moral stature that we once had.

The great democracies are not free because we are strong and prosperous. I believe we are strong and influential and prosperous because we are free.

Throughout the world today, in free nations and in totalitarian countries as well, there is a preoccupation with the subject of human freedom, human rights. And I believe it is incumbent on us in this country to keep that discussion, that debate, that contention alive. No other country is as well-qualified as we to set an example. We have our own shortcomings and faults, and we should strive constantly and with courage to make sure that we are legitimately proud of what we have. . . .

Let me conclude by summarizing: Our policy is based on an historical vision of America's role. Our policy is derived from a larger view of global change. Our policy is rooted in our moral values, which never change. Our policy is reinforced by our material wealth and by our military power. Our policy is designed to serve mankind. And it is a policy that I hope will make you proud to be Americans.

Thank you.

FURTHER READINGS

Bill, James, *The Eagle and the Lion: The Tragedy of American Iranian Relations* (New Haven, Conn.: Yale University Press, 1988).

Mower, A. Glen, *Human Rights and American Foreign Policy: The Carter and Reagan Experiences* (New York: Greenwood Press, 1987).

Muravchik, Joshua, *The Uncertain Crusade: Jimmy Carter and the Dilemma of Human Rights Policy* (Landham, Md.: Hamilton Press, 1986).

Rosati, Jerel, *The Carter Administration's Quest for Global Community* (Columbia: University of South Carolina Press, 1987).

Schoultz, Lars, *Human Rights and United States Policy toward Latin America* (Princeton, N.J.: Princeton University Press, 1981).

Smith, Gaddis, *Morality, Reason and Power: American Diplomacy in the Carter Years* (New York: Hill and Wang, 1986).

DOCUMENT 63

The Panama Canal Treaty

President Jimmy Carter and Panama's General Omar Torrijos Herrera signed the Panama Treaty and the Treaty Concerning the Permanent Neutrality and Operations of the Panama Canal on 7 September 1977. The Senate approved the Panama Canal Treaty by a vote of 68-32 on 18 April 1978.[63]

ꙮꙮꙮ

THE UNITED STATES OF AMERICA AND THE REPUBLIC OF PANAMA,

Acting in the spirit of the Joint Declaration of April 3, 1964, by the Representatives of the Governments of the United States of America and the Republic of Panama, and of the Joint Statement of Principles of February 7, 1974, initialed by the Secretary of State of the United States of America and the Foreign Minister of the Republic of Panama, and

Acknowledging the Republic of Panama's sovereignty over its territory,

Have decided to terminate the prior Treaties pertaining to the Panama Canal and to conclude a new Treaty to serve as the basis for a new relationship between them and, accordingly, have agreed upon the following:

ARTICLE I

ABROGATION OF PRIOR TREATIES AND ESTABLISHMENT OF A NEW RELATIONSHIP

1. Upon its entry into force, this Treaty terminates and supersedes:
   a. The Isthmian Canal Convention between the United States of America and the Republic of Panama, signed at Washington, November 18, 1903;
   b. The Treaty of Friendship and Cooperation signed at Washington, March 2, 1936, and the Treaty of Mutual Understanding and Cooperation and the related Memorandum of Understandings Reached, signed at Panama, January 25, 1955, between the United States of America and the Republic of Panama;
   c. All other treaties, conventions, agreements and exchanges of notes between the United States of America and the Republic of Panama

---

[63]William J. Jorden, *Panama Odyssey* (Austin, Texas: University of Texas Press, 1984), Appendix D, 705–17, passim.

concerning the Panama Canal which were in force prior to the entry into force of this Treaty; and

d. Provisions concerning the Panama Canal which appear in other treaties, conventions, agreements and exchanges of notes between the United States of America and the Republic of Panama which were in force prior to the entry into force of this Treaty.

2. In accordance with the terms of this Treaty and related agreements, the Republic of Panama, as territorial sovereign, grants to the United States of America, for the duration of this Treaty, the rights necessary to regulate the transit of ships through the Panama Canal, and to manage, operate, maintain, improve, protect and defend the Canal. The Republic of Panama guarantees to the United States of America the peaceful use of the land and water area which it has been granted the rights to use for such purposes pursuant to this Treaty and related agreements.

3. The Republic of Panama shall participate increasingly in the management and protection and defense of the Canal, as provided in this Treaty.

4. In view of the special relationship established by this Treaty, the United States of America and the Republic of Panama shall cooperate to assure the uninterrupted and efficient operation of the Panama Canal.

ARTICLE II

RATIFICATION, ENTRY INTO FORCE, AND TERMINATION

1. This Treaty shall be subject to ratification in accordance with the constitutional procedures of the two Parties. The instruments of ratification of this Treaty shall be exchanged at Panama at the same time as the instruments of ratification of the Treaty Concerning the permanent Neutrality and Operation of the Panama Canal, signed this date, are exchanged. This treaty shall enter into force, simultaneously with the Treaty Concerning the Permanent Neutrality and Operation of the Panama Canal, six calendar months from the date of the exchange of the instruments of ratification.

2. This Treaty shall terminate at noon, Panama time, December 31, 1999.

ARTICLE III

CANAL OPERATION AND MANAGEMENT

1. The Republic of Panama, as territorial sovereign, grants to the United States of America the rights to manage, operate, and maintain the Panama Canal, its complementary works, installations and equipment and to provide for the orderly transit of vessels through the Panama Canal. The United States of America accepts the grant of such rights and undertakes to exercise them in accordance with this Treaty and related agreements. . . .

ARTICLE IV

PROTECTION AND DEFENSE

1. The United States of America and the Republic of Panama commit themselves to protect and defend the Panama Canal. Each Party shall act, in accordance with its constitutional processes, to meet the danger resulting from an armed attack or other actions which threaten the security of the Panama Canal or of ships transiting it.
2. For the duration of this Treaty, the United States of America shall have primary responsibility to protect and defend the Canal. The rights of the United States of America to station, train, and move military forces within the Republic of Panama are described in the Agreement in Implementation of this Article, signed this date. The use of areas and installations and the legal status of the armed forces of the United States of America in the Republic of Panama shall be governed by the aforesaid Agreement. . . .

ARTICLE XIII

PROPERTY TRANSFER AND ECONOMIC PARTICIPATION BY THE REPUBLIC OF PANAMA

1. Upon termination of this Treaty, the Republic of Panama shall assume total responsibility for the management, operation, and maintenance of the Panama Canal, which shall be turned over in operating condition and free of liens and debts, except as the two Parties may otherwise agree.

FURTHER READINGS

Gaddis, John Lewis, *The United States and the End of the Cold War* (New York: Oxford University Press, 1992).

Glad, Betty, *Jimmy Carter* (New York: Norton, 1980).

LaFeber, Walter, *The Panama Canal: The Crisis in Historical Perspective* (New York: Oxford University Press, 1978).

McLellan, David, *Cyrus Vance* (Totowa, N.J.: Rowman & Allanheld, 1985).

Moffett, George, *The Limits of Victory: The Ratification of the Panama Canal Treaties* (Ithaca, N.Y.: Cornell University Press, 1985).

Ryan, Paul B., *The Panama Canal Controversy* (Stanford, Calif.: Hoover Institution Press, 1977).

DOCUMENT 64

The Carter Doctrine

President Jimmy Carter responded to the Soviet invasion of Afghanistan on 23 January 1980 by announcing that the United States would consider a Soviet attempt to control the Persian Gulf "an assault on the vital interests of the United States of America."[64]

᭥᭥

MR. PRESIDENT, MR. SPEAKER, MEMBERS OF THE 96TH CONGRESS, FELLOW CITIZENS:

This last few months has not been an easy time for any of us. As we meet tonight, it has never been more clear that the state of our Union depends on the state of the world. And tonight, as throughout our own generation, freedom and peace in the world depend on the state of our Union.

The 1980's have been born in turmoil, strife, and change. This is a time of challenge to our interests and our values and it's a time that tests our wisdom and our skills.

At this time in Iran, 50 Americans are still held captive, innocent victims of terrorism and anarchy. Also at this moment, massive Soviet troops are attempting to subjugate the fiercely independent and deeply religious people of Afghanistan. These two acts—one of international terrorism and one of military aggression—present a serious challenge to the United States of America and indeed to all the nations of the world. Together, we will meet these threats to peace.

I'm determined that the United States will remain the strongest of all nations, but our power will never be used to initiate a threat to the security of any nation or to the rights of any human being. We seek to be and to remain secure—a nation at peace in a stable world. But to be secure we must face the world as it is.

Three basic developments have helped to shape our challenges: the steady growth and increased projection of Soviet military power beyond its own borders; the overwhelming dependence of the Western democracies on oil supplies from the Middle East; and the press of social and religious and economic and political change in the many nations of the developing world, exemplified by the revolution in Iran.

---

[64]*Public Papers of the Presidents: Administration of Jimmy Carter, 1980* (Washington, D.C.: U.S. Government Printing Office, 1981), 194–97.

Each of these factors is important in its own right. Each interacts with the others. All must be faced together, squarely and courageously. We will face these challenges, and we will meet them with the best that is in us. And we will not fail. . . .

But now the Soviet Union has taken a radical and an aggressive new step. It's using its great military power against a relatively defenseless nation. The implications of the Soviet invasion of Afghanistan could pose the most serious threat to the peace since the Second World War. . . .

The region which is now threatened by Soviet troops in Afghanistan is of great strategic importance: It contains more than two-thirds of the world's exportable oil. The Soviet effort to dominate Afghanistan has brought Soviet military forces to within 300 miles of the Indian Ocean and close to the Straits of Hormuz, a waterway through which most of the world's oil must flow. The Soviet Union is now attempting to consolidate a strategic position, therefore, that poses a grave threat to the free movement of Middle East oil.

This situation demands careful thought, steady nerves, and resolute action, not only for this year but for many years to come. It demands collective efforts to meet this new threat to security in the Persian Gulf and in Southwest Asia. It demands the participation of all those who rely on oil from the Middle East and who are concerned with global peace and stability. And it demands consultation and close cooperation with countries in the area which might be threatened.

Meeting this challenge will take national will, diplomatic and political wisdom, economic sacrifice, and, of course, military capability. We must call on the best that is in us to preserve the security of this crucial region.

Let our position be absolutely clear: An attempt by any outside force to gain control of the Persian Gulf region will be regarded as an assault on the vital interests of the United States of America, and such an assault will be repelled by any means necessary, including military force.

During the past 3 years, you have joined with me to improve our own security and the prospects for peace, not only in the vital oil-producing area of the Persian Gulf region but around the world.

FURTHER READINGS

Gaddis, John Lewis, *The United States and the End of the Cold War* (New York: Oxford University Press, 1992).

Garthoff, Raymond L., *Détente and Confrontation: American-Soviet Relations from Nixon to Reagan* (Washington, D.C.: Brookings Institution, 1994).

Glad, Betty, *Jimmy Carter* (New York: Norton, 1980).

Jones, Charles O., *The Trusteeship Presidency: Jimmy Carter and the United States Congress* (Baton Rouge: Lousiana State University Press, 1988).

McLellan, David, *Cyrus Vance* (Totowa, N.J.: Rowman & Allanheld, 1985).

DOCUMENT 65

Reagan and the Soviet Union

At a press conference on 29 January 1981 President Ronald Reagan indicated that he would take a harder line in dealing with the Soviet Union which began a process that would ultimately lead to the end of the Cold War.[65]

㊟㊟

GOALS OF THE SOVIET UNION

Q. Mr. President, what do you see as the long-range intentions of the Soviet Union? Do you think, for instance, the Kremlin is bent on world domination that might lead to a continuation of the cold war, or do you think that under other circumstances détente is possible?

The President. Well, so far détente's been a one-way street that the Soviet Union has used to pursue its own aims. I don't have to think of an answer as to what I think their intentions are; they have repeated it. I know of no leader of the Soviet Union since the revolution, and including the present leadership, that has not more than once repeated in the various Communist congresses they hold their determination that their goal must be the promotion of world revolution and a one-world Socialist or Communist state, whichever word you want to use.

Now, as long as they do that and as long as they, at the same time, have openly and publicly declared that the only morality they recognize is what will further their cause, meaning they reserve unto themselves the right to commit any crime, to lie, to cheat, in order to attain that, and that is moral, not immoral, and we operate on a different set of standards, I think when you do business with them, even at a détente, you keep that in mind.

FURTHER READINGS

Gaddis, John Lewis, *The United States and the End of the Cold War* (New York: Oxford University Press, 1992).

Garthoff, Raymond L., *Détente and Confrontation: American-Soviet Relations from Nixon to Reagan* (Washington, D.C.: Brookings Institution, 1994).

Johnson, Haynes, *Sleepwalking through History: America in the Reagan Years* (New York: Norton, 1991).

---

[65]*Public Papers of the Presidents: Administration of Ronald Reagan, 1981* (Washington, D.C.: U.S. Government Printing Office, 1982), 57.

Shaller, Michael, *Reckoning with Reagan* (New York: Oxford University Press, 1992).
Talbott, Strobe, *Reagan and Gorbachev* (New York: Vintage Books, 1987).

DOCUMENT 66

Reagan and the Evil Empire

In an address before the Annual Convention of the National Association of Evangelicals on 8 March 1983, President Reagan urged those discussing nuclear freeze proposals not "to ignore the facts of history and the aggressive impulses of an evil empire." Instead of a nuclear freeze, the president argued that the United States "must find peace through strength."[66]

There is sin and evil in the world, and we're enjoined by Scripture and the Lord Jesus to oppose it with all our might. Our nation, too, has a legacy of evil with which it must deal. The glory of this land has been its capacity for transcending the moral evils of our past. For example, the long struggle of minority citizens for equal rights, once a source of disunity and civil war, is now a point of pride for all Americans. We must never go back. There is no room for racism, anti-Semitism, or other forms of ethnic and racial hatred in this country.

I know that you've been horrified, as have I, by the resurgence of some hate groups preaching bigotry and prejudice. Use the mighty voice of your pulpits and the powerful standing of your churches to denounce and isolate these hate groups in our midst. The commandment given us is clear and simple: "Thou shalt love thy neighbor as thyself."

But whatever sad episodes exist in our past, any objective observer must hold a positive view of American history, a history that has been the story of hopes fulfilled and dreams made into reality. Especially in this century, America has kept alight the torch of freedom, but not just for ourselves but for millions of others around the world.

And this brings me to my final point today. During my first press conference as President, in answer to a direct question, I pointed out that, as good Marxist-Leninists, the Soviet leaders have openly and publicly declared that the only morality they recognize is that which will further their cause, which is world revolution. I think I should point out I was only quoting Lenin, their guiding spirit, who said in 1920 that they repudiate all morality that proceeds from supernatural ideas—that's their name for religion—or ideas that

---

[66]*Public Papers of the Presidents: Administration of Ronald Reagan, 1983* (Washington, D.C.: U.S. Government Printing Office, 1984), book I, 362-64.

are outside class conceptions. Morality is entirely subordinate to the interests of class war. And everything is moral that is necessary for the annihilation of the old, exploiting social order and for uniting the proletariat.

Well, I think the refusal of many influential people to accept this elementary fact of Soviet doctrine illustrates an historical reluctance to see totalitarian powers for what they are. We saw this phenomenon in the 1930's. We see it too often today.

This doesn't mean we should isolate ourselves and refuse to seek an understanding with them. I intend to do everything I can to persuade them of our peaceful intent, to remind them that it was the West that refused to use its nuclear monopoly in the forties and fifties for territorial gain and which now proposes [a] 50-percent cut in strategic ballistic missiles and the elimination of an entire class of land-based, intermediate-range nuclear missiles.

At the same time, however, they must be made to understand we will never compromise our principles and standards. We will never give away our freedom. We will never abandon our belief in God. And we will never stop searching for a genuine peace. But we can assure none of these things America stands for through the so-called nuclear freeze solutions proposed by some.

The truth is that a freeze now would be a very dangerous fraud, for that is merely the illusion of peace. The reality is that we must find peace through strength.

I would agree to a freeze if only we could freeze the Soviets' global desires. A freeze at current levels of weapons would remove any incentive for the Soviets to negotiate seriously in Geneva and virtually end our chances to achieve the major arms reductions which we have proposed. Instead, they would achieve their objectives through the freeze.

A freeze would reward the Soviet Union for its enormous and unparalleled military buildup. It would prevent the essential and long overdue modernization of United States and allied defenses and would leave our aging forces increasingly vulnerable. And an honest freeze would require extensive prior negotiations on the systems and numbers to be limited and on the measures to ensure effective verification and compliance. And the kind of a freeze that has been suggested would be virtually impossible to verify. Such a major effort would divert us completely from our current negotiations on achieving substantial reductions.

A number of years ago, I heard a young father, a very prominent young man in the entertainment world, addressing a tremendous gathering in California. It was during the time of the cold war, and communism and our own way of life were very much on people's minds. And he was speaking to that subject. And suddenly, though, I heard him saying, "I love my little girls more than anything—" And I said to myself, "Oh, no, you don't You can't—don't say that." But I had underestimated him. He went on: "I would rather see my little girls die now, still believing in God, than have them grow up under communism and one day die no longer believing in God."

There were thousands of young people in that audience. They came to their feet with shouts of joy. They had instantly recognized the profound truth in what he had said, with regard to the physical and the soul and what was truly important.

Yes, let us pray for the salvation of all those who live in that totalitarian darkness—pray they will discover the joy of knowing God. But until they do, let us be aware that while they preach the supremacy of the state, declare its omnipotence over individual man, and predict its eventual domination of all peoples on the Earth, they are the focus of evil in the modern world.

It was C. S. Lewis who, in his unforgettable "Screwtape Letters," wrote:

The greatest evil is not done now in those sordid "dens of crime" that Dickens loved to paint. It is not even done in concentration camps and labor camps. In those we see its final result. But it is conceived and ordered (moved, seconded, carried and minuted in clear, carpeted, warmed, and well-lighted offices, by quiet men with white collars and cut fingernails and smooth-shaven cheeks who do not need to raise their voice.

Well, because these "quiet men" do not "raise their voices," because they sometimes speak in soothing tones of brotherhood and peace, because, like other dictators before them, they're always making "their final territorial demand," some would have us accept them at their word and accommodate ourselves to their aggressive impulses. But if history teaches anything, it teaches that simple-minded appeasement or wishful thinking about our adversaries is folly. It means the betrayal of our past, the squandering of our freedom.

So, I urge you to speak out against those who would place the United States in a position of military and moral inferiority. You know, I've always believed that old Screwtape reserved his best efforts for those of you in the church. So, in your discussions of the nuclear freeze proposals, I urge you to beware the temptation of pride—the temptation of blithely declaring yourselves above it all and label both sides equally at fault, to ignore the facts of history and the aggressive impulses of an evil empire, to simply call the arms race a giant misunderstanding and thereby remove yourself from the struggle between right and wrong and good and evil.

I ask you to resist the attempts of those who would have you withhold your support for our efforts, this administration's efforts, to keep America strong and free, while we negotiate real and verifiable reductions in the world's nuclear arsenals and one day, with God's help, their total elimination.

While America's military strength is important, let me add here that I've always maintained that the struggle now going on for the world will never be decided by bombs or rockets, by armies or military might. The real crisis we face today is a spiritual one; at root, it is a test of moral will and faith.

Whittaker Chambers, the man whose own religious conversion made him a witness to one of the terrible traumas of our time, the Hiss-Chambers case, wrote that the crisis of the Western World exists to the degree in which the West is indifferent to God, the degree to which it collaborates in communism's attempt to make man stand alone without God. And then he said, for Marxism-Leninism is actually the second oldest faith, first proclaimed in the Garden of Eden with the words of temptation, "Ye shall be as gods."

The Western World can answer this challenge, he wrote, "but only provided that its faith in God and the freedom He enjoins is as great as communism's faith in Man."

I believe we shall rise to the challenge. I believe that communism is another sad, bizarre chapter in human history whose last pages even now are being written. I believe this because the source of our strength in the quest for human freedom is not material, but spiritual. And because it knows no limitation, it must terrify and ultimately triumph over those who would enslave their fellow man. For in the words of Isaiah: "He giveth power to the faint; and to them that have no might He increased strength. . . . But they that wait upon the Lord shall renew their strength; they shall mount up with wings as eagles; they shall run, and not be weary. . . ."

Yes, change your world. One of our Founding Fathers, Thomas Paine, said, "We have it within our power to begin the world over again." We can do it, doing together what no one church could do by itself.

God Bless you, and thank you very much.

FURTHER READINGS

Gaddis, John Lewis, *The United States and the End of the Cold War* (New York: Oxford University Press, 1992).

Garthoff, Raymond L., *Détente and Confrontation: American-Soviet Relations from Nixon to Reagan* (Washington, D.C.: Brookings Institution, 1994).

Johnson, Haynes, *Sleepwalking through History: America in the Reagan Years* (New York: Norton, 1991).

Shaller, Michael, *Reckoning with Reagan* (New York: Oxford University Press, 1992).

Talbott, Strobe, *Reagan and Gorbachev* (New York: Vintage Books, 1987).

DOCUMENT 67

The Reagan Doctrine

In his State of the Union Address of 6 February 1985 President Reagan asked Congress for continued funding for the "freedom fighters" attempting to topple the Marxist Sandinista regime in Nicaragua.[67]

We cannot play innocents abroad in a world that's not innocent; nor can we be passive when freedom is under seige. Without resources, diplomacy cannot succeed. Our security assistance programs help friendly governments defend themselves and give them confidence to work for peace. And I hope that you in the Congress will understand that, dollar for dollar, security assistance contributes as much to global security as our own defense budget.

We must stand by all our democratic allies. And we must not break faith with those who are risking their lives—on every continent, from Afghanistan to Nicaragua—to defy Soviet-supported aggression and secure rights which have been ours from birth.

The Sandinista dictatorship of Nicaragua, with full Cuban-Soviet bloc support, not only persecutes its people, the church, and denies a free press, but arms and provides bases for Communist terrorists attacking neighboring states. Support for freedom fighters is self-defense and totally consistent with the OAS and U.N. Charters. It is essential that the Congress continue all facets of our assistance to Central America. I want to work with you to support the democratic forces whose struggle is tied to our own security.

FURTHER READINGS

Draper, Theodore, *A Very Thin Line: The Iran-Contra Affairs* (New York: Wang and Hill, 1991*)*.

Gaddis, John Lewis, *The United States and the End of the Cold War* (New York: Oxford University Press, 1992).

Garthoff, Raymond L., *Détente and Confrontation: American-Soviet Relations from Nixon to Reagan* (Washington, D.C.: Brookings Institution, 1994).

Johnson, Haynes, *Sleepwalking through History: America in the Reagan Years* (New York: Norton, 1991).

Shaller, Michael, *Reckoning with Reagan* (New York: Oxford University Press, 1992).

Talbott, Strobe, *Reagan and Gorbachev* (New York: Vintage Books, 1987).

---

[67]*Public Papers of the Presidents: Administration of Ronald Reagan, 1985* (Washington, D.C.: U.S. Government Printing Office, 1988), 1:135.

DOCUMENT 68

The Intermediate-Range Nuclear Forces Treaty

On 6 December 1987 President Reagan and Communist Party Chairman Mikhail Gorbachev signed the Intermediate Nuclear Force Treaty which called for the elimination of U.S. and Soviet INF missiles in Europe.[68] The Senate approved the treaty by a 93–5 vote in May 1988.

ভ঵঵঵

REMARKS ON SIGNING THE INTERMEDIATE-RANGE NUCLEAR FORCES TREATY, DECEMBER 8, 1987

The President. Thank you all very much. Welcome to the White House. This ceremony and the treaty we're signing today are both excellent examples of the rewards of patience. It was over 6 years ago, November 18, 1981, that I first proposed what would come to be called the zero option. It was a simple proposal—one might say, disarmingly simple. Unlike treaties in the past, it didn't simply codify the status quo or a new arms buildup; it didn't simply talk of controlling an arms race.

For the first time in history, the language of "arms control" was replaced by "arms reduction"—in this case, the complete elimination of an entire class of U.S. and Soviet nuclear missiles. Of course, this required a dramatic shift in thinking, and it took conventional wisdom some time to catch up. Reaction, to say the least, was mixed. To some the zero option was impossibly visionary and unrealistic; to others merely a propaganda ploy. Well, with patience, determination, and commitment, we've made this impossible vision a reality.

General Secretary Gorbachev, I'm sure you're familiar with Ivan Krylov's famous tale about the swan, the crawfish, and the pike. It seems that once upon a time these three were trying to move a wagonload together. They hitched and harnessed themselves to the wagon. It wasn't very heavy, but no matter how hard they worked, the wagon just wouldn't move. You see, the swan was flying upward; the crawfish kept crawling backward; the pike kept making for the water. The end result was that they got nowhere, and the wagon is still there to this day. Well, strong and fundamental moral differences continue to exist between our nations. But today, on this vital issue, at least, we've seen what can be accomplished when we pull together.

---

[68]*Public Papers of the Presidents: Administration of Ronald Reagan, 1987* (Washington, D.C.: U.S. Government Printing Office, 1989), 2:1455–56.

The numbers alone demonstrate the value of this agreement. On the Soviet side, over 1,500 deployed warheads will be removed, and all ground-launched intermediate-range missiles, including the SS-20's, will be destroyed. On our side, our entire complement of Pershing II and ground-launched cruise missiles, with some 400 deployed warheads, will all be destroyed. Additional backup missiles on both sides will also be destroyed.

But the importance of this treaty transcends numbers. We have listened to the wisdom in an old Russian maxim. And I'm sure you're familiar with it, Mr. General Secretary, though my pronunciation may give you difficulty. The maxim is: *Dovorey no provorey*—trust, but verify.

The General Secretary. You repeat that at every meeting.

The President. I like it.

This agreement contains the most stringent verification regime in history, including provisions for inspection teams actually residing in each other's territory and several other forms of onsite inspection, as well. This treaty protects the interests of America's friends and allies. It also embodies another important principle: the need for *glasnost*, a greater openness in military programs and forces.

We can only hope that this historymaking agreement will not be an end in itself but the beginning of a working relationship that will enable us to tackle the other urgent issues before us: strategic offensive nuclear weapons, the balance of conventional forces in Europe, the destructive and tragic regional conflicts that beset so many parts of our globe, and respect for the human and natural rights God has granted to all men.

FURTHER READINGS

Gaddis, John Lewis, *The United States and the End of the Cold War* (New York: Oxford University Press, 1992).

Garthoff, Raymond L., *Détente and Confrontation: American-Soviet Relations from Nixon to Reagan* (Washington, D.C.: Brookings Institution, 1994).

Johnson, Haynes, *Sleepwalking through History: America in the Reagan Years* (New York: Norton, 1991).

Shaller, Michael, *Reckoning with Reagan* (New York: Oxford University Press, 1992).

Talbott, Strobe, *Reagan and Gorbachev* (New York: Vintage Books, 1987).

DOCUMENT 69

The Shattering of the Eastern Bloc

In his State of the Union Address on 31 January 1990, President George Bush summarized the dramatic changes that had taken place in Eastern Europe during the previous year.[69]

Tonight I come not to speak about the state of the Government, not to detail every new initiative we plan for the coming year nor to describe every line in the budget. I'm here to speak to you and to the American people about the state of the Union, about our world—the changes we've seen, the challenges we face—and what that means for America.

There are singular moments in history, dates that divide all that goes before from all that comes after. And many of us in this Chamber have lived much of our lives in a world whose fundamental features were defined in 1945; and the events of that year decreed the shape of nations, the pace of progress, freedom or oppression for millions of people around the world.

Nineteen forty-five provided the common frame of reference, the compass points of the postwar era we've relied upon to understand ourselves. And that was our world, until now. The events of the year just ended, the Revolution of '89, have been a chain reaction, changes so striking that it marks the beginning of a new era in the world's affairs.

Think back—think back just 12 short months ago to the world we knew as 1989 began.

One year—one year ago, the people of Panama lived in fear, under the thumb of a dictator. Today democracy is restored; Panama is free. Operation Just Cause has achieved its objective. The number of military personnel in Panama is now very close to what it was before the operation began. And tonight I am announcing that well before the end of February, the additional numbers of American troops, the brave men and women of our Armed Forces who made this mission a success, will be back home.

A year ago in Poland, Lech Walesa declared that he was ready to open a dialog with the Communist rulers of that country; and today, with the future of a free Poland in their own hands, members of Solidarity lead the Polish Government.

---

[69]*Public Papers of the Presidents: Administration of George Bush, 1991* (Washington, D.C.: U.S. Government Printing Office, 1991), 1:129–34, passim.

A year ago, freedom's playwright, Václav Havel, languished as a prisoner in Prague. And today it's Václav Havel, President of Czechoslovakia.

And 1 year ago, Erich Honecker of East Germany claimed history as his guide, and he predicted the Berlin Wall would last another hundred years. And today, less than 1 year later, it's the Wall that's history.

Remarkable events—events that fulfill the long-held hopes of the American people; events that validate the longstanding goals of American policy, a policy based on a single, shining principle: the cause of freedom. . . .

I began tonight speaking about the changes we've seen this past year. There is a new world of challenges and opportunities before us, and there's a need for leadership that only America can provide. Nearly 40 years ago, in his last address to the Congress, President Harry Truman predicted such a time would come. He said: "As our world grows stronger, more united, more attractive to men on both sides of the Iron Curtain, then inevitably there will come a time of change within the Communist world." Today, that change is taking place.

For more than 40 years, America and its allies held communism in check and ensured that democracy would continue to exist. And today, with communism crumbling, our aim must be to ensure democracy's advance, to take the lead in forging peace and freedom's best hope: a great and growing commonwealth of free nations. And to the Congress and to all Americans, I say it is time to acclaim a new consensus at home and abroad, a common vision of the peaceful world we want to see.

Here in our own hemisphere, it is time for all the peoples of the Americas, North and South, to live in freedom. In the Far East and Africa, it's time for the full flowering of free governments and free markets that have served as the engine of progress. It's time to offer our hand to the emerging democracies of Eastern Europe so that continent—for too long a continent divided—can see a future whole and free. It's time to build on our new relationship with the Soviet Union, to endorse and encourage a peaceful process of internal change toward democracy and economic opportunity.

We are in a period of great transition, great hope, and yet great uncertainty. We recognize that the Soviet military threat in Europe is diminishing, but we see little change in Soviet strategic modernization. Therefore, we must sustain our own strategic offense modernization and the Strategic Defense Initiative.

But the time is right to move forward on a conventional arms control agreement to move us to more appropriate levels of military forces in Europe, a coherent defense program that ensures the U.S. will continue to be a catalyst for peaceful change in Europe. And I've consulted with leaders of NATO. In fact, I spoke by phone with President Gorbachev just today.

I agree with our European allies that an American military presence in Europe is essential and that it should not be tied solely to the Soviet miltary presence in Eastern Europe. But our troop levels can still be lower. And so, tonight I am announcing a major new step for a further reduction in U.S. and Soviet manpower in Central and Eastern Europe to 195,000 on each side. This level reflects the advice of our senior military advisers. It's designed to protect American and European interests and sustain NATO's defense strategy. A swift conclusion to our arms control talks—conventional, chemical, and strategic—must now be our goal. And that time has come.

Still, we must recognize an unfortunate fact: In many regions of the world tonight, the reality is conflict, not peace. Enduring animosities and opposing interests remain. And thus, the cause of peace must be served by an America strong enough and sure enough to defend our interests and our ideals. It's this American idea that for the past four decades helped inspire this Revolution of '89.

FURTHER READINGS

Beschloss, Michael and Talbot, Strobe, *At the Highest Levels* (Boston: Little, Brown, 1993).

Hogan, Michael, editor, *The End of the Cold War* (New York: Cambridge University Press, 1992).

Document 70

The New World Order

President Bush responded to Iraq's invasion of Kuwait by organizing an international coalition that successfully liberated the victim of aggression. On 6 March 1991 the president told Congress, "We can see a new world coming into view. A world in which there is the very real prospect of a new world order."[70]

🎵🎵

Speaker Foley. Mr. President, it is customary at joint sessions for the Chair to present the President to the Members of Congress directly and without further comment. But I wish to depart from tradition tonight and express to you on behalf of the Congress and the country, and through you to the members of our Armed Forces, our warmest congratulations on the brilliant victory of the Desert Storm Operation.

---

[70]*Public Papers of the Presidents: Administration of George Bush, 1991* (Washington, D.C.: U.S. Government Printing Office, 1992), 1:218–22.

Members of the Congress, I now have the high privilege and distinct honor of presenting to you the President of the United States.

The President. Mr. President. And Mr. Speaker, thank you, sir, for those very generous words spoken from the heart about the wonderful performance of our military.

Members of Congress, 5 short weeks ago I came to this House to speak to you about the state of the Union. We met then in time of war. Tonight, we meet in a world blessed by the promise of peace.

From the moment Operation Desert Storm commenced on January 16th until the time the guns fell silent at midnight 1 week ago, this nation has watched its sons and daughters with pride, watched over them with prayer. As Commander in Chief, I can report to you our armed forces fought with honor and valor. And as President, I can report to the Nation aggression is defeated. The war is over.

This is a victory for every country in the coalition, for the United Nations. A victory for unprecedented international cooperation and diplomacy, so well led by our Secretary of State, James Baker. It is a victory for the rule of law and for what is right. . . .

Tonight, I come to this House to speak about the world—the world after war. The recent challenge could not have been clearer. Saddam Hussein was the villain; Kuwait, the victim. To the aid of this small country came nations from North America and Europe, from Asia and South America, from Africa and the Arab world, all united against aggression. Our uncommon coalition must now work in common purpose: to forge a future that should never again be held hostage to the darker side of human nature.

Tonight in Iraq, Saddam walks amidst ruin. His war machine is crushed. His ability to threaten mass destruction is itself destroyed. His people have been lied to, denied the truth. And when his defeated legions come home, all Iraqis will see and feel the havoc he has wrought. And this I promise you: For all that Saddam has done to his own people, to the Kuwaitis, and to the entire world, Saddam and those around him are accountable. . . .

The consequences of the conflict in the Gulf reach far beyond the confines of the Middle East. Twice before in this century, an entire world was convulsed by war. Twice this century, out of the horrors of war hope emerged for enduring peace. Twice before, those hopes proved to be a distant dream, beyond the grasp of man. Until now, the world we've known has been a world divided—a world of barbed wire and concrete block, conflict, and cold war.

Now, we can see a new world coming into view. A world in which there is the very real prospect of a new world order. In the words of Winston Churchill, a world order in which "the principles of justice and fair play protect the weak against the strong. . . ." A world where the United Nations, freed from cold war stalemate, is poised to fulfill the historic vision of its founders. A world in which freedom and respect for human rights find a home among all nations.

The Gulf war put this new world to its first test. And my fellow Americans, we passed that test. . . .

Tonight, as our troops begin to come home, let us recognize that the hard work of freedom still calls us forward. We've learned the hard lessons of history. The victory over Iraq was not waged as "a war to end all wars." Even the new world order cannot guarantee an era of perpetual peace. But enduring peace must be our mission. Our success in the Gulf will shape not only the new world order we seek but our mission here at home. . . .

We went halfway around the world to do what is moral and just and right. We fought hard and, with others, we won the war. We lifted the yoke of aggression and tyranny from a small country that many Americans had never even heard of, and we ask nothing in return.

We're coming home now—proud, confident, heads high. There is much that we must do, at home and abroad. And we will do it. We are Americans. May God bless this great nation, the United States of America. Thank you all very, very much.

FURTHER READINGS

Beschloss, Michael and Talbot, Strobe, *At the Highest Levels* (Boston: Little, Brown, 1993).

Freedman, Lawrence and Karsh, Efraim, *The Gulf Conflict, 1990–1991* (Princeton, N.J.: Princeton University Press, 1992).

Hogan, Michael, editor, *The End of the Cold War* (New York: Cambridge University Press, 1992).

DOCUMENT 71

The End of the Cold War

With the apparent demise of the communist regime in Russia President Bush was able to declare on 28 January 1992: "By the grace of God, America won the cold war."[71]

We gather tonight at a dramatic and deeply promising time in our history and in the history of man on Earth. For in the past 12 months, the world has known changes of almost Biblical proportions. And even now, months after

---

[71]*Public Papers of the Presidents: Administration of George Bush, 1991* (Washington, D.C.: U.S. Government Printing Office, 1993), 1:156–58.

the failed coup that doomed a failed system, I'm not sure we've absorbed the full impact, the full import of what happened. But communism died this year.

Even as President, with the most fascinating possible vantage point, there were times when I was so busy managing progress and helping to lead change that I didn't always show the joy that was in my heart. But the biggest thing that has happened in the world in my life, in our lives, is this: By the grace of God, America won the cold war.

I mean to speak this evening of the changes that can take place in our country, now that we can stop making the sacrifices we had to make when we had an avowed enemy that was a superpower. Now we can look homeward even more and move to set right what needs to be set right.

I will speak of those things. But let me tell you something I've been thinking these past few months. It's a kind of rollcall of honor. For the cold war didn't end; it was won. And I think of those who won it, in places like Korea and Vietnam. And some of them didn't come back. Back then they were heroes, but this year they were victors.

The long rollcall, all the G.I. Joes and Janes, all the ones who fought faithfully for freedom, who hit the ground and sucked the dust and knew their share of horror. This may seem frivolous, and I don't mean it so, but it's moving to me how the world saw them. The world saw not only their special valor but their special style: their rambunctious, optimistic bravery, their do-or-die unity unhampered by class or race or region. What a group we've put forth, for generations now, from the ones who wrote "Kilroy was here" on the walls of the German stalags to those who left signs in the Iraqi desert that said, "I saw Elvis." What a group of kids we've sent out into the world.

And there's another to be singled out, though it may seem inelegant, and I mean a mass of people called the American taxpayer. No one ever thinks to thank the people who pay a country's bill or an alliance's bill. But for half a century now, the American people have shouldered the burden and paid taxes that were higher than they would have been to support a defense that was bigger than it would have been if imperial communism had never existed. But it did; doesn't anymore. And here's a fact I wouldn't mind the world acknowledging: The American taxpayer bore the brunt of the burden and deserves a hunk of the glory.

So now, for the first time in 35 years, our strategic bombers stand down. No longer are they on 'round-the-clock alert. Tomorrow our children will go to school and study history and how plants grow. And they won't have, as my children did, air raid drills in which they crawl under their desks and cover their heads in case of nuclear war. My grandchildren don't have to do that and won't have the bad dreams children had once, in decades past. There are still threats. But the long, drawn-out dread is over.

A year ago tonight, I spoke to you at a moment of high peril. American forces had just unleashed Operation Desert Storm. And after 40 days in the desert skies and 4 days on the ground, the men and women of America's Armed Forces and our allies accomplished the goals that I declared and that you endorsed: We liberated Kuwait. Soon after, the Arab world and Israel sat down to talk seriously and comprehensively about peace, an historic first. And soon after that, at Christmas, the last American hostages came home. Our policies were vindicated.

Much good can come from the prudent use of power. And much good can come of this: A world once divided into two armed camps now recognizes one sole and preeminent power, the United States of America. And they regard this with no dread. For the world trusts us with power, and the world is right. They trust us to be fair and restrained. They trust us to be on the side of decency. They trust us to do what's right. . . .

There are those who say that now we can turn away from the world, that we have no special role, no special place. But we are the United States of America, the leader of the West that has become the leader of the world. And as long as I am President, I will continue to lead in support of freedom everywhere, not out of arrogance, not out of altruism, but for the safety and security of our children. This is a fact: Strength in the pursuit of peace is no vice; isolationism in the pursuit of security is no virtue.

FURTHER READINGS

Beschloss, Michael and Talbot, Strobe, *At the Highest Levels* (Boston: Little, Brown, 1993).

Hogan, Michael, editor, *The End of the Cold War* (New York: Cambridge University Press, 1992).

Index

About the Editor

STEPHEN J. VALONE is Associate Professor of History at St. John Fisher College in Rochester, New York. He is the author of *"A Policy Calculated to Benefit China": The United States and the China Arms Embargo, 1919–1929* (Greenwood, 1991).

ISBN 0-275-95324-6

EAN

HARDCOVER BAR CODE